TIME CHANGER'S TAROT IS A NEW LOOK AT AN OLD SYSTEM, AND ONE DESIGNED FOR THE AGE IN WHICH WE LIVE. Learning Tarot is a way to begin to understand our roles in these changing times. Diving deeply into Tarot it is possible to develop an understanding of the invisible powers and forces that surround us. There is comfort in knowing that there are benevolent guides that wish us well.

Caitlín Matthews brilliantly offers a view with both personal and global significance. This deck can help us open to the Knowing Field, to the ever-present guidance that is always around us. Standing bravely in the present moment, each one of us can attune to the unfolding future by using strategies for our human continuance. How wise to look at the world from a larger perspective attuning not only our personal destinies, but also becoming increasingly aware of the ways in which our families, communities and the globe are also changing.

Time Changer's Tarot presents a way to live with wisdom in chaotic times. It is for all who wish to see a kinder, safer, and wiser planet from both a personal and global perspective. Having a sense of where we are going helps each one of us prepare inwardly so we can align with our everchanging world.

—Ayn Cates Sullivan, PhD, creator of Imaginosophy

THIS IS A PARTICULARLY RELEVANT BOOK FOR TODAY, WHICH INCLUDES SEVERAL NEW CONCEPTS FOR ALL TAROT READERS—INDEED, ALL THINKING HUMANS ON EARTH. IT IS ESSENTIAL READING, FOR ALL OF US, BUT OF COURSE IN PARTICULAR FOR "TAROMANCERS" (the author's terms for readers). Her concept of the "Household of the Earth" points out that Tarot cards should be seen as the spiritual patterning of the universe. Caitlín considers how the Tarot needs a wider focus than an individual's current situation or psychological issues: in other words, that a reading should look at the client in relation to their community and environment which, given the serious problems facing the world, is vital. She points out that there are of course no black and white answers, but the cards can be used to offer mythic suggestions and possibilities.

The deck she uses throughout is the Waite-Smith Tarot whose images have become so widespread that it is the only choice for this book, which is thorough and encyclopaedic. Her interpretations of the cards are thorough and cover most questions a taromancer might wish to see, particularly within the "oikeiosis"—the circles of life on the planet.

What I found most fascinating in the book were the later chapters, beginning with Groups, Institutions and Collectives. Caitlín's point, that it is not necessarily an institution itself that is at fault, it is the uses to which its powers have been put. However, it is often extremely difficult not to become complicit when you are part of that institution. Using the cards to regain some objectivity, you may see how you can best work to clear its problems. The example she gives, of how the models of Peace and Reconciliation practices worked in South Africa and Ireland, are

CAITLÍN MATTHEWS

the TIME CHANGER'S TAROT

Reading for Yourself,
Your Community, and Your World
with the Waite-Smith Tarot

REDFeather

MIND | BODY | SPIRIT

Printed in China

interesting—though I did wonder about how that might apply when you see your own government falling hopelessly short of ideals it professed to enshrine when it was voted into power. To see how the cards might help to correct it, the next section, on "Community," which, again, is extremely useful. Caitlín suggests that, after analysing where the organization or institution has deviated from its core principles, you might wish to invite the spirit or founding principle back into the institution, given that every organisation will have its own original spiritual agency. The examples of how readings can shine a light on problems within an intitution or group, are very helpful, as are suggestions for readings on "the prevailing conditions."

I particularly liked the section on the "knowing field." This is an issue I've looking into recently from a semi-scientific point of view. Caitlín's suggestions here—using a modification of Etteila's cartomancy methods—are fascinating. I will use her reading regarding world events to see what the cards say about the serious problems currently facing the world. It will be interesting to see what the cards' suggestions will be!

Caitlín also uses the "knowing field" to include animals, plants, even an entire habitat, to speak from their point of view. This is unique and the concept should be included in every taromancer's (indeed every human's) resources. Our ignorance, and disregard of these other "fields" is now coming home to roost, and we must adjust our thinking now, before it is too late. I think this book is an essential study, not only for taromancers, but for every thinking human on the planet.

—Cilla Conway, author of *The Old Gods Tarot*,
    and the artist of *Byzantine Tarot* by John Matthews.

Cover and interior design by Brenda McCallum
Type set in Minion/New Hero

ISBN: 978-0-7643-6695-6
Printed in China

Published by REDFeather Mind, Body, Spirit
An imprint of Schiffer Publishing, Ltd.
4880 Lower Valley Road
Atglen, PA 19310
Phone: (610) 593-1777; Fax: (610) 593-2002
Email: Info@redfeathermbs.com
Web: www.redfeathermbs.com

ACKNOWLEDGMENTS

I want to thank all my teachers for widening my mind to the *oikei-osis,* or "the household of the earth," particularly to Daan van Kamp-enhout, and to Tim Addey of the Prometheus Trust. Also, to my peers and colleagues of the Spirits of Institutions Group who have met together since 2010, thanks from the bottom of my heart for helping bring to the surface those understandings of collective and institutional relationship that are so elusive when you are actually also part of an institution! Together, you have helped turn on a light in the hidden places and upon the treasures that lie at their heart. Thank you to Linda Henery for her thoughtful foreword and kind companionship on the Tarot journey. Thanks to Sévérine Jeauneau, who put this book on the road, and to Schiffer Publishing and RED-Feather Mind, Body, Spirit for roadside assistance when the way ahead looked blocked. Thank you so much to Tero Goldenhill for kind permission to share his wonderful Hazmat Suit spread. To John, thanks for reading and editing the manuscript, and for helping to unfailingly maintain things during times of particular stress: of all people, you understand what it is to live between the worlds, and the balancing act that this requires. Thanks to all those, both online and in person, who allowed me to share their readings, with changes of name and details. Gratitude also to all my Tarot family across the world: though we meet up but seldom, you keep faith with the es-sential core of Tarot so that we can all experience it in a variety of helpful ways.

CONTENTS

FIGURES

FOREWORD
THE CARDS STEP FORWARD

Having used the *Waite-Smith Tarot* as my primary tool for my reading and teaching for several decades, I became aware during the world events of the past few years of a new depth that this Tarot had to offer. This same observation was also being made by other Tarot readers and students with whom I was in regular communication. Toward the end of a Tarot course in 2021, a student emailed me with great excitement to share a dream she had experienced featuring her *Waite-Smith Tarot* deck. She saw the cards being shuffled and spread, and, after the question was asked, all the cards started talking to each other, encouraging certain cards to step forward to be chosen since they would be able to answer the question so well. They were particularly supportive of the shy cards, and all were friends, working together as a supportive, harmonious community, wanting to be of the highest service to the reader and the querent.

The *Waite-Smith Tarot* had taken on a life of its own outside time, as we experience it, stepping onto a new and broader stage to perform roles that extended their ability to take on more challenging workloads. The student's dream aligned with the purpose and content of Caitlín's book *The Time Changer's Tarot*, which explains how

Tarot can enable us to bring hope and help "shine the lantern of wisdom" in times of despair, by adopting an attitude of service and gratitude to match that of the cards in the dream. This book explains not only the holistic view of what we were experiencing, but how as Tarot readers we can change to meet the needs of those who seek solutions, to become changers of our times, not mere, powerless witnesses.

This book enables us to see our world through different models, beginning with the ancient understanding of the "Household of the Earth" with its concentric circles that make up life on earth, inviting us as readers to work with the conjoining of physical and spiritual reality. The gratitude and service we have for the earth is an essential requirement for reading for our community and our world, beyond just our own needs, and the questions we ask through the ritual of the reading are answered by the universe from the Knowing Field, where it ripples out to find answers.

Many years ago, while speaking at a Tarot conference here in Australia, Caitlín explained how, as Tarot readers, we dwelt on the fringe of society, and that when individuals became overwhelmed at the centre, they headed for the edge, and that is whence they would find us. That is where we needed to be. While that statement resonated deeply with me at the time, in retrospect it was such a prophetic statement, spoken so many years ago, given the global events and circumstances that people have experienced over these past few years. At that edge, Tarot has the ability to provide insight, comfort, reassurance, and solutions through a language of timeless images and symbols that has evolved accordingly, with the *Waite-Smith Tarot* performing through the decades. Making personal changes in life is often extremely difficult, but unpredictable times have amplified this dilemma. Fear and uncertainty paralyses. Such times call for the courageous and patient approaches Caitlín offers in this book.

The *Waite-Smith Tarot* has connected like-minded people around the world, speaking a common language through images, a source of great richness in emotional, intuitive, and creative expression. As a teacher of deaf education, I am aware that visual language is limited only by the depth of the questions asked, the nature of the ideas expressed, and the ability to interpret the communication. Caitlín addresses all these aspects of the *Waite-Smith Tarot* in this book, broadening their horizons in every direction to deal with current challenges faced by individual organizations, communities, and countries alike.

The Time Changer's Tarot gives confirmation of what I had been observing, bringing clarity to jumbled thoughts on how these Waite-Smith cards were communicating at a deeper level, expanding their range during our years of dealing with the COVID-19 pandemic and its associated restrictions and rules. As we were being locked down, teaching and meeting online, the cards were revealing another level of meanings. While we were being restricted, they found a stronger and insightful voice. The cards themselves seemed to be initiating this expansion, asking with insistence to be heard. Change has arrived at great and continuing speed in our world. History shows that when change occurs suddenly, many people become disconnected from their communities, falling by the wayside. The Tarot cards became a trusted voice, a means of helping and giving hope.

Was it the cards, was it us, or was it the source from where the messages came? Something was changing, as though this deck was created for these times. Her explanation of the four different ways that each Major Arcana card can be read explained my experience during late 2019, when it seemed that readings for clients and students in a group would all feature the Tower! What was it that was coming to affect so many? This was clearly a "signpost of change" that was going to affect what Caitlín refers to as "the Household of the Earth."

With her understanding of the importance of asking the right question, guidance is given on how to pose it effectively for the individual querent, for an organization or government. Caitlín provides comprehensive meanings of the cards relevant to how the questions may be asked. During the challenges of the past few years, it is as though the cards want to help us cope with circumstances that we have never faced before, revealing their hidden depth to help us access ours. Caitlín's experience and wisdom has enabled her to decode more information from these cards, which she describes in her book through meanings, strategies, skills, and spreads for working not only with individuals, but with groups and organizations of varying sizes and complexities, for as she explains, every thought, attitude, word, and action creates a ripple that spreads through time and space and in every direction.

The pandemic, with its lockdowns and the accompanying isolation, taught us much about ourselves and our place in our families, our communities, and the world. In isolation we learned about connection, a concept at the core of Indigenous cultures and so insightfully expressed in this book. While we are all alone, we are all connected to everything in our universe, past, present, and future and made of the same materials. The Tower taught and warned us that you can't keep building on unsound foundations. Complexity and fragility endure, and we are all in unchartered waters, but the cards understand the bigger picture. The cards know, and we can access that knowledge through what she describes as the Knowing Field. Caitlín skillfully incorporates her years of study and teaching of cartomancy, her profound knowledge and skill in Tarot, to bring ritual and depth to the experience of accessing wisdom from beyond this plane. This enables us to tap into the signs of the natural world, connecting to our ancestors and the knowledge of our many lineages, to access the source of wisdom.

Not only is *The Time Changer's Tarot* a comprehensive guide to deepening your Tarot-reading skills, but it also unlocks keys to further learning for the enthusiastic Tarot student. Most importantly, the skills and strategies revealed herein express the importance of reading with hope and finding ways to deal with change and challenges, as well as understanding our connection to the past and to future generations by acting with courage in the present. By adopting the pathways of the four virtues, Temperance, Fortitude, Justice, and Wisdom (represented by Temperance, Strength, Justice, and the Hermit or the World card in the *Waite-Smith Tarot*), we can stabilize the way ahead.

This is the challenge for the Tarot community in the twenty-first century. *The Time Changer's Tarot* gives us the skills to move forward with a deck valued and respected by the Tarot community for over a century, to honour its wisdom and allow it to perform to its full potential, while elevating our own skills as readers to meet these exceptional times. All we need now is the desire and dedication.

Linda Henery
The Tarot Conservatory

PREFACE

CHANGING TIMES IN TAROT

We have become too powerful to live thoughtlessly.

—Tim Addey,
the Prometheus Trust's Essentials Course

TAROT DEVELOPMENTS

Divination by Tarot is an art that has adapted itself to many times and traditions, but at this present moment, we are having to adapt to some of the fastest-moving changes into an unfolding future. *The Time Changer's Tarot* has been written to help negotiate the times through which we are living, when we need to read not only for personal guidance, but for our community, and with an eye on the wider issues that affect us all. We are all time changers: people who not only are living through changing times but can also note time's changes from a much wider perspective, looking for handholds, strategies, and timeless wisdom to help those who consult us.

To help us with this work, and to accompany this book, we have the *Waite-Smith Tarot,* first published in 1909: this influential Tarot was written by A. E. Waite, a magician, freemason, and scholar, and illustrated by Pamela Colman Smith, an artist and storyteller with a background in theatre design. It has been with us for over one hundred years, but it can help us catch up with some of the changes that have been happening and continue to develop, both in the Tarot and in the world.

Published just before World War 1, the *Waite-Smith Tarot* was in circulation before women were allowed to vote in the United Kingdom and the United States, before television was created, before racial integration and sexual equality were regarded as socially normal. With hindsight, we can see this Tarot as a prophetic herald of a world that would change irrevocably. After the war, all the older values underpinning the world entered into a process of severe breakdown: patriarchal values shaped through colonialization, financial control, social regulation, and religious dogmas were countered by movements that supported social and economic justice, national self-determination, universal suffrage, racial and sexual liberation, and a host of spiritual, psychological, and magical pathways, both ancient and modern, that brought a freedom of mind and soul to overthrow the rigid dogmas that had shaped the world for so long.

These movements had their roots in much earlier eras, of course, but since Waite wrote the *Pictorial Key to the Tarot*, the self-view of humanity has changed in extraordinary ways; we sense the foreshadowing of these in the way in which Pamela Colman Smith painted her Tarot images, presenting its people as standing upon the stage of life, as if they might have their own part to play. The tempering movements that have sought to modify life on Earth in more equitable ways have not gone uncontested: forces of repression, censure, and control made everyone fight harder for the freedoms that today we take for granted. At the beginning of the twentieth century, women were expected to keep to their place in the home, workers were largely powerless to change the terms of their employment, and people from other countries or with other skin colours were frequently treated as inferior, while lack of education kept people small and without agency. Social and religious values were rigorously policed—not only by those in authority, but by society itself, so that it was easy to fall foul of the opinion or respect of one's own peer group if you stepped outside the normal boundaries. Of course, there are places in the world where even today people are living under similar conditions, powerless to better their lot due to repressive regimes or restrictive religions and ideologies. The fight for freedom, equitable treatment, and respect for the universal commonwealth continues into and beyond our own times.

We now enter a time when many of the institutions that were reformed during the nineteenth and twentieth centuries are needing a fresh approach: we now want to live in a world where everyone can thrive, where laws serve human and animal rights, where the research of science can serve us ethically, and where truth and equality uphold people of all conditions.

All these things have also shaped our way of using Tarot, as a quick look at a historical Tarot deck will show. Historical Tarot cards, pre-*Waite-Smith*, consisted of 40 pip cards with no pictorial scenes upon them, only suit emblems, like playing cards; with the 22 Major Arcana and 16 court cards, they showed, respectively, the mundane, the deeply mythic, and a range of personality aspects. Court cards looked to the left or right, but never full face—for these were the cards that represented the querent or questioner, and the people associated with them. Because the Major Arcana depicted powerful and sometimes frightening things, these cards also looked to one side or the other, so as not to be confrontational. Only a handful of Major Arcana cards faced forward to the viewer, representing those inevitable forces that cannot be avoided or are essential to everyone, such as Justice, Judgement, the Devil, the Sun, and the Hanged Man.[1]

Modern Tarots, dating from the *Waite-Smith Tarot* onward, now feature a pictorial Minor Arcana showing scenes with which anyone can easily identify. While more familiar modes of artwork have modified the greater powers and forces of the Major Arcana into more contemporary and fantastic forms—to the extent that people no longer shy away from these powerful cards—now taromancers (the people who read Tarot) and their querents (or clients), often actively identify themselves not just with the court cards—but also with the Major Arcana themselves, speaking of themselves as a "High Priestess" or "Strength with her lion." This kind of self-identification has arisen not only through the evolution of consciousness wrought by social change, and the growing application of psychological values to the cards, but also because of the magical development of Tarot, whereby its cards are seen as part of the spiritual patterning of the universe. These more ancient values of a universal cosmology sit alongside psychological factors, sometimes in a rather mismatched way because the coordinating virtues that used to accompany the traditional practice of divination and esotericism are not often learned in an integrative way.

While psychology may unfold the inner and hidden workings of the human psyche and its effect upon behaviour, we still also need the abiding values of ethical discernment that psychology did not entirely integrate, constellating as it did in the most materialistic and mechanistic end of the nineteenth century. Without the coordinating help of the Cardinal Virtues of Temperance, Fortitude, Wisdom, and Justice, some Tarot use can sink to a level of self-focus that is less than healthy, occasionally bordering on the narcissistic. Of course, the *Waite-Smith Tarot* was conceived at a time when psychology was just coming to the fore, but A. E. Waite was more interested in how he might discreetly convey the fruits of his magical training without breaking his oaths to the lodges within which he worked. He would probably not now recognize the roots of his magical teachings among the many cards and commentaries of today, which often focus more on the everyday aspects of social life and the psychological inferences now derived from his cards. Over the last seventy years, Tarot has largely developed into a divinatory tool that has adopted a form of psychological evaluation that speaks almost entirely about the individual, but the cards now need a much wider focus than this.

AVOIDING THE WASTELAND

It is no longer sufficient to read just for ourselves: we also have to include our community and our world. In the twenty-first century, social responsibility and accountability have come to prominence, along with a sense of how we impact our world by our behaviour, lifestyle, and intentions. Each one of us is discovering the balancing act of being an integrated person of self-knowledge, adapting sensitively and sensibly to the field of diverse social interaction, as well as learning how we can be environmentally responsible. The essential art of considering *all* of our world as a living entity is now a vital requirement for the survival of every being within it.

We live in a time where everything we thought certain is once more in rapid flux, subject to sudden change and alteration just as alienating and confusing as those faced by people about to enter the First World War. To make things even more difficult, the problems facing us are not ones that have black-and-white solutions: the paradoxes foremost in our time include the way we interact with our endangered environment, how we deal with the mass movement of displaced people, the uneasy interference in daily life by corporate interests that collude with and have influence upon many of our institutions, the pending crisis in energy and food shortages, and an increased uncertainty surrounding the veracity of media reportage. In times where exigency and a lack of resources cause short-term inequities that will have an effect upon the world in the future, the rights and treatment of people and animals are as important as ever. In a time where large corporate interests control many of our activities, when accountability, human dignity, and personal freedom are being endangered in the regions of health, science, media, and communication, as well as having an impact on justice and the environment, we need to pay better attention. Education itself seems intent on producing "oven-ready minds" rather than cultivating the actual potentialities of students. Many people, like the Fool himself, are stepping out of mainstream society in order to consider the truth of things for themselves: they are time changers whose findings will guide us forward, but at present many of them are ridiculed and demonized for being different or out of step.

In such times, reliable messengers and practical oracles have never been more needed. With so many big businesses, political factions, and social groups manipulating the news, we increasingly need to know how to identify and assess the impact of many issues on our lives, especially when it is hard to read the subliminal and sometimes manipulated messages of mainstream media. Where conspiracy theories are rife on social media, where the official policies of some countries militantly suppress their racial and LGBT minorities, where the closure or control of the internet shuts down social interaction, it is even more important that the cards of the

Tarot be free to speak and advise people who may have no better information than the Tarot under their hands to guide them.

All these matters have the potential to change our lives, not just by the daily inconveniences and diversions that change brings, but the way in which they influence and alter social interaction, and the way we have to cope with the vaster changes that affect everyone, where the climate, energy, and environmental crisis is altering our world and impacting all lives. With the stark prospect of environmental degradation, we are looking Wasteland in the face. In the Grail legends, the Wasteland was what resulted from not living in tune with the ancient contracts of life, from abusing and neglecting the agreements that hold our universe in place.[2] The people who restored the fertility of the earth by going on quest for the Grail—the ultimate vessel of regeneration—were the Grail seekers or, as we could say, the time changers of that myth. In changing times, we, like them, need to ask skilful questions. The world does not have to become a Wasteland if we begin to ask the Grail question "Why are things like this?" By seeking answers and the guidance to live through uncertain times, we gain the knowledge to change our lives.

The hopelessness and despair generated by many world issues that affect ourselves and our communities are not the only response that there is. By taking the issue out of time and looking at it in timelessness, we can draw mythic possibilities and envisage new visions for our future. By working together and seeing ourselves as part of the bigger picture of the universe, we have the ability to become the time changers ourselves. The way we use Tarot now matters.

Because we are all becoming travellers moving through a world of change, *The Time Changer's Tarot* is presented as a means of negotiating our way across the world: not only for personal guidance, but for our community, and with an eye on the wider issues that are all around us. No life is lived without impact: we simultaneously inhabit the nesting boxes of self, family, friends, community, environment, nature, and universe, so at the heart of the book is a new way of addressing the meanings of the cards, methods that enable us to live with greater respect and conscious understanding.

WHY THE WAITE-SMITH TAROT?

This book, using the familiar cards of the *Waite-Smith Tarot* in a simple travel-format size, offers practical ways of mapping this uncertain terrain, by expanding the choices of reading methods and meanings, offering the reader opportunities to intelligently explore each card's possibilities so that they can help signpost the way through the challenging times in which we live. The cards can show us not only the difficulties but also the solutions, and how we can be part of them.

So, if we are moving into a future upon which we might make a more responsible impact, why use a Tarot from another era? It is my belief that in order to find ways to couch the great welter of contemporary issues into one Tarot, a familiar deck like the *Waite-Smith Tarot* has the power to guide us. Waite employed Pamela Colman Smith to illustrate his ideas by depicting the people and scenarios that appear in these cards in medieval clothing. There was nothing very radical about that, of course, because nearly every pack of playing cards today is still dressed in the style of the Renaissance era, however atavistic that may seem. The past is forgiving, providing us with templates that help our understanding. And yet, every Tarot reader knows that the currency of every reading is always about what is happening now, what consequences it will have, and how the querent will come out of it.

Waite wrote, "The Tarot cards . . . drawn and coloured by Miss Pamela Colman Smith, will, I think, be regarded as very striking and beautiful, in their design alike and execution . . . They differ in many important respects from the conventional archaisms of the past and . . . it remains for me to justify their variations so far as the symbolism is concerned. That for once in modern times I present a pack which is the work of an artist does not, I presume, call for apology. For the variations in the symbolism by which the designs have been affected, I alone am responsible. In regard to the Minor Arcana, they are the first in modern, but not in all times, to be accompanied by pictures, in addition to what is called the 'pips'—that is to say, the devices belonging to the numbers of the various suits. These pictures respond to the divinatory meanings, which have been drawn from many sources."[3]

The *Waite-Smith Tarot* cards have a familiarity about them, used as they are by countless Tarot teachers worldwide to inculcate their wisdom, which is why I have chosen to use them to accompany this book. But you can use *any* Tarot cards with this book, using the imagery depicted on your cards to guide you to inclusive and flexible meanings. In uncertain times, we appreciate the familiar, which is why I have used them to illustrate these new ways of working with the Tarot. These smaller, travel-sized cards are also a conscious choice: in shifting times and in many places, we can take these cards as our *vade-mecum* (literally, our "go with me") oracle, which help us map the way ahead for ourselves, our family and friends, and our world.

In these pages, I have addressed the cards on their own terms, without stressing the esoteric associations that have built up around them, including astrological ascriptions, since I feel that the cards can speak for themselves and stand on their own without being manipulated or interpreted by ascriptions that have become attached to them in the modern era. Divination with Tarot has its own craft, and I have striven to serve it well, so that any person may use Tarot cards without having to learn other disciplines. My focus is on the way we live with and in the world. I encourage the reader to look at and work closely with the images of Pamela Colman Smith, which is how I was first introduced to this Tarot, and how I learned to practically read with it.

I also introduce a unique use of the cards to stand as representatives of powers and resources that can help support the querent or to reveal the help available in readings about groups or world issues. By using the cards as resources or reservoirs of help, and as representatives, we are enabled to read "out of time" for those things that are being experienced "in time," thus revealing the mythic and ritual dignity of the cards. This powerful method of reading with support for the querent and their issue is one that I find works well in the times through which we living, where people often feel so isolated and disempowered.

While I am aware that this is not a handbook for beginners, I do know that everyone who reads Tarot can gain much from working with the concepts in this book, which challenge the taromancer to broaden and deepen their practice in ways that meet the world's needs.

In chapter one, we explore the idea of spreading the reading cloth wider to include the whole world. In chapters two and three, I have given different ways of considering the cards from the point of view of the individual as well as from a relationship between lovers, friends, or colleagues, and from the standpoint of how our words, thoughts, and actions affect the world. Here also, you will find aspects of environment issues that surround our questions. In chapter four, I give some general strategies for reading these cards in a more efficient way. In chapters five and six, we find ways of reading for our community and the world. In chapter seven, we look deeper at the spiritual and holistic aspects of reading Tarot and how it can be used in ritual, prayer, and mediation, as we do our part to mend the world.

This work takes us back to the most ancient use of oracles, when kings, rulers, and governments used to ask the gods and spirits of the divine oracles for practical help and guidance in national affairs, how to deal with enemies upon their borders, what crops to sow, or how a policy or course of action would play out.

Whatever decisions we each make will have impact somewhere in the world, just as the decisions that politicians, artists, and trendsetters make will ultimately also affect us. By using the skills given in *The Time Changer's Tarot,* we can all adapt our readings to spread our reading cloth wider, so that our questions on life guidance become better calibrated with the much larger events within our community and world.

By reading with responsibility and accountability, we too enable the world's changes in a supported way, becoming prophets of the future world we hope to inhabit. By becoming time changers in our Tarot reading, we will find that rather than being passively changed by the times, the times will actively change with us as a more balanced world evolves.

NOTES:

*In this book, I have used "querent" to signify the questioner of the cards: the one for whom the reading is being done. I have also used the word "taromancer" for a Tarot user or Tarot reader.

*Throughout, I encourage you to lay out the examples of spreads or use the readings and layouts for yourself, so that you can practically understand how they work.

*Throughout, the custom of laying one card upon one position is not often used. You are encouraged to read by the context of the question within whichever portion of the spread or layout the cards have fallen. Usually there will be guidance for a line or column to be read. If you are reading a line, then read it across in forward narration, like a story, sentence, or statement. When cards click together in a merged meaning, include that too. Don't be put off by what look like large clumps of cards together; these can be read simply and quickly, without the reading taking an age to comprehend.

BELONGING TO THE HOUSEHOLD
OF THE EARTH

Self-love but serves the virtuous mind to wake,

As the small pebble stirs the peaceful lake,

The centre moved, a circle straight succeeds,

Another still, and still another spreads,

Friend, parent, neighbour first it will embrace,

His country next, and next all human race.

Wide and more wide the o'erflowings of the mind,

Take every creature in of every kind.

—Alexander Pope, *Essay on Man*

BECOMING TIME CHANGERS

We are not just people who passively live through changing times—we can also be the ones who change our times. How can Tarot address the changes that are sweeping through our world? How can we become responsible time changers in our readings and Tarot work? First of all, by acknowledging that we are not alone in the world, by becoming aware of those with whom we share the world. By starting from this outlook, we are able to include "all that is."

Perhaps, as a schoolchild, you wrote in the front cover of your notebook your name, your street, and your town, locality, and country, followed by the world, the universe, the cosmos, etc.? Most young human beings understand themselves as being at the centre of an ever-expanding universe, in a series of nesting circles; very near are the familiar faces and places of home and family, and farther away are those we hear of but do not see often. As we grow up, that relationship changes and stretches, as we locate ourselves—not as being selfishly at the centre of everything—but rather as one living being who interrelates with the wider world.

In the second century, the Greek Stoic philosopher Hierocles developed the notion of *oikeiôsis,* or a concern for "the household of the earth." He wrote, "We are surrounded by many circles, some smaller that are included within the larger, and some larger which include the others. . . . The nearest circle is the one which everyone draws about their own mind, which surrounds their body. . . . The next circle surrounds it and is made up of parents, brothers and sisters, spouse and children. The third circle contains uncles and aunts, grandparents, nieces and nephews. Then the circle of more distant relatives. Beyond this is the circle containing people of the same tribe, then the one that contains citizens, those that live near the capital city, and another circle of those who all live in the same province or county. The outermost and largest circle is that which includes all the other circles, made up of the whole human race."[4] This theory took it as read that every living person had a correct relationship to the gods as well. Hierocles was proposing that the way we conduct ourselves to our nearest and most distant kindred could be modelled toward our fellow and sister beings in ever widening circles of familiarity.

FIG. 1 *Hierocles's concept of the household of the earth*

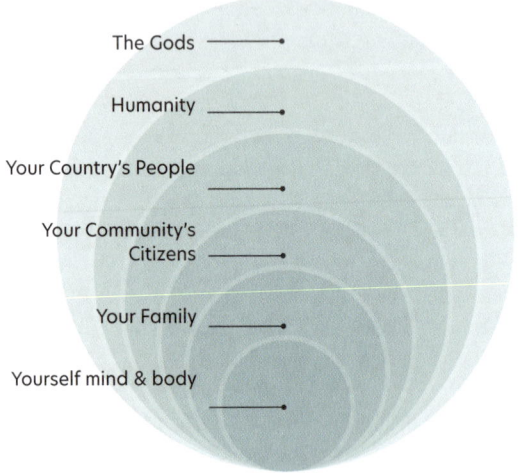

The Gods

Humanity

Your Country's People

Your Community's Citizens

Your Family

Yourself mind & body

Hierocles's idea practically enables us to ethically consider our relationship to the ever-widening circles of the universe that surround us, and how we might conduct ourselves with those inside each circle: yourself, with your family, your fellow citizens, your country people, humankind as a whole, and the gods. His concept was based on the way we care about our close family and how it might be expanded to include strangers as friends, friends as relatives, and so on. He was first drawn to this understanding of endearment and affinity from his own study of animals, and the way that they care for their offspring and each other. Hierocles also wrote about how the inclusion of these different kinds of relationship with people might be acknowledged by calling strangers "brother" or "sister."

We see similar constructs at work today in traditional, transmigratory, and tribal societies who live at close quarters with each other: to maintain equitable relations in sometimes stressful living situations, it is common to respectfully call all elders "grandmother" or "grandfather," while people older than yourself are called "uncle" or "aunt," and people of your own age become "cousin" or "brother" and "sister," while those younger than yourself are called "niece" or "nephew" or "son" or "daughter." This custom equalizes everyone as a family member, even if they are visitors or strangers to the group.

Of course, Hierocles's concept of "the household of the earth," being predicated on just human beings, is different from our own sense of the world now, because today we are adopting a more animist view, where we may think of that household as including all living beings, from rocks, plants, and animals to trees, interrelated ecosystems, and habitats, with all the zones and landscapes of the earth. Science has been continuously stretching our view of the universe ever wider, and, were Hierocles living now, he would undoubtedly add to his concentric circles of affinity to include the environment, the distant stars of other galaxies, as well as to the bacterial life that was unseeable before the coming of the microscope.

This way of considering things encourages the making of relations between all beings, establishing a peaceful interaction that strengthens bonds, values affinity, and builds friendships. It is a means of welcoming everyone and everything, seeing all life as belonging, with us, to a wider family. The Greeks, positioned as they were among the many islands and polities around the eastern Mediterranean, which was home to a myriad of different cultures, sagely practiced the art of *philoxenia,* or "kindness to strangers," as a cultural law to ensure that strangers felt at home: when you have eaten at someone's table and been treated as family, you are less likely to harm them.

For us today, though the population of our own locality or country has more people than we can relate to in so easy a way, we can still hold in our hearts all the world in an act of hospitality by considering how our own "household of the earth" might look. This might include yourself (the person doing the considering); your family and ancestry (the people from whom you derive your life); your community, group, tribe, or nation (those who live in the same region as yourself or who share your views); and, last, the wider universe and the environment of the earth itself (all that is living on Earth, and all that is unseen in the spiritual world).

Drawing upon Hierocles's concepts for our times, we can understand the reality of these nesting boxes, both from the diagram on the next page and from the cards of The Fool, Ten Pentacles, Six Wands, and The World below, with each aspect of our life resting within larger and wider circles, where our personal existence nests within the context of family and our sphere of work, which is set within the wider community and country that we inhabit, which is, in turn, set within our environment and the universal circle of life.

FIG. 2 *The ripples and circles of each life*

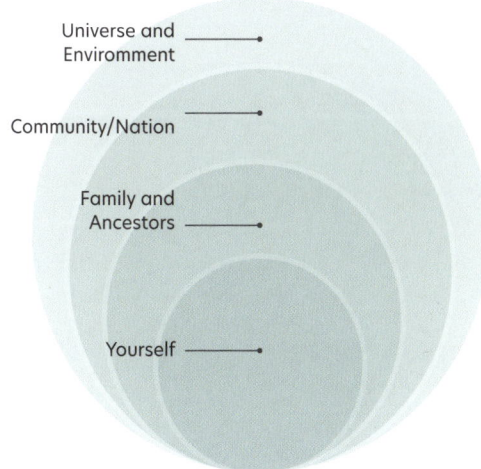

Universe and Enviromment

Community/Nation

Family and Ancestors

Yourself

YOURSELF

The thoughts, deeds, and words of each personal life are like stones thrown into a pool. The ripples spread wide, affecting those whose lives receive its ripples. These ripples also come back to us from the rest of the nesting realities in which we live. As individuals, we have agency and opinion, whose effect we cannot always comprehend.

FIG. 3   *The nesting boxes of influence*
These nesting boxes of influence make up the household of the whole world and can become a powerful way of reading for any situation.

FAMILY AND ANCESTORS

The context of our family and ancestry also affects us, enabling us to grow up with family values that give us our initial formation. We later acquire peer influences and work ethics that may differ from those of our family. The values of our society are made up from a mixture of these aspects

COMMUNITY, GROUP, TRIBE, NATION

The community, group, tribe, or nation in which we live includes all its inhabitants, who imbue it with group or national values. The manner in which we live affects and is affected by our wider community and our country; its way of making decisions will determine how our life is shaped. How we respond matters.

UNIVERSE, NATURE, ENVIRONMENT, SPIRIT

The wider universe encompasses us all and includes our whole environment. The world of nature was here before us, in all its variety. The unseen world of spirit is not unknown and is also included here. Our relationship with the universal realm is ongoing, stretching beyond into the great world of spirit.

RIPPLES IN TIME: THE CONSEQUENCES OF CAUSE & EFFECT

The ripples that we experience from all these different circles that make up our lives are effecting changes all the time. But because human beings mostly desire things to remain constant and comfortable, we tend to see most changes as harmful and upsetting, and we require reassurance about them. Since we have to live with the consequences of decisions that we make, and tend to ignore what caused them or where the ripples of those actions might run, we seek out diviners who can give us the bigger picture. Alternatively, we may be undergoing the effect of changes and are actively seeking how to deal with those consequences, discovering how we can live in a better, safer, or more stable way. Even this wish will have consequences. We both cause and suffer from the ripples that flow from our thoughts, words, and actions, and from those of others. An understanding of these ripples and their effect is essential in divination, which is why tarotmancers need to be skilful time changers—

people who are able to contextualise a querent's question in helpful ways, both from within time and outside it. (See chapter 4, p. 247.)

Tarot divination shows us a snapshot of the whole picture of a question from the standpoint of a moment in time: a view of "where/how the ripples are reaching / will reach you." Some of those ripples come from the distant past and are still affecting us, shaping both opinion and attitude even now. For example, we have unconsciously inherited several beliefs from the theological developments of western Christian belief that are affecting our world today, such as that all creation is somehow seen as soiled by the Fall from Grace, while, from Darwinian evolutionary theory, many harbour a view that humanity masters the whole universe, and that everything within it is a resource for us to use, without much consideration. These two concepts alone have left our planet open to abuse and exploitation, since they tend to erode our respect for other forms of life, encouraging us to believe that everything in the universe is a commodity for us to use, without thought for the consequences. Such attitudes have effect in our world, as does the kind of modernist belief that this life is the only one we have, and so it doesn't matter how we behave; this belief encourages blunt, short-term policies that put the current needs of the present generation above any wiser legacies left to us by ancestors while, at the same time, completely ignoring the needs of future generations and the world at large.

Contrast this with the Indigenous view of the world, where it is generally held that the duty of humans is to maintain spiritual health and strength by caring for the earth, so that it can be enabled to care for us.[5] Indigenous and traditional societies have a reciprocal relationship, where their ancestors include all life forms, as well as everything and every being in the natural world, from rocks and mountains, through animals, trees, and flowers, to celestial objects in the sky. The maintenance of that relationship enables such societies to continually evolve. Their sense of belonging to the planet, rather than the planet belonging to them, ensures humility and a sense of kinship with everything on it, so that poor decision-making is less likely to happen, because they will deeply consider what it means to bring change to future generations.

In times of radical change, we can emulate the wisdom of Indigenous peoples by being aware of our ancestors—not just as human beings from a few generations ago, but as a vast and interlinked family of life who perceive each of us as kin: human, animal, plant, rock. When we see ourselves as partaking of this wider kinship, our whole relationship with the world changes. It ceases to be a "them and us" relationship and become one of "us." By acknowledging this wider ancestry, we begin to feel less abandoned ourselves, becoming aware of a well-being and support that is ours forever. Whatever the changes that may come, the shared wisdom within the network of that vast circle of life remains our heritage forever, but we have to actively engage with it.

We can become time changers when we ask our ancestors to stand behind us in our endeavours, to witness, support, commiserate, mourn, or celebrate, because our life is part of a wider weaving. By considering those who will come after us, we take responsibility for passing on what we have inherited. Ancestors are not only about those who live in the past, but also about those who live in the futur—because, even though you have no children of your body, you too will have collateral human descendants, to whom *you* will be the ancestor. The changes made in our time will ripple through to them. The decisions and action we take will have consequences on all of them, which we can envisage in this shrine mat that shows one person and seven generations of ancestors or descendants.

FIG. 4 *Seven generations of ancestors or descendants*

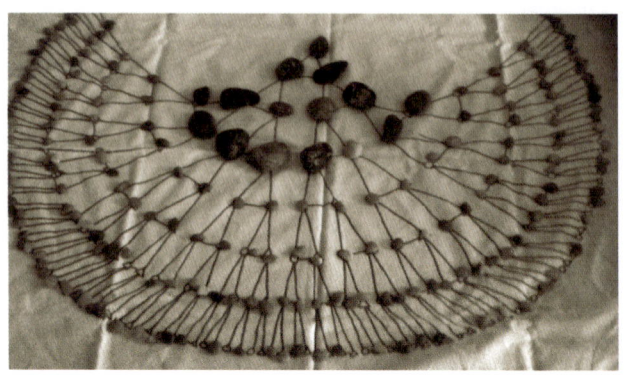

To acknowledge and experience this ancestral wisdom is also to generate love for all that is, because we can steer—not solely by own exigencies and needs—but by the guidance of the ancestors behind us, and with care for those descendants who lie ahead of us in time. And this is what leads us to be of service. The concept of service is something we often think belongs to some other group, a belief that arises from a culturally perceived idea of service as "menial work." Yet, every skill, talent, and aptitude we possess is actually a way of serving the world and our community.

Interpenetrating ripples of mutual help and support surge through the great weaving of life. We see how, in many folk stories, when the hero or heroine of the tale finds themselves cast out of their home, left to their own resources or set impossible quests, they inevitably find that the world of nature asks them for some simple help or service: later in the story, that help is returned in miraculous ways, often enabling the hero to achieve over terrible odds. This is a representation of the reciprocation that can be between ourselves and our world. In every Tarot reading we can look for similar help for the querent, since, whatever their situation, help and support stand close to them.

By beginning to view the whole world as kin, we also draw closer to the concept that the apparent reality about us is connected to the unseen reality that interpenetrates and is wound with it, something that also has consequences.

SPIRITUAL AND PHYSICAL REALITY
ARE CONJOINED

Spiritual and physical reality are conjoined, like the weaving of a cloak whose warp-and-weft interweave to make one garment: just because we don't see the side of the cloak that is worn next to the wearer's body doesn't mean to say it is not there. This subtle inter-meshing of reality is also involved in the cause and effect that we experience as change. Whenever we forget to relate to the unseen realm of spirit or to the timeless and eternal present, we also tend to forget to relate to the beings with whom we share the apparent realm of the physical world, often leading us into injustice or into lack of consideration or compassion. We see this everywhere: in governments that focus policies solely on expedient policies, rather than on the ancestral heritage and the impact on future generations; selfish actions that irrevocably damage lifestyle and environment of many creatures, plants, and natural habitats; a mentality of greed where people grab all available resources because "this life is all we have."

What we experience when we consider the whole world as kin—both the seen and unseen sides of it—is an unconditional love, that mysterious medium that draws us together. Unfortunately, because of many historical and personal factors, a working sense of spiritual reality has become optional or even fictional to many in society today. However, when we read for querents, we need to consider the widest circle of spiritual reality for them: not to impose or infer belief, but so we can see them as they essentially are, at the fullest potential of their soul, not just as the sum of their body or their physical circumstances at the time of the consultation. This is a witnessing and hospitality of spirit that enables the querent to settle down and attend to the question that is concerning them in the widest context, where both change and possibility can be invited onto the reading cloth.

Our sense of belonging to the household of the earth opens to us a much more expansive realm than any religious dogma. We are part of a universe that weaves us into everything that is, that perceives us and supports us. This sense of spiritual reality is more hospitable and inclusive than a religion: it is the landscape of our soul's knowing that no one can take from us. Taromancers everywhere understand that the querent usually comes for a consultation when they have fallen out of that knowing and need reminding what holds them in being, so that they can be once more an agent in their own story.

Holistic context is what querents are seeking—their sense of the interweaving of all things that makes life worthwhile. While they are not coming for conventional religious advice or wise spiritual council, necessarily, they are seeking a way to stand in a changing world that threatens to knock them off balance. This is why there is space throughout this book for a different way of looking at things, ways to deepen how we read. These can show us how to widen the reading cloth to include factors that enable the querent to be witnessed as someone who is part of that greater weaving, and not a random individual who is helplessly abandoned on the seas of fate.

This spiritual context is near to us and is not about dogma or religion: it can be as simple as the way a wren looks into you when you step out your front door, the joy as you stand on a hillside at sunset, the song that rises in you when you are released from a time of trial, the sense of an ancestor standing with you when you are suffering or unhappy. These are all real experiences of the whole world both in time and timelessness connecting with us, not delusions. Disconnection from the household of the earth may be the mainstream view, but no one can deny you or forbid you from belonging to it. You have *always* been connected, you have always belonged, and you will always belong.

DRAWING OUT THE MEANING: FINDING THE CONTEXT

The context of Tarot readings can include the self, the family, our ancestors, our community, the nation, the environment, and the spiritual reality of the universe. This is why this book presents much fuller categories from which you may read, understand, and interpret the card. This context is often completely absent from a classic reading but is much more to the fore in our own era, giving the taromancer a unique set of tools with which to explore the cards in depth and draw out both the meaning and the helpful possibilities.

Each of the 22 Major Arcana cards can include different ways of reading:

1. as an opportunity that presents itself at this time
2. as a signpost of change that flags up things we need to be aware of
3. as a prompt to clear the way and to more radically reevaluate things
4. as a manifestation of the ripples that are moving and changing the whole universe, and as a means of finding kinship with the household of the earth

Each of the 40 Minor Arcana cards can be read as offering clarification on

1. the querent's personal lifestyle
2. the querent's interaction with another person
3. the querent's wider impact within their community or country
4. the querent's spiritual context and the wider community impact within their environment or it upon them

Each of the 16 Court Cards can be read as

1. a person known to or involved with the querent
2. a process that is playing out in the querent's life
3. an event that is unfolding as a context to the querent's question
4. the moral and spiritual context of the wider environment

The ripples or consequences of something in the question can be read in all these categories as either upright and reversed, showing ways where we correspond closely to the theme of each card, or ways where we divert from it. This might vary from question to question, so please feel free to investigate any part of the categories to draw out helpful themes, and don't be afraid of looking into the reversed as well as the upright meanings when something seems contrary, unseen, or unspoken.

These meanings are not definitive or fixed, as we will see. They are mutable, ready to be applied to any question. The meanings given in chapters 2 and 3 are not the only possibilities that the cards can give. If you are an experienced reader, you will already appreciate this. When you are a beginner, it takes awhile to fully comprehend how flexible the cards can be and how eloquent in answering your question, where each card reshapes itself to accommodate and answer the question. Read with the question in mind and be prepared to work with the visual clue, the metaphor, and the way the cards shape themselves like actors who stand ready to enter our drama and represent it for us.

A TEMPLATE FOR THE SPIRIT:
MAJOR ARCANA

Human beings are a compendium
of the whole universe because they contain all the
powers of the cosmos.

—Photinus, *Life of Pythagoras*

The Major Arcana speak with the archetypal voice that governs all beings on Earth. Each card will automatically show you the bigger, collective picture of your question, revealing where the larger influences are at work within it. These may erupt into your life as irresistible forces of fate, as prevailing conditions that govern the world, or as influences that cause you to change or struggle. But they can also reveal to you the power to deal with current problems and dilemmas, how that power can help you withstand, or how a community can harness the virtues that each Major Arcana offers.

Each card entry in this chapter describes the card itself and gives some sayings that typify the card in the "Focus" section. It ends with questions whereby the card questions you. The deeper you engage with these questions, the more you will uncover: please adapt these questions to help reveal more about your issue.

The arrangement of the meanings is completely reenvisaged in this book. Each of the 22 Major Arcana cards offers four different ways of reading:

1. as an opportunity that presents itself at this time
2. as a signpost of change that flags up what we need to be aware of
3. as a prompt to clear the way and more radically re-evaluate things
4. as a manifestation of the ripples that are moving and changing the whole universe, and as a means of finding kinship with the household of the earth

To discover which of the four different entries will best answer your question, follow these steps:

1. Choose *Opportunity* when you want to take the opportunity of your question to engage more deeply. This level offers you the supportive freedom of your talents and imagination. It can also

help you find resources and ways through difficult times.

2. Choose *Change* when you need to see the possibilities that change might bring. This level offers you suggestions and approaches to make those changes. This level is challenging because we all hate change, but it enables us to be part of the changing times we live through.

3. Choose *Clearing the Way* when you need to adopt a more radical approach. Sometimes we have to start over or clear the decks for new things to come into our lives. This level speaks very truthfully and challengingly. Use it to cut away old habits, to support growth in the long term, or to understand what is involved when a new wave sweeps away the known and familiar landmarks.

4. Choose *Environmental* when you are reading to include the whole of nature or movements within the world at large; use it too to understand the more spiritual and moral principles that are at work in your question, and to see which virtues the card supports and which you can adopt or draw upon while undergoing changes, taking opportunities or clearing the decks for more radical living.

The first three options come with upright ⬆ and reversed ⬇ entries. But in the Environmental section, the topics and qualities associated with them have been mixed together, since paradox often plays a part in these issues where you must use your own judgment. Remember to use the reversed entries not only for physically reversed cards but also when an upright card appears to be conflicted or difficult on its particular position or when it falls in juxtaposition with another card. Sometimes you may find helpful answers in more than one entry to the card you are reading: be flexible in your approach, because all questions can have more than one answer.

THE CARD BACK

The card back originates from a stone that is one of the internal lining stones of Cairn Holy 1, one of two fourth-century BCE chambered cairns near the south coast of Dumfries and Galloway, in southwest Scotland. This stone, with its seven concentric rings, would have been facing the ancestor laid within the cairn tomb, an eternal remembrance of the widening circle of life. It reminds us that every life form is a compendium of the whole universe, having relationship to all the powers of the cosmos.

FIG. 5 *Cairn Holy*

THE FOOL .

0 THE FOOL

Image: Against a yellow sky, a youth in a short, dark-green tunic patterned with orange flowers stands on the brink of a precipice in a mountainous place, with a white dog at his heels. In his right hand is a stick with a wallet attached to it. In his left hand is a white rose.

Focus:
"I leap without a second glance into my destiny."
"I play the fool in order to become wise."
"I follow the vision with all my heart."

Background: The Fool is ready to follow his dream, spurred on by his imagination; he wants to enter into the world of possibility. He doesn't yet know much or how he will achieve his dream, but his steps are guided. The Fool is innocent and uncomplicated, holding all the possibilities in his heart in a childlike way, and just wants to implement what his vision promises. This is the card of following your dream, an innate sense of adventure, throwing caution to the winds. In the game of Tarocchi, the Fool card was "the excuse"—the card you played when you literally couldn't "follow suit." Waite also suggests, "Folly, mania, extravagance, intoxication, delirium, frenzy, bewrayment. While reversed, negligence, absence, distribution, carelessness, apathy, nullity, vanity."

Opportunity: ⬆ The chance to try things out for yourself is offered to you. By trusting your vision, you may experience carefree enthusiasm and youthful energy. By questioning the process, you learn your skills. Follow your dream or your heart's desire with enthusiasm. Trying things out, adventuring, risking but trusting, the jumping-off point. Following your vision.

⬇ Being unduly naive leads you into dangerous places. Foolhardy bravado beckons you to the edge. Behaving idiotically or thoughtlessly endangers you and others. Intoxication and extravagance lead you astray.

Change: ⬆ Prepare to play with the possibilities that present themselves. You are able to strike out into new areas due to changes. A sense of optimism and adventure will see you through. Whatever you are starting out on, follow the promise of your potential. Stepping out of line, even appearing foolish. Taking a risk.

⬇ Inappropriate levels of engagement leave you open to loss of innocence. Reactionary impulses can lead into sophisticated paths or exploitative ways. Beware of revealing your agenda in self-exposing ways. Your trust is likely to be abused.

Clearing the Way: ⬆ Needing the spontaneity or curiosity to go deeper. Seeking the heart's desire leads to obsession or mania. Thus far, blessed ignorance protects you, but don't push your luck. Life is a serious business for you, so work playfully but play with enthusiasm.

⬇ A sense of being ostracized or marginalized. Not wanting to look like a fool. Escaping into childlike states brings feelings of security. Being too careful means you never leave home. Distrusting the unknown or scorning the simple options. Anarchy is getting in the way of clear intent.

Environmental: Having the childlike sense and love of nature. The wisdom to know that environmental problems cannot be solved alone. Not being afraid of making mistakes, because this is the edge where experience grows. Being led by the instinctive wisdom of animals. Dogs, and pets. The humility of kinship of all life. Honouring the spontaneity of the moment.

Questions:
What chance is being taken?
What impels your heart?
What is driving things to this edge?

I THE MAGICIAN

Image: Against a yellow sky, the Magician holds a double-ended wand upright in his right hand, while his left hand points to the earth. Over his head is a lemniscate, symbol of eternity. He is dressed in a white robe that is girdled by a serpentlike belt, with a red overrobe. Before him stands a wooden table upon which are the four emblems of the Tarot suits: the pentacle, cup, sword, and wand. In the foreground are lilies and red roses.

Focus:
"I channel the power between heaven and earth."
"I keep faith with the potential of life."
"My ingenuity is in the service of all."

Background: Originally called the *Bateleur* or *Bagatto* or the Juggler, he becomes the Magician in the *Waite-Smith Tarot*, a conduit for elemental power, the master of spiritual attainment in the mysteries. The power that he mediates is the bright spark at the heart of all creation, the dynamo of its power, which comes down to Earth in inventive ways. Mind is his natural medium. The capacity to hold and remember is held in the memory theatre of his brain, the knowledge that bridges all manner of possibilities. Waite also suggests these meanings: "skill, diplomacy, address, subtlety; sickness, pain, loss, disaster, snares of enemies; self-confidence, will, signifying the Querent, if male. Reversed: Physician, Magus, mental disease, disgrace, disquiet."

Opportunity: ⬆ Here you are called to use all your talents and skills, to make an impact with every ounce of your potential. Creative initiative and clarity of mind translates into skill of hand. When you actively grasp your power and follow its creative lead, you feel powerful and dynamic. Your concentration and engagement initiates connections that will transform your life. You can become a conduit for magic.
⬇ Overconfidence can lead to megalomania and arrogance to the corruption of power. Use your imaginative insight to feed creativity and compassion. Beware of the trickery or cleverness that scams you.

Change: ⬆ Engage with the task in hand. Learn or practice a skill. This is the time to be single-minded and determined. Believing in yourself, you will not be afraid to act decisively. Self-confidence aligns you with life's ebb and flow. Make a strong connection with your core motivations. Get down to the practical tasks. Fire up your synapses, brainstorm solutions, use your ingenuity.
⬇ Overreaching the mark is risky. Self-doubt causes plans to stall or fall apart. Discover the correct focus and concentrate.

Clearing the Way: ⬆ You and your mind are one: whatever you conceive or ponder is manifesting around you. Blockages may be caused by being too clever or confident, becoming traps. Examine what has become too complicated and theoretical. The potential for self-sabotage, deception, and manipulation is present.

🔽 A charlatan or trickster tries to trick you. Check whether you might be believing something you have uncritically accepted. Denying the power that is innately yours causes the flow of energy to be disrupted. Accurate perception and reading the patterns clearly can help train your will to get started.

Environmental: How we balance our use of technology and its by-products, with their effect upon the earth. Considering how to take the initiative wisely. The magic of invention and ingenuity. Reverse engineering. Nuclear power. Issues of clean energy. Developing technology. Dealing with nonbiodegradable waste products. The willingness to make connection. Honouring the potentialities of life.

Questions:
What needs to come into manifestation?
What comes of using your skills wisely?
How will the earth receive it?

II THE HIGH PRIESTESS

Image: Against a night blue sky, a moon-crowned woman sits dressed in watery robes with a waxing crescent moon at her feet. She has an equal-armed cross upon her breast, and a scroll bearing the words *Tora* under her right arm. To her left is the white pillar of mercy with the *J* of Jachin, while to her right is the black pillar of severity with *B* for Boaz. Behind her is a veil of pomegranates and palms, signifying the Tree of Life.

Focus:
"I veil the mystery for the time of revelation."
"I initiate and conceive the weaving."
"I guide the seeker along the trackless path."

Background: The original figure of Papesse or female pope was replaced by eighteenth-century Tarot commentator Court de Gebelin with the High Priestess. Waite sees her as the Shekinah, the holy presence of God. She sits as the initiator into knowledge and deeper wisdom. The moon is her crown and gives forth the outgoing tides of wisdom at her feet, enabling us to steer by nighttime consciousness. As an oracular sibyl, she backs onto the world of dreams and archetypes. Her task is to reveal the truth behind appearances or to veil things from sight until the revelation can be imparted. As the mistress of the right moment, she lightly holds ideas and concepts, shaping them ready for manifestation by modelling them virtually. Her intelligent silence fosters inspiration. When you listen to the inner voice within your soul, you can find the answers to the most important questions. Allow yourself to enter and be held by that silence: within the ocean of the creative stars, self-knowledge swims closer to you. Silence and tenacity keep faith with all the generations to be born.

Opportunity: ⬆ You have the opportunity to seek at a deeper level, to consult the innate knowledge of your soul. The ability to educate, to give instruction or advice, is needed now, maybe to foster or support the dreams of others. You may give or receive counsel. By receiving guidance from your deepest dreams and visions, you are able to read the hidden messages
⬇ Ignoring your intuition. Disrespecting the wisdom within does you damage. Purposeful secrecy mystifies and obscures things. Broken confidences or hoarded knowledge isolates you.

Change: ⬆ In preparation for transition, you enter a period of restraint, quietness, or consideration, so slow down to honour what is emerging. Examine your dreams for meanings that will light the way forward. You are led more by your inspiration or intuition than by reason. Moving forward without clear knowledge, by intuition.
⬇ Escaping into psychism, guesswork, or ungrounded divination, losing touch with your common sense. A time of licence after restraint or austerity. Working from shallow or superficial knowledge. Scrutinizing and examining your motives.

Clearing the Way: ⬆ The council of soul guidance is needed: seek out a wise friend or expert to help you unclutter the way. The omens and portents you notice are becoming the writing on the wall that cannot be ignored. Feeling suddenly vast with vision or potential, you can clearly see what doesn't serve you any longer. Enter lucid dreaming for guidance. Needing scientific rigour in research.
⬇ Secrets are revealed in an untimely or embarrassing fashion. Compromised values hem you in; so, time to return to what you believe. Being easily captivated by signs and symbols, you miss the real meaning of life.

Environmental: The seed of all ideas, DNA, patterns in nature, blueprints of the cosmos: the unwritten codes that determine all life. The ability to read the omens and portents, holding the essence in balance, revealing or veiling what is hidden. A culture of secrecy. Keeping faith with all generations. Reading, journalism, curating knowledge.

Questions:
What waits to be revealed or remains secretly guarded?
Where will the seeds of the past germinate in the future?
Where is the wisdom to be found in the question?

III THE EMPRESS

Image: Against a yellow sky, a woman in a starry crown sits upon a cushioned throne, dressed in a loose robe. On the ground at her feet is a heart-shaped shield with the symbol of Venus upon it. In her right hand is a sceptre, on which is a globe. A field of wheat is before her, while behind her is a forest and a stream that waterfalls to her left.

Focus:
"I am the gate of life."
"I lead the senses to explore and learn."
"I rejoice in the beauty of the world."

Background: The Empress cherishes the life and well-being of the universe with mutual respect and pleasure. Her abundance and fertility nourishes all, bestowing a sense of prosperity and plenty. She bestows elegance, beauty, and fruitfulness to everything that is made, sharing her gifts generously, to enrich the world about her. She speaks through the gateways of the senses, the medium by which we enjoy pleasures, also enabling us to be receptive to the information that is all around us. When we engage with life at the deepest level, everything we touch can be made beautiful. This card also signifies the door of life, the realm of women, motherhood, and a long life. Waite gives, "Fruitfulness, action, initiative, length of days; the unknown, clandestine; also difficulty, doubt, ignorance. Reversed: Light, truth, the unravelling of involved matters, public rejoicings; vacillation."

Opportunity: ⬆ Creativity is a pleasure where you can concentrate on the growth or fulfilment of something dear to your heart. In the process of nurturing or giving birth to something. Abundance and fertility are lined up to support your plans. Giving and receiving tenderness or compassion. Material and spiritual wealth help you feel prosperous. You have the chance to bring harmony.

⬇ Wild growth, extravagance, or too much of a good thing. Thwarted passion or abuse of the feminine diminishes your self-image. Frustrated creativity turns inward.

Change: ⬆ Appreciating beauty after a phase of being surrounded by the mundane, the plain, or the unadorned. Physical well-being comes online for you. Social events and gatherings help you affirm life's pleasures. A feeling of richness and pleasure helps you feel expansive. Passion is in the air, so prepare to attract and be attractive. Sharing your resources generously. Doing things in a feminine way. A time of public rejoicing.

⬇ Expedient measures circumscribe resources. A period of dearth after plenty. An inability to share. Failure to respond reciprocally. Superficial attractions lure you in.

Clearing the Way: ⬆ Spending your resources on creating a good impression is wasteful and time consuming. Luxury and opulence for their own sake. You are out of phase with nature and natural rhythms. Be careful that you are not too demanding. Is your self-image becoming overly conventional? Maternal love becomes smothering. Where are you led to foster creativity in yourself or others?

⬇ Overindulgence or letting yourself go. Having to cut back on pleasures or extravagances. Feeling left out of the circle. Not taking care of yourself. Things are running wild.

Environmental: Tending to or wastefulness of Earth's resources. Wheat or grain production. Staple foodstuffs. Mother Nature. Exploitation of women and girls. Honouring the gift of life. Reverence for all life-forms. Honouring the abundance and variety of life.

Questions:
To what is the door of life opening?
Where is abundance or gratitude needed?
What is ripening now?

IV THE EMPEROR

Image: Against a red sky, the Emperor in an imperial crown holds a crux ansata in his right hand and the globe in the left, as he sits upon a throne decorated with ram's heads. Under his red robes, he is clad in armour. Behind him runs a small stream, while in the background, under an orange-red sky, are rocky outcrops.

Focus:
"I rule with authority and mercy."
"I maintain the paths of life with justice."
"I guard life with benevolence."

Background: The Emperor oversees the commonwealth with responsible oversight of the earth, with courage and vision, stability and commitment. He defines and defends his realm humanely, wielding authority with responsibility. His stabilizing strength becomes a protection to others because he establishes clear structures and helpful boundaries. His virility and verve guide and regulate the world. The Emperor enables you to take the lead and get organized, helping you follow a regime, maintain a schedule responsibly, and set standards. When you take up your life with courage, you can have natural authority and hold the boundaries without wavering. This card also signifies the male realm and fatherhood. Waite gives, "Stability, power, protection, realization; a great person; aid, reason, conviction; also authority and will. Reversed: Benevolence, compassion, credit; also, confusion to enemies, obstruction, immaturity."

Opportunity: ⬆ Your leadership qualities mean you can turn ideas into reality, lead the field, or bring the plan through to its goal. Making a secure environment gives protection to others. Responsible love heads up the workplace, family, or environment. Authoritative energy and delight in potency bring organization. Authenticity is the result of you taking up the challenge. Time to employ systematic structures. The power to be authentic lies in your hands. ⬇ Arrogance or perfectionism mars the enterprise. Immaturity, weakness, or lack of authority leaves things in a disorganized mess. The inability to get organized just puts off the challenge to another day. Megalomania or delusions of grandeur begin to crowd out common sense.

Change: ⬆ You may find yourself holding power or securing boundaries for the benefit of all, rather than just serving yourself. Consider what changes when you approach things in a responsible way. Organising things with courage. Taking a more pragmatic or realistic attitude toward life. Taking charge of your life rather than aimlessly following.

⬇ Censorious attitudes or overly rigid structures make life feel narrow. Indecisiveness or sitting on the fence means that others have to do your work. Failure to lead leaves things in disarray. Having been in control, you leave the field to another.

Clearing the Way: ⬆ Allowing things to be administrated or organized fairly frees up things. Check that your governing qualities don't become too domineering. Paternalistic or chauvinistic attitudes can restrict the authority or liberty of others. Scrambling for position immerses you in competition for dominance or hierarchy. Where do you need to set stronger boundaries or structures?
⬇ Authoritarian tyranny is in control. Abuse of the masculine or failure to maintain good boundaries diminishes your self-image. Autocracy stifles progress.

Environmental: Authentic guardianship of the wild. Paternalistic governments or structures. Maintaining good borders, policing territory. The official or elected government. The dominant species. The exploitation of men and boys. Global warming, the greenhouse effect. Sovereignty or its loss. Honouring the boundaries of every life-form.

Questions:
Who needs to take the authority?
What is the best way for things to be ordered?
How are you called to be authentic and responsive?

V THE HIEROPHANT

Image: Against a grey sky, a pope in a triple crown sits on a throne between two pillars. He is dressed in a red cope and pallium and raises his right hand in blessing, while he carries a patriarchal cross in his left hand. Before him kneel two tonsured clerics in copes with roses and lilies. Between them, at the pope's feet, are crossed golden keys.

Focus:
"I bless the whole of life."
"I mediate the sacred powers."
"I teach the doctrine of grace."

Background: The Hierophant's deep understanding supports and upholds all with a sacred focus. Learning the rules and conventions of anything doesn't mean you have to become a slave to them, merely their master: those spiritual guidelines are there to support the soul. When you have learned the basics, your own specialisms and style will dictate how you change and influence things for yourself. This card provides sacred guidance, reminding everyone of the spiritual dimension of life. Traditionally, the pope governed marriage and alliances, as well as education and learning. Waite also gives, "Marriage, alliance, captivity, servitude; by another account, mercy and goodness; inspiration; the man to whom the Querent has recourse. Reversed: Society, good understanding, concord, overkindness, weakness."

Opportunity: ⬆ Inspired by excellence, you can add something of value to the tradition, re-enthusing conventionally-held codes with powerfully supportive concepts. Preserving or reinstating the heritage with style. Skilful insights or professing a skill enables you to inspire others. You can give wise advice or counsel to the uncertain.

⬇ Doing things by the book. Imbuing guilt in others. Intergenerational friction. Clinging to outmoded ways stultifies things. Traditional methods are compromised.

Change: ⬆ By transforming the mundane into the spiritual, you lift the whole way that people live. Revelatory ideas, initiation into ritual patterns, or following a spiritual way gives you a sense of expansion. Instructing or mentoring the young or inexperienced, you can bring things alive. You can bridge two divides by your skill. Reappreciate or reform your union or agreements.

⬇ Holding fixed or dogmatic views limits your potential. Beware of becoming enthralled by a self-appointed guru or by popular opinion. Unprincipled behaviour leads to ostracism. Be prepared to break your agreements or union.

Clearing the Way: ⬆ Being spiritually or morally coercive, you can limit the blessing. Abiding by the narrow rules of the institution or social mores, you fail to inspire. How can you be of better service to the community? Failing to practice what you preach opens you to accusations of hypocrisy.

⬇ Throwing over the traces or flouting the conventions can bring freedom. Iconoclasm breaks down barriers or old figureheads. Holding unorthodox views. Rebellion or civil disobedience opens the way to better social life.

Environmental: Blessing the work. Sacred power or dominant religion. Conventional piety. Fundamentalism. Deep ecumenism. Intergenerational friction over shared values. Forming alliances and unions

to strengthen things. Spiritual principles that sustain good relationships between species. Living as if everything was holy or had a soul
and consciousness. Honouring all life as sacred.

Questions:
Where is a blessing needed?
What spiritual values need to be upheld in this situation?
How do you bridge your gifts and the world needs?

VI THE LOVERS

Image: Against a yellow sky in which the
sun is fully radiant, a naked Adam regards
Eve, while she regards a red-winged,
purple-clad angel who appears from a
cloud above them. Behind Eve is a snake
wound around the Tree of the Knowledge
of Good and Evil, while behind Adam
is the Tree of Life. Behind them is a
single mountain.

Focus:
"We hold the balance of choice and desire."
"We find the place of meeting."
"Between us, we fulfil life's promise."

Background: When love strikes, no one can ever predict the result.
When you make a decision of your own free will, you can experience
the freedom to fulfil your heart's desire. This is a card of choice and
of pledge, where desire and attraction are sifted until there is either

a perfect equilibrium or a harmonious union of opposites. Waite changed the Lovers card to portray the Garden of Eden with the Angel, rather than showing a man between two women and the arrow of Eros. Despite his notions of antediluvian innocence, the card is very much about the physical attraction between people, from the instinct to mate with the right partner to the heart's impulse to follow something that gives fulfilment. Waite also gives, "Attraction, love, beauty, trials overcome. Reversed: Failure, foolish designs. Another account speaks of marriage frustrated and contrarieties of all kinds."

Opportunity: ⬆ Love is in the air. The marriage of true minds and hearts or a real bond of friendship is in the cards. Unions, mergers, contracts, or the agreements you enter into have a special magic. Emotional ties develop into full-blown relationships. The fulfilment of desire or the satisfaction of passion.
⬇ Unreliable partners or the betrayal or friends. You suffer unrequited love or else stalk the uninterested. Broken contracts or promises. Separation or divorce. Jealousy, envy, or possessiveness limits the scope of a relationship.

Change: ⬆ You have your hands on the magical attractor that holds things together or makes them work. The opportunity to test how things or people gel together is here. You need to find the way to communicate and relate in a simple or artless way. Prepare to make a choice or important decision.
⬇ Inharmonious gatherings as a result of mixed agendas. Poor or confused choices endanger your stability. You are stuck on the horns of a dilemma. Misunderstandings between close friends or partners.

Clearing the Way: ⬆ The way you explore or fail to register loyalty and commitment defines the relationships you will have. Issues of trust need to be re-negotiated. Ambivalent relationships or mere infatuations may need clarification. Determine your own values before merging with those of another.

⬇ You engage in a struggle for dominance. Divergent goals divide you both or split up relationships. Repulsion or infatuation switches the relationship on and off in succession. Staying true to yourself guides you through. Listen to your innermost heart.

Environmental: Tending the garden. Recognizing the gifts of all species. The mating season. The natural attraction and interdependency of nature. Population increase. Genetic manipulation, DNA mapping. Making choices that will honour future generations. Welcoming love into the equation. Hearkening to the song of the universe. Honouring the messages of the heart.

Questions:
Where is your love bestowed?
What is being reciprocated?
What can be fulfilled?

VII THE CHARIOT

Image: Against a yellow sky, a charioteer is in the cockpit of a chariot drawn by a pair of black-and-white sphinxes. He is dressed in armour with dish-shaped epaulettes upon his shoulders, shaped like the moon. In his right hand is a wand, while on the front of the chariot is a shield showing a spinning top. Over him is a starry canopy, and on his head, a starry diadem.

Focus:
"I have perfect faith in myself."
"The mind triumphs when discipline drives."
"I hold a steady course."

Background: The Chariot prevails over obstacles, with the energy and confidence to see things through. It has the drive that fuels plans and enterprises and keeps them on the road. Victory and success do not arrive overnight: they come by mastering adversities, by maintaining discipline and vision. By establishing an identity in your field, you step closer to your own triumph and have your hands upon the reins. Whether challenged by competition or rising above distractions, you can keep focus and maintain stamina to come through. The Chariot is based upon the triumphal chariot of a Roman commander's victorious return as well as upon the Renaissance procession float. Waite also gives, "Succour, providence also war, triumph, presumption, vengeance, trouble. Reversed: Riot, quarrel, dispute, litigation, defeat."

Opportunity: ⬆ Mastery brings victory. Self-confidence and self-discipline enable you to harness your abilities toward a great purpose. Harnessing your resources helps you attain your goal. Navigating life with controlled steering. Travel broadens your outlook and brings prestige. Determination and courage ensure that you beat the competition. Ambition to succeed.
⬇ Plans come unstuck. Things are unworkable in their present state. Tests and trials are needed to get things moving. Overconfidence is deflated by setback or failure. Overambition is self-defeating.

Change: ⬆ You are making a great leap forward and getting your hands upon the reins or steering wheel. Success and fame are the rewards of achievement, so be prepared to handle them. Setting yourself a goal will keep your forward momentum steady and sustain your efforts.

⬇ Failure of imagination or fears run you off the road. Rash judgments change the way ahead. Stalemate. Journeys are delayed or cancelled. Letting your anger get the better of you.

Clearing the Way: ⬆ Being grimly determined can make you grip the steering wheel rather too humourlessly. How much faith do you have in your enterprise? Admiration and influence keep you on the road: have you enough interest to continue without these to propel you?

⬇ Letting go of the controls for good or ill. Overshadowed or threatened by another's success. Usurping another's power to get ahead. Curbing your impulses keeps you on the road.

Environmental: Public celebrations. The progress of an army. Making an inspection of land. Transport. Entering the course of a development phase. Finding the right way for things to unfold. Yoking together disparate groups in union for the common good. Honouring the power to move forward.

Questions:
Where is your will directed?
What keeps you on the road?
Where are things veering off course?

VIII STRENGTH

Image: Against a yellow sky, a white-robed woman with a garland on her head places her hands upon the jaws of a lion, closing its mouth. Over her head is a lemniscate, symbol of eternity.

Focus:
"I endure and overcome."
"I use moral courage to persevere."
"I master myself first."

Background: Fortitude arises from the moral power within. When the coin of fear is face-uppermost, it locks down power. When the reverse of the coin is uppermost, then power is in control, enabling the fortitude to cope with things with conviction and courage. When you connect to the power within, you can be encouraged and supported. Waite swapped cards 8 and 11 in the Tarot sequence to accord with Golden Dawn astrological ascriptions to Libra and Leo. Strength was originally one of the cardinal virtues, Fortitude. Waite also gives, "Power, energy, action, courage, magnanimity; also, complete success and honours. Reversed: Despotism, abuse of power, weakness, discord, sometimes even disgrace."

Opportunity: ⬆ Enduring strength sees you through. You have the confidence that there's enough fuel to keep you going. Having the strength of mind or moral courage to engage with things. Struggling with or taming the forces of life.
⬇ Letting things get on top of you. Things are out of control, and so you fall back on enforcement, bribes, or persuasion. Meeting opposition with brutality. Debility has you beaten.

Change: ⬆Things are building to a crescendo that will change your life. Your inner conviction will help you navigate your way. Take courage and fortitude to accept challenges. You have the capacity for whatever transpires. Show forbearance and keep calm as the pace increases.

⬇ Self-righteous vindication is taken as weakness. Allowing things to power down quietly is the best course. Going into overkill when a smaller effort will have the same effect. Audacity and risk-taking are needed. Appeasement and compliance are not going to work.

Clearing the Way: ⬆ Taming the beast takes resolution and careful handling. Check up on the health of your mind, body, and spirit. Don't stay in survival mode too long without refreshing resources. Finding help, or burnout may result. Hubris will lead you into biting off too much.

⬇ Enforced compliance may only be as deep as lip service. Feeding your fears makes them grow. When the odds are overwhelming, learn to delegate or seek help. Acknowledging your limitations may be sensible.

Environmental: Taming the unruly. Caring for animals in captivity. Introducing species back into the wild. Animal-breeding programmes. Master and servant. Introducing civilizing influences. Soothing mental or physical distress. Enforced measures. Finding inner strength and fortitude in times of trials. Going for overkill, despotism, or missionary zeal. Honouring the power of life.

Questions:
Where is restraint called for?
What urges must be reined in?
What needs the courage of your convictions?

IX THE HERMIT

Image: Against an evening blue sky, a bearded elder in a hood and long grey robe walks in the snow, holding a lantern high in his right hand and a staff in his left. The light of the lantern is in the form of a star.

Focus:
"I follow the eternal light."
"I think first before I act."
"I let wisdom guide me."

Background: Returning to the centre and the stillness brings wisdom. The Hermit has the wisdom to wait and let things mature in their own time, and the concentration to allow things to develop at the proper time. By the light of his lantern, you can find the wisdom that you seek. No one is ever alone, for the soul's *daimon* or genius walks ever beside you, guiding you by its original vision. When it is hard to find the best possible way forward, you can enter the stillness and perceive more possibilities. Waite gives, "Prudence, circumspection; also, and especially treason, dissimulation, roguery, corruption. Reversed: Concealment, disguise, policy, fear, unreasoned caution."

Opportunity: ⬆ Searching for guidance, spiritual truth, illumination, or wisdom, you can find a mentor, idea, or role model. A good time for a necessary space of reassessment or introspection. Communing with your *daimon,* or genius, happens in the quiet spaces. Originality and inventiveness give you the edge. Exercising prudence.

⬇ Seeking for guidance or wisdom from inferior or misleading sources. The premature exposure of your plans. The fear of being alone or unwanted haunts you. Operating without a guide or compass unfocuses you. The pursuit of perfectionism leads you to procrastinate.

Change: ⬆ As your plans mature, you will need a fallow period to allow further creation to flow. Prepare to withdraw, rest, or recover. Taking the advice of an older or wiser person will help. Someone you trust gives you the opportunity to be yourself.
⬇ Entering society again after a period of withdrawal means picking up the tempo. Going into sullen reclusive mode or retreating into a private world after a rejection. Claiming a skill you don't actually possess. Heavy with depressive thoughts. Stepping out of unhelpful ideologies.

Clearing the Way: ⬆ Giving a listening space to a friend or allowing an idea space to expand can clear the present impasse. Prudent reflection stops you from making a bad choice. What is the voice of your conscience telling you? Denying what's obvious or hiding it away is a useless affectation.
⬇ Refusing to mature or act your age. Failure to listen to your inner promptings. Furtively concealing something. Compulsive avoidance. Struggling alone with something. Over-caution leads to loss of opportunity.

Environmental: A contemplative retreat, a hermetic existence. Solitary species. Self-abnegation, asceticism. Tightening your belt, living within your means. Intentional communities. Over-caution in creating efficient policies. Providence. Silence, sound pollution. Keeping a low profile. Micro-solutions. Arctic regions. Honouring the wisdom within.

Questions:
What does prudence dictate?
What arises from the silence?
How can discretion help now?

WHEEL *of* FORTUNE.

X WHEEL OF FORTUNE

Image: Against a blue sky with clouds, a disk engraved with sigils and the word TARO turns in the air. At the top of it sits a blue sphinx with a sword, to its left is a yellow serpent, while at its base is a red, dog-headed god. In the four corners are the four winged holy creatures of angel, eagle, lion, and ox.

Focus:
"I turn and ever shall."
"Who loses will rise again; who wins will fall."
"I teach by every experience."

Background: The Wheel of Fortune is the original time changer of all phases and cycles, giving us the wisdom of experience as an everyday opportunity. The cyclic nature of the universe ensures that nothing lasts forever, except as a restatement or variation of a previous theme. Whatever decisions, actions, or words arise from you, they open a new and different door every time to a path that will teach you much. When you step into the present moment, you can find the appropriate opening of opportunity. Waite changed Fortuna's wheel into one with the serpent of Typhon, the Sphinx, and the dog-headed Hermanubis. While these beings whirl around the wheel, the four holy creatures at the corners remain constant. Waite gives the meanings as, "Destiny, fortune, success, elevation, luck, felicity. Reversed: Increase, abundance, superfluity."

Opportunity: ⬆ Fateful encounters and experiences await timely discovery. You flow with the creative possibility of the cycle. Cyclic changes move you to the next place. Evolutionary forces mean you cannot keep changes from happening.

⬇ Unpredictable patterns mean you are unable to line things up as you would wish. You are caught in a run of mishaps or bad luck. A sense of being stuck on a treadmill or whirligig.

Change: ⬆ Ideas, projects, or relationships pass into their next phase. Taking the chance while it's offered means never regretting. Fortune's changes come in quick succession. Things are on their way up or about to surprise. Be prepared to adapt or to be flexible or versatile. Suddenly feeling lucky.

⬇ Realising that things are out of phase or past their best. Mood swings make it hard to get perspective. A sense of being out of time or in the wrong place. You keep missing the opportunities.

Clearing the Way: ⬆ The ripples resulting from your actions, words, or decisions are already stirring and changing things. Consider what you are setting in train and its effects. Being fatalistic keeps you turning on the wheel. The opportunities you've neglected come home to roost or fester. Where can you start afresh?

⬇ Speculation or gambling comes to grief. Recurrent events that haven't been laid to rest. A sense of justice or rightness. Blaming your bad luck. Putting the past behind you.

Environmental: Understanding cause and effect. The turning and cycles of time. Maintaining balanced government. Ebb and flow of tides. The exigencies of the present moment. Composting the old to renew the new. Honouring the cycles of life.

Questions:
What have you set in motion?
Where in its cycle is the current situation?
Which experience is ready to be grasped?

XI JUSTICE

Image: Against a yellow sky, a crowned woman sits upon a throne between two pillars. In her right hand is an upraised sword; in her left hand is a pair of scales. Behind her, between the pillars, is a purple curtain.

Focus:
"I am utterly impartial."
"I serve the truth above all."
"I vindicate the innocent."

Background: The neutrality of Justice allows her to clearly see the truth, so that no one suffers oppression: her human counterparts, the judges, listen for her oracle, so that the workings of justice bring equality to all. Knowing yourself is a great part of this process, as well as standing up for what is of value. It is not just a matter of apportioning blame or innocence, but taking personal responsibility that enables you to be objectively fair. When you discern the balance point, you can be yourself authentically as well as speak the truth and act equitably. This was originally the executive virtue within the four cardinal virtues. Waite gives, "Equity, rightness, probity, executive; triumph of the deserving side in law. Reversed: Law in all its departments, legal complications, bigotry, bias, excessive severity."

Opportunity: ⬆ Justice, truth, and honesty are your friends. Your integrity is vindicated or your case upheld. You enjoy balanced partnerships or make an equitable contract. Making a fair assessment or account of a project. You mediate or arbitrate between two disaffected parties.

⬇ Seeking representation or an advocate to plead your case. Legal difficulties or false accusation means you must clear your name. The rule of law is overset.

Change: ⬆ Negotiate contracts clearly. Be prepared to arbitrate on legal matters or take advice. Measuring up to the situation or perceiving your motives is required. Seeking justice or vindication for yourself or another. You seek to give or receive fair exchange or good measure. Prepare to be impartial rather than to take sides.

⬇ Someone wants to play the blame game. You have to deal with corrupt individuals or institutions. Negotiations break down. Something needs to be adjusted. Trying to do the right thing makes it worse.

Clearing the Way: ⬆ A legal case, tribunal, or examination means you have to account for yourself. Where do you have to be true to your nature? The need to avenge or get even may be blinding you to the truth. Rational decisions may be leaving mercy out of the picture. Self-justification is alienating someone.

⬇ Unfairness or injustice persists until an advocate or mediator is appointed. You can own up to your mistakes or misdemeanours and face the consequences.

Environmental: Truth, both inconvenient and necessary. Taking into account the rights and wrongs. Measuring and sifting what serves the ethical balance of the world. Propaganda, media-speak, prejudice, or presumption, which clouds the situation. Investigative tribunals into corruption and misrepresentation. Transformative justice. Restoration of agency to victims. Recognition of the rights of all beings. Honouring the eternal truth.

Questions:
How is equity and fairness best served?
What is true here?
What is the fairest course of action for you now?

XII THE HANGED MAN

THE HANGED MAN.

Image: Against a grey sky, a man hangs by his right foot from a cross-pole that is garlanded with ivy. The man's left leg crosses behind his right leg, while his two hands are fastened behind him. Around his serene face, a nimbus of light shines.

Focus:
"I am changed by suffering."
"I am prepared to transform."
"I await what comes next."

Background: The Hanged Man explores the dedication to our destiny. Maturity of outlook and a consent to let things be themselves often result in a totally different perspective, although nothing else seems to have outwardly changed. When the world is turned upside down, you have to have streetwise senses to find your way. What looks or feels like sacrifice or inconvenience can actually be the gap through which you emerge into greater freedom or a new perspective that will change your life. By moving into a place of commitment, you risk everything but you can also gain everything. The traditional card of the traitor is rendered by Waite into something nearer martyrdom or an initiatic sacrifice. Waite gives, "Wisdom, circumspection, discernment, trials, sacrifice, intuition, divination, prophecy. Reversed: Selfishness, the crowd, body politic."

Opportunity: ⬆ Trusting the process or entering into rapport, you gain insight. Letting something go in order to heal. Pausing to review your options or finding alternatives. Your self-sacrifice is in aid of higher principles or better conditions. Commitment to your principles makes you a role-model for others. Aligning yourself with your destiny.

⬇ Prior agendas or obligations must be dealt with first. Things are currently stuck or waiting. A feeling of restraint or dancing to someone's else tune. Enjoying the acclaim of the martyr or moaner. Entering deeply into the process requires calm surrender.

Change: ⬆ You need to look at things from a different perspective during this period of your life. As you undergo the stripping away of inessentials, the real you can emerge completely. The wisdom you gain will be proportionate to your hardship and experience. Tests and trials change your life. You pay the full price for commitment to your destiny.

⬇ Being under pressure to change how you do things. On the horns of a dilemma, there's little point trying to control the outcome. Larger forces are guiding events.

Clearing the Way: ⬆ Getting hung up on your illusions or suspicions weaves a web in which you get stuck. Sitting on the fence is of no avail; only your total engagement will get you through. How are you letting other people's projections dictate your life? When you feel restricted by fate, try exploring your destiny instead.

⬇ Ignoring or neglecting your duty. Conformity to others' opinions leaves you no liberty. Allowing yourself to be painted into a corner by events. You have to attend to the details before you can proceed.

Environmental: The pain of climate change. The consequence of poor governmental decisions upon every level of life. Blaming other causes than the obvious ones. Retrenchment of privileges to bring better solutions. Pollution and its clearing. Inevitable suffering as a result of bad choices. Re-educating ourselves to live in a better way. Betrayal of the kinship of life. Punishment. Vengeance. Blood feuds. Allowing others to decide or act for you. Honouring the consequences of every action, word, or thought.

Questions:
What is held up, delayed, or suspended?
What needs to change and what will it involve?
What is your duty or obligation in this situation?

XIII DEATH

Image: Against a grey sky, the skeleton of Death, attired in black armour, rides a white horse over a field of dead and dying people of all ranks and ages. In his left hand is a black banner on which is a white rose. In the middle ground is a river with a ship sailing in the between light. In the distance the sun rises or sets between two towers.

Focus:
"I come for all mortal beings."
"Let me remove what is decaying."
"I clear the way for new life."

Background: Without change and evolution, things stultify and stagnate. The world is cleared of decay lest it become full of corruption. However glorious your status, Death clears it all away to make things new. Death brings the sharpest change, yet many try to become members of the living dead by their inability to change. When you let go of things willingly and with full knowledge, you can cleanse the path ahead. Waite gave this card a banner of the mystic rose of life, rather than the more traditional scythe, to remind us that death's change makes room for life. Waite gives, "End, mortality, destruction, corruption also, for a man, the loss of a benefactor for a woman, many contrarieties; for a maid, failure of marriage projects. Reversed: Inertia, sleep, lethargy, petrifaction, somnambulism; hope destroyed."

Opportunity: ⬆ Endings bring change and transformation. The overturning of outworn ideas or situations or the disruption of old patterns brings you relief from worry. After clearing the way, you can make a new beginning. Saying goodbye to what you've loved or known. Undergoing a state of loss or bereavement.

⬇ Shoring up the appearances, despite the pain. The shock of change. Struggles are at an end. A near-death experience.

Change: ⬆ The dismemberment of your ordered life ensures that decisions have been taken out of your hands. You may have to take ruthless yet compassionate action. Accepting the inevitable, you can prepare to welcome change. Accept Death's embrace like a lover and refresh your life.

⬇ Dicing with death or trying to get through the door as it closes. Changes that make little difference. Hanging on without much avail. Deaths or endings are deferred. Inertia sets in.

Clearing the Way: ⬆ If you are hanging on to things rather than letting go of what is fading or ending, consider how can you make space for renewal. Resistance to change merely brings stultification. Eliminate some old attitudes that have been shoring you up.

⬇ Cheating or deluding yourself can bring you a living death. By avoiding the burning issues of your life, you risk being haunted by anxiety. Health issues emerge as a result of ignoring the mainspring of your vocation.

Environmental: The downfall and ending of reputations, institutions, people, and species. The clearing away of waste or pollution. The extinction of a species. Radical solutions to environmental problems. Having to let go of forms of behaviour or habits in the face of great change. Massacre. Pandemic. Honouring death as the renewer of life.

Questions:
What outworn principles are you clinging to?
What needs to come to an end?
What do you finally need to let go of?

XIV TEMPERANCE

Image: Against a grey sky, a white-clad angel with dark-rose and purple wings and a shining diadem pours water from one chalice into another. On his chest is a square with a yellow triangle within it. The left foot is on the land, while the right is in the water of a pool. To the right grow wild irises, while to the left, a path leads to distant mountains where the sun rises.

Focus:
"I am the reconciler of all things."
"I temper the anger and foster peace."
"I mediate the healing."

Background: The reconciliation of opposites and their synthesis are met in this card. When you learn to adapt and negotiate, you can find the balancing point. The synthesis of all that you are capable of being or doing is the cutting edge of life. Temperance is the least heeded of all the cardinal virtues in our time, and one of the most needed. Waite gives this card of traditional restraint and moderation a more esoteric overtone of eternal life, after the visitation of Death. Waite gives, "Economy, moderation, frugality, management, accommodation. Reversed: Things connected with churches, religions, sects, the priesthood, sometimes even the priest who will marry the querent; also, disunion, unfortunate combinations, competing interests."

Opportunity: ⬆ Your chance to bring the harmonious fusion of complementary forces helps you adapt or moderate your plans. You can find creative solutions that lead to compatibility and balanced living. Your part in the healing of the environment is to find the centre where everyone and everything can flourish together.
⬇ There is a conflict of interests or a clash between opposites. Lack of moderation spoils the environment. Anger creates misunderstanding between people. There is a failure of flow.

Change: ⬆ The chance to mitigate extremes also enables you to combine resources or potentials. Your own creative flow of ideas grows and changes as you blend or merge with different ideas. By mediation or arbitration, you can create a united front out of a disparate group of people. This requires delicacy of touch and the ability to respect disparate views.
⬇ You become acrimoniously enmeshed in other people's affairs. Things go to extremes and pull apart a working relationship.

Clearing: ⬆ Self-indulgence or addictive behaviour can take your physical, mental, and spiritual health out of balance. Merging with every new or popular idea scatters your potential. Find your balance point or create your own gauge of personal warning signs that herald you down the path to excess: they also chart the way back to balance.
⬇ Reactionary living or exploring the extremes becomes your raison d'être. Your polarised views antagonize others or create conflict. A disharmonious life leaves you with few friends or a sense of frustration that spills over aggressively.

Environmental: The world slews out of balance as greed or excess dominates. Recycling. Rivers and water courses. Water filtration and clarity. Rewilding nature. Peace and reconciliation after excess and brutality. The priesthood of humanity as an agency of adaptation and health for the world. Reconciling those in opposition. Reconsidering mainstream mindsets. Honouring the healing that results from moderation.

Questions:
Where do you need to show restraint or moderation?
Where is healing needed?
What can be brought peaceably together?

XV THE DEVIL

Image: Against a black sky, a goat-headed and horned being with bat wings crouches upon a black altar, where a ring holds bound a naked woman and man who have neck rings attached to its chain. The devil has an inverted pentagram on its head, while the human pair have horns and tails. The devil's right hand is raised in the mockery of a blessing while it holds an inverted torch in its left. His lower quarters are shaggy, and he has clawlike feet.

Focus:
"I bind everyone to my service."
"I forge the chains of fear and subversion."
"I foster self-delusion."

Background: The loss or lessening of humanity in any situation is also the loss of common sense and compassion. When we make habitual links without realizing the consequences, we become enslaved, but when our humanity reasserts itself, we find freedom. Engaging with what is dangerous for you may lead to instant gratification, but it may not deal with what lurks beneath. The Devil challenges us to see our own distorted image. By refusing to be sucked deeper into unhealthy habits and ways of behaving and believing that sap our power, we can overthrow obsessions. Waite gives, "Ravage, violence, vehemence, extraordinary efforts, force, fatality; that which is predestined but is not for this reason evil. Reversed: Evil fatality, weakness, pettiness, blindness."

Opportunity: ⬆ When you allow the limitation of fear or the colonization of obsession, you enter into an indulgent captivity. Inflexibility is leading to stagnation, imprisonment, or bondage. Ignorance, pessimism, or self-limitation is dominant. You feel limited by being in the shadow of something fearful. A chance to resist violence and coercion.
⬇ Things are released from bondage. You are liberated from concepts and ideas. Recovering your common sense or humanity brings reality to the situation and helps you overcome fear.

Change: ⬆ It begins by a slight bending of the rules to your personal requirement, and before you know where you are, you are ruled by your demons and habits. Addictive gratification is often the neglect of creative possibilities. Being caught up in the appearances, you can neglect what really matters.

⬇ You recover from a close shave or avoid temptation. By rechecking your motivations, you return to your proper coordinates. You can free yourself from doubts and fears by spontaneity and humour.

Clearing the Way: ⬆ Obstacles that must be overcome take on gigantic stature. Past traumas may be dictating your reactions. Finding a scapegoat for your blame ignores your part in the matter. A fatal attraction is sapping your forces. What wisdom do you reclaim as yours from the sea of fear?
⬇ The overthrow of illusions may lead you to extremes. Mockery and laughter deflate pomposity or bugaboos. Codependent entanglements have the power to press your buttons, but you can resist reacting.

Environmental: Coercion and collusion. Force majeure. War. Forging the chains of human habit. Addiction, manipulation, the distortions of self-interest or false belief. The defilement and neglect of nature. Demonization of the other. The greed and fear that enslave. Pornography. The desacralization of spirituality. The bloating of those unprincipled individuals in power who project images of their own all-powerfulness. Enslavement. Bonded servitude. Honouring the consent of all life-forms.

Questions:
Where must you show your humanity?
What are the chains that bind you?
What collusion or dependency holds sway?

XVI THE TOWER

Image: Against a black sky filled with grey clouds, the crown upon a solitary tower built on a rock is struck by lightning, and fire issues forth. Two robed figures fall headlong to the earth. From the lightning, sparks of fire shine.

Focus:
"I level all things to the ground."
"Pride goes before a fall."
"I overwhelm and reduce."

Background: The Tower is the liberator who breaks down the boundaries when things become insupportable and reveals the cracks. Old conditionings, ancient régimes, and proud plans all go to the wall when their time has come. Whatever has been shoring up the walls, they can no longer stand. When we let go of control or reject ideas that control your mind, we can experience the release of pressure and the relief. This is the traditional card of the disaster, the upheaval or the unexpected crash that inevitably comes. Waite gives, "Misery, distress, indigence, adversity, calamity, disgrace, deception, ruin. It is a card in particular of unforeseen catastrophe. Reversed: The same but in a lesser degree; also, oppression, imprisonment, tyranny."

Opportunity: ⬆ Sudden and unexpected change is here. There is a breakdown of the system or natural forces at work to bring things down. You may be lucky to anticipate this, but be vigilant, since it strikes fast as lightning! You receive a flash of revelation that changes everything. The transfiguration of your hopes or plans cleanses the way. Pretence is stripped away to reveal reality. You suffer a blow to your self-esteem. Cultivate humility in the face of great changes. ⬇ Disaster is narrowly averted or you get out in time. A period of upheaval and little rest or relief. Setbacks intensify. Things need to be detoxified.

Change: ⬆ A reversal of energies is coming quickly. You may be subliminally aware of the changes to come but are still ignoring them. Loss of your cosy security or routine or the realisation of your limitations is bringing you into an unknown land. Institutions or empires fail or fall. A physical collapse or economic crash means you have to approach things differently.
⬇ Crisis still threatens. Clearing up after a breakdown or break-in. You accept the changes, trimming your sails to new winds.

Clearing the Way: ⬆ Painful self-awareness or sudden news may leave you petrified by shock. Whatever you've been shoring up finds its downfall, and no amount of hubris will maintain it. Reputations are tarnished or masks fall away. What have you been hiding from?
⬇ Things fruitlessly hang on or don't come to pass. A sense of being under a cloud that never rains relief. Denying what needs release or continuing to turn a blind eye to things. Change is desperately needed or the cracks will extend.

Environmental: Breakdown of a civilization, the collapse of régimes. Environmental or natural disaster. Dismantling outworn values over generations. Human hubris. Tyranny ends in overthrow. Bankruptcy. Humility after pride. Networks fail. The legacy of generational traumas. Starting again from a levelled society after disaster. Honouring the breakdown of out-worn patterns and values in exchange for ones that work.

Questions:
What has been shoring things up?
What is the real state of affairs?
What will radical change entail?

XVII THE STAR

Image: Against a blue sky, in a green landscape, a naked woman kneels upon the bank of a pool, with her right foot in the water. She pours out two jugs of water, one upon the land, the other upon the water. To her left is a small tree with a bird in it. Above her in the sky is a large, yellow, eight-pointed star, with seven smaller white stars.

Focus:
"I pour out life more abundantly."
"I restore faith and hope."
"I clothe everything with beauty."

Background: The Star restores the natural ease to daily life after difficult times and revitalizes things, pouring out life afresh. When you feel dinted after a long struggle, The Star reminds you to allow the natural cycles and processes to refuel and refresh you. Your innate destiny can pour forth and be revitalized by the renewal of hope and vision. This card gives the refreshment and beauty back after hard times and can speak about prophecy, vision, and blessing. Waite gives an uncharacteristically dour set of meanings to begin his list: "Loss, theft, privation, abandonment; hope and bright prospects, Reversed: Arrogance, haughtiness, impotence."

Opportunity: ⬆ Hope and inspiration bestow their peace and promise. There is a raising of popular consciousness that supports a new vision in which everyone can share. You are invited to respond with altruistic compassion. Things come around to a better place. Your expectations and aspirations are confident.

⬇ Ideas are not ready to be exposed or plans are too diffuse. Inspiration has dried up and needs to be refreshed. Conditions are too unstable to make headway. Your aspirations seem unrealistic.

Change: ⬆ This is the beginning of a new cycle with the prospect of brighter tomorrows. Prepare to perceive the bigger picture and be optimistic. Emotional expansiveness enables you to enjoy refreshment, healing, or renewal. Things go with ease and grace. With faith in the future, you can see your way clear.

⬇ Repressing your emotions after abuse or ingratitude. False hopes are aroused or dashed. You are unable to find the right guidance. By refusing to look up, you miss the moment. Immersing yourself in unattainable projects or relationships.

Clearing the Way: ⬆ You scour the sky for omens of a change for the better and yet fail to welcome them. Self-esteem is at low ebb, and the prospect of receiving a gift or being recognized is overwhelming. Find a place of sanctuary and allow a time of recovery and rebuilding. What is the hope that you keep ever before you?

⬇ Living off hope gone stale, you are looking in the wrong part of the sky. Credulously following every sign leads to confusion. Problems with your self-image continue, so seek help.

Environmental: Reconnection to sources of refreshment returns after the storm or upheaval. Purifying the waters. Irrigating the earth. Allowing the larger view to bring hope. Going back to nature. Lakes, pool, and wells. Simplicity. Neglect of beauty. Keeping faith with the discouraged. Returning to your true self, after a period of scattering. Rededication, forgiveness. Honouring the harmony at the heart of all things.

Questions:
Where are you being guided?
What hope or expectation shimmers on the horizon for you?
How is life returning?

XVIII THE MOON

Image: Against a blue sky, the old moon, with the new moon in its arms, shines down sparks of light upon a sleeping landscape. In the foreground, a crayfish arises from the pool, while the path leading from it stretches into the distance, passing two towers. On either side of the path are a dog and wolf.

Focus:
"I shine my reflected light by night."
"My phases influence every cell of life."
"I guide you by my deep influences."

Background: The Moon is the keeper of the mysterious and unconscious tides that govern this whole world. Its lunar influence heightens emotion, stirring the deep evolutionary tides to new growth. When we admit fantastic or intuitive impressions, we may strengthen our power to visualize, but we may also be overwhelmed by deeply submerged fears about the unknown. Daydreams and night dreams can be pleasurable or scary, but they provide the creative medium that bring your plans from the unconsciousness of the crayfish's pool into manifestation. The French expression "between dog and wolf" denotes the half light of twilight, when it is difficult to distinguish forms or colour, and informs the two canines here. Waite gives, "Hidden enemies, danger, calumny, darkness, terror, deception, occult forces, error. Reversed: Instability, inconstancy, silence, lesser degrees of deception and error."

Opportunity: ⬆ Dreams and visions are reflected and enhanced by your imagination in this cycle. Validate your intuition or psychic intimations by testing the information by trial and error. You may need a period of fallowness or introspection. By observing the cyclic patterns of growth, your plans can land in a creative medium.
⬇ Swimming in a stream of consciousness, you are drawn from personal into collective views. In the grip of unfounded surmise or rumour. Waning influences restore you to reality.

Change: ⬆ Cycles of birth and generation are turning, and something is trying to be born. A strong synchronicity shows you the way forward. This is a time to indulge your speculations and imaginings creatively. The seasonal round and the tides of time gear you into new activities or plans.
⬇ There are submerged dangers ahead. You feel psychically exhausted or played out. Flux and reflux leave you between the tides. You welcome alternative or irrational views.

Clearing the Way: ⬆ Fantasies or nightmares have you in their grip. Being under the influence of a strong compulsion or powerful, inchoate emotion, you are unable to see forward. A sense of bewilderment or confusion makes you step warily. Fluctuation of mood is clouding your judgment.

⬇ Unconscious impressions freak you out or make you insecure. A sense of being stalked or staked out. Mental confusion, paranoia, or derangement. When labouring under powerful illusions, check out what is real and what is not. Stop sleepwalking.

Environmental: Evolution. Light pollution. Exploring intuitive inscapes to reveal the spiritual tides that flow through you. Entering unknown territory. Following the guidance of dreams. Steering by instinct or intuition. Mutability, and degrees of change over time.
Collective viewpoints. Unconscious prejudices. Nighttime. Fear and suspicion. Honouring the unseen influences.

Questions:
What is waxing and what is waning?
Where are your instincts leading?
What unknown terrain is revealed by your dreams?

XIX THE SUN

Image: Against a blue sky, a many-rayed sun beams down upon a naked child who sits upon a white pony. The child has a feather in its hair and clutches a red banner. Behind the child is a wall, behind which sunflowers grow.

Focus:
"I shine upon all life."
"I bring health and happiness."
"I am grateful every day."

Background: Finding life's simple pleasures and allowing yourself to enjoy them without guilt is one of the delights of existence. While the sun shines, you can bathe in optimism, raise your spirits, and revel in physical pleasure. The Sun brings joy, health, and energy to all, as a gift that is simple and direct. Friendships, relationships, and plans flourish, and fortunes are restored. Here you can be carefree and open, without fear of compromise. Innocence and simplicity enable you to be true to yourself. When you allow yourself to experience simple enjoyment, the path can become clear and open before you. A sense of gratitude for all good things is the basis of radiant health. Waite gives, "Material happiness, fortunate marriage, contentment. Reversed: The same in a lesser sense."

Opportunity: ⬆ Health and energy are abroad, shedding radiance on everything. Your true vocation is realised at last. Clarity and directness enter into your dealings. You experience joy, freedom, or happiness. Recovery after illness or reconciliation after dispute also means the return of pleasure.

⬇ Happiness has a fly in its ointment. You are overshadowed by or overshadowing another. You miss the pleasure or the promise. Rationalist solutions outshine the simple and obvious.

Change: ⬆ Prepare to receive a radiant vitality in your life. A sense of enlightenment and wholeness comes to expand your views. Your generous sharing of good fortune gives joy to others. You enjoy recreation or holiday. A sense of accomplishment is yours. Doing things naturally brings satisfaction.
⬇ An enforced stay indoors. A heavy schedule obscures your happiness. You experience burnout or exhaustion. Confidence wanes or enthusiasm drains away. Doing things synthetically alienates yourself or others.

Clearing the Way: ⬆ Things come to light or out into the open in ways that expose you. The good fortune of others puts you into the shadow. You are unable to be transparent in your dealings with others. You long to have your innocence restored or to enjoy things with simplicity.
⬇ Gullible naivety leads you astray. You are expecting something for nothing, and that gets in the way of your good fortune. Your intolerance or sense of rightness is unjustified. Try to cultivate a loving heart by seeking the consolations of nature.

Environmental: Solar power. Solar flares disrupt. Desertification. Recognizing all life as kindred. The light behind all spiritual paths. Material benefits. Sharing your good fortune with community. Social media. Gladdening the circle of life. Thankfulness. Honouring the potential in every seed of life.

Questions:
What brings you into a healthier communion with life?
With whom can you share your joy?
For what do you give thanks?

XX JUDGEMENT

Image: Against a blue sky, an angel with dark-rose and purple wings emerges from a cloud to blow a trumpet, from which hangs a white flag with a red cross upon it. Below, naked forms arise from their graves and from their resting places in the waters: they raise their arms to the angel.

Focus:
"I restore and regenerate all things."
"I call forth potential from sleep."
"I awaken the wisdom of the ages."

Background: Judgement provides the chance for a new beginning and calls you to wake up. It can also recall something that is at the heart of your life but that you once set aside or thought moribund: you are encouraged to re-examine and make space for it again. Judgement is the great awakener of all that lies dormant. When it is time to move on, re-evaluate or come out of a situation where you've been stuck, this card opens the way. When the options shrink and there seems no way forward, you can redeem the energy and opportunity by transforming your life. Ridding yourself of burdens, you can forgive yourself and others, to bring transformation to all. Waite gives, "Change of position, renewal, outcome, total loss through lawsuit. Reversed: weakness, pusillanimity, simplicity; also, deliberation, decision, sentence."

Opportunity: ⬆ The regenerative influences around you bring renewal or transformation. After laying aside the past, you make a great leap forward. You are fulfilling what your ancestral heritage has invested in you. Awakening to new possibilities or re-evaluating your options.

⬇ You take a chance to clear the consequences of the past. The disbanding or dispersal of old groups and associations. By resisting the call to transform, you postpone healing and choose an illusory security.

Change: ⬆ The impulse to change or reform your life is coming. You experience a recapitulation of events or ideas in a new form. A vision that changes society completely is underway, and you are a part of it. You recover something you've lost sight of. You can stop checking your tally and forgive or let go.

⬇ You procrastinate while you check the options. Rejecting innovations, you stick with what you know. You experience a sense of alienation with new movements. You hang on for a better but illusory chance.

Clearing the Way: ⬆ Forgiveness or adjustment is difficult when you feed the grudge. You are now reaping what you once sowed. Someone digs up your past, and you are exposed. You need to reprogramme your outlook or ideas in order to move on.

⬇ Choosing to stay and be nourished by the drama rather than accepting change. Running apocalyptic scenarios in your mind hastens the end of your life. Painful memories still hold you hostage. Accept what needs to be laid down, and make your way without it.

Environmental: Restoring habitats, dormant species re-emerge. Silencing, criticism, and "being judged." Moving from torpor or ignorance into action and usefulness. Reclaiming land and potential. The cumulative heritage of the ages that waits to be found. Archaeology.

Restoring the sacred places. Giving voice and agency to Indigenous cultures. Ancestors. Taking up a conscious path that renews everything in your life. Honouring the regeneration of all things.

Questions:
Which of your long-held dreams is possible?
What needs to re-awaken?
Where is the hidden potential?

XXI THE WORLD

Image: Against a blue sky, a naked hermaphrodite, draped in a purple cloth, dances in the air, holding a double-ended wand in either hand. It is surrounded by a green garland. In each corner are the heads of the four holy creatures: the man, eagle, lion, and ox.

Focus:
"I dance for the promise of every life."
"I open every possibility for the good of all."
"I regard every part of the world at once."

Background: The World enables things to find their ultimate achievement and attain the wholeness of their encoded promise. By synthesising the gifts of all the elements, it opens up the possibilities to their greatest extent. It is encoded within all things and being, and its gift is the flowering of the promised potential. The World is able to draw upon all the resources and find the point where they can combine and be made available. When you pass beyond your own limitations and stand in your confidence, you can attain your goals harmoniously. The commonwealth of the Imperium is held together by mutual support and a collective commitment, inviting you to step beyond the merely personal and enter into all of it. Waite gives, "Assured success, recompense, voyage, route, emigration, flight, change of place. Reversed: Inertia, fixity, stagnation, permanence."

Opportunity: ⬆ Things reach their culmination, attainment, or perfection in this cycle. You are moving into the centre of things, where the recognition of rewards and honours is extended. The integration of your potential with the needs of the world creates the perfect medium for your talents.

⬇ Obligations drag you down. Work fails to reach completion. You never want this moment to end, and so you catch it by the tail. The honours are slow in arriving.

Change: ⬆ The right time and place is here. By pushing back the limits, you enter a wider arena. The possibility of perfect alignments or meetings is dancing all about you. By becoming totally engaged with the essence of your plans, you can reach a satisfactory conclusion.

⬇ You become distracted by the task in hand and miss the bigger picture. Emotional restrictions leave you out of the harmonious loop. There are delays or postponements.

Clearing the Way: ⬆ Your triumph over challenges, fears, or limitations seems very distant. It is time to choose action rather than inertia or stagnation. Contemplate your heart's desire and make one practical step toward it. Don't be afraid of combining with others in order to achieve what you want.

⬇ An over-protective environment or relationship is hemming you in. Perfectionism ultimately disappoints. Clinging to limitations saps the savour of success. Getting out of your own way, you can see the whole picture.

Environmental: The atmosphere of the earth. The sacred cordon protecting the planet. The opportunity to bring everything together in completion. Bisexual and transgender people. Unity among the nations. Institutions dedicated to cultural interchange and harmonious fulfilment. Roundtable gatherings, and world councils. Collective consciousness. The World Soul. The commonwealth of all beings. Universal concord. Honouring life from a planetary and holistic viewpoint.

Questions:
How are you called to manifest your plans or ideas?
What is coming to a conclusion?
How is the universe served here?

THE MINOR ARCANA:
FOUR PATHS TO UNDERSTANDING

The world dreamed you as well (as me),
it dreamed everything, and everyone.

—Donny Woolagoudja,
aboriginal elder

The Minor Arcana speak with the voice of the world at large and govern the everyday ways that we live, giving us meanings that speak of personal, daily, and community issues. A. E. Waite drew most of his Minor Arcana meanings from the work of the eighteenth-century cartomanancer Etteilla, the pre-revolutionary Frenchman to whom we look as the father of modern cartomancy, someone to whom every taromancer should be grateful, since he wrote the first "how to divine with cards" book. The four suits of Swords, Wands, Cups, and Pentacles offer us four different paths of understanding. Looking through the sequences of each suit from Ace to Ten, we can discern some of the stories that they seem to relate: you may find and see other kinds of stories.

SWORDS: The Path of Struggle

The Sword is the emblem of the warrior who fights or defends. It deals with ethics, thoughts, and words, and how we clarify or come to grips with the contractions and difficulties of life. One of the story sequences we can see in the Swords is that of conflict.

1. Taking up the sword.
2. Not taking either side in the conflict.
3. The inevitability of sorrow and loss.
4. Rest after conflict or struggle.
5. The ambiguities of taking sides.
6. Removing yourself from strife.
7. Stealing a march on the opponent.
8. Excluded or made helpless by the other.
9. The fear and anxiety of unrelieved struggle.
10. The consequences of conflict.

WANDS: The Path of Power

The Wand or Baton is the emblem of the commander, the one who leads and directs proceedings. Many of the themes of the Wands suit show us patterns of growth and expansion, where we can have agency in our lives, as well as the ambition, competition, and responsibility of pursuing this path. It shows the consequences of wielding power.

1. The power of life and growth.
2. Power seen from the lonely top.
3. Daring to be enterprising.
4. Celebrating some success.
5. Competition and practice.
6. The victory of success and achievement.
7. Defending a position.
8. Accelerating the action.
9. Persevering in the face of overwhelming forces.
10. The responsibility of carrying power.

CUPS: The Path of Loving

The Cup is the vessel of hospitality and communion with what nourishes us physically and spiritually. The major themes of the Cups are the home, the familiar, emotions, feelings, reactions, influences, satisfactions, and disappointments.

1. The power of love.
2. The reciprocal exchange of love.
3. Celebrating the first fruits of the season.
4. Familiarity breeds discontent

5. The swings and roundabouts of loving.
6. The comfort of the familiar.
7. Handling illusions and influences.
8. Moving away from old influences.
9. The satisfaction of fulfilment.
10. The love of the family circle.

PENTACLES: The Path of Provision

The Pentacle is Waite's reworking of the Coin as a suit emblem. Coins are about providing material benefits, insecurities, as well as our income and ancestral values. A pentacle was originally intended as a magical talisman; the word itself derives from the nineteenth-century French magician Eliphas Lévy, whose "pantacle" [*sic*] was his reinvention of the "pentagram." Pentacles retain the sense of the values, benefits, and belongings, but in Pamela Colman Smith's images, we also see the themes of work, employment, and occupation unfolding: just one of the stories that we see unfolding in this sequence.

1. A vocational opening.
2. Deciding what work to do.
3. Professional training and excellence.
4. Keeping resources carefully or to yourself.
5. What it is to have no income or home.
6. Applying for support in need.
7. Work satisfaction; a week's work over.
8. The repetition of work and the ability to provide a service.
9. The leisure enjoyed after work.
10. Retirement in the bosom of the family.

Each Minor Arcana card has four different entries to help you approach your question:

1. The querent's personal lifestyle
2. The querent's interaction with another person
3. The querent's wider impact within their own community or country
4. The querent's spiritual context and the wider impact within the world and upon their environment

1. Choose *Lifestyle* when the question is about your own actions, behaviour, thoughts, or opinions.
2. Choose *Interaction* when the question concerns members of your friends or family or your interaction with a partner, work colleague, or someone else.
3. Choose *Impact* when the question has wider consequences or effect upon the locality, community, your country, or the world at large.
4. Choose *Environmental* when you need to look at the longer-term implications of an action or decision, as well as when you want to spiritually discern what teaching the card is offering you.

As with the Major Arcana, the entries give both upright and reversed possibilities, but you can still use the reversed meanings if a card reveals itself as conflicted or problematic in its position or in juxtaposition to another card in a reading.

COURT CARDS

The 16 Court Cards of Page, Knight, Queen, and King are the pillars of the community, as well as the representatives of institutional powers and ethical principles, and the influencers whose acts and views set the tone in any society. Each can be read as

1. a person known to or involved with the querent
2. a process that is playing out in the querent's life
3. an event that is unfolding as a context to the querent's question
4. the moral and spiritual context of the wider environment

Each has entries showing their appearance as a person, process, or event:

1. Choose *Person* when your question shows the court card as a person or the influence of a person in your reading.
2. Choose *Process* when there is some movement that is being undergone by yourself or when there is need for a change.
3. Choose *Event* when a happening, plan, or process is causing reaction or necessitating a response.
4. Choose *Environmental* when you need to explore the impact upon the community or the world at large, as well as to understand the moral and spiritual lessons that each court card offers.

Sometimes you will need to move freely between these entries to find solutions to your question. Again, please remember that the entries given here are not set in stone, nor are they exhaustive in possibility. You will undoubtedly discover alternative as well as specific meanings and applications that will be dictated by the question.

ACE OF SWORDS

Image: Against a grey sky, a disembodied hand shrouded by cloud, holds a sword, while around the upright point is a crown garlanded by greenery. Six yods of power shine from it.[6] Beneath it, there stretches blue and grey hills.

Focus:
"I have the inspiration."
"My words can make it so."
"Clear thought creates honest speech."

Background: The Ace of Swords comes with the power of the wind, showing you how to cut through confusion or red tape or represent the seeding of a new idea. You can face your challenges because you've looked at all the facts clearly and know the terrain.

As on a clear-blue winter day, your thoughts are almost visible on the wind, and your clarity of mind stands behind the words you utter: a sense of incisive energy and clarity. This card speaks of the power to act, to speak up for yourself, to use your judgment to good effect. Appreciate the power of your mind to work things out clearly! When reversed, Ace of Swords can bring excess and crisis. Waite gives, "Great prosperity or great misery. Reversed: Marriage broken off, for a woman, through her own imprudence."

Lifestyle: ⬆ Clarity and power are yours. New ideas arise. Truth and ethics keep you principled. The power of the intellect and sharp analysis reveals things clearly. Your single-mindedness pays off.
⬇ Surrendering to the inevitable or feeling cut off. In the grip of negative influences. Suffering mental instability or clouded thoughts.

Interaction: ⬆ Your sense of fair play gives objectivity in relationships. Assert yourself or speak out about what moves you.
⬇ Hypercritical words wound. Manipulation is a form of aggression. Exaggeration or self-detraction makes you swamp or fail to take up your place. Words that you cannot take back.

Impact: ⬆ Your championship helps things take off. By committing to see things through, illusions are dispersed or mysteries unravelled. Things line up exactly. Taking an ethical approach to life.
⬇ Expect some turbulence ahead. There's little or no power to push things forward. Confusion. A decision is not followed through.

Environmental: Air quality or pollution. Wind power. Integrity in environmental decision or thought. Words of power. The power of thought and ideas. Decisiveness in your undertakings. Honouring the power of the mind and the word.

Questions:
Where or to whom do you need to speak the truth?
What clarity is being brought?
Where has power turned to excessive force?

TWO OF SWORDS

Image: Against a dark-blue sky, a blind-folded woman dressed in white sits on a stone bench with the sea at her back. Her arms are crossed over her chest, and she holds a sword in either hand. A waxing moon is in the sky.

Focus:
"I cannot see the way ahead or decide right now."
"I will do my best to bring the peace by being impartial."
"I look within at night."

Background: Blindfolded at the shore, with two swords equally poised, the Two of Swords combines the stillness of the High Priestess and the forbearance of Justice. Peace is a possibility, but so is resumption of hostilities or differences. Sometimes, provoking strife is the only way when you fight for those who have no voice. It all depends on whatever has brought you to this moment. This card encourages you to communicate with whomever you are at loggerheads. Call a truce, suspend hostilities, exchange views. Diplomacy can bring reconcil-iation or balance. The act of taking a moment to explore peaceful possibilities or to seek mediation is not a weakness. Waite also gives, "Gifts for a lady, influential protection for a man in search of help. Reversed: Dealings with rogues."

Lifestyle: ⬆ Analysis of the situation is required before action. Sitting on the fence or avoiding commitment. Compromise, indecision, or hesitation. Looking deeper within. ⬇ Closing yourself off. Suspension of deeply held beliefs. Ignoring the writing on the wall.

Interaction: ⬆ Dialogue or mediation is needed. Making a pact or alliance with someone. Laying aside competitiveness in your relationships. Impartiality.
⬇ Unequal contracts or a sense of disrespect strains relations. Communications break down between you. Fearful of the changes a decision may bring.

Impact: ⬆ Amnesty, truce, or peace. Acknowledging an impasse and other possibilities. Ambivalence about public policy. Allowing each side to have its say.
⬇ Questioning or uncovering the wrongs of society. Plaguing the powers that be. Resuming the conflict. A numbness of response. Conformity.

Environmental: Weighing up the cost of environmental decisions for all species. A sense of truce, suspension of hostilities, stalemate, with neither side having advantage. Protecting the habitat of the sea. Making environmental decisions. Passivity. Being unable to look. Not taking sides or engaging in the debate. Honouring both sides of a viewpoint.

Questions:
What are you hesitating about?
What is to be gained by abetting or denying neither side?
What reconciliation is needed?

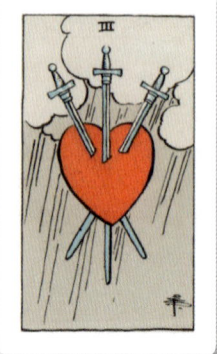

THREE OF SWORDS

Image: Against a grey, cloudy sky from which rain falls, a red heart is transfixed by three swords.

Focus:
"There are no words, my grief is so great."
"Why does it always rain on my parade?"
"My heart is riven through."

Background: The three swords that pierce the heart refer to the saying of prophet Simeon when the Blessed Virgin brought her son to the temple for circumcision: "Yes, and a sword shall pierce through thine own soul; that the thoughts from many hearts may be revealed" (Luke 2: 35). Over time, sorrow transmutes slowly into understanding. This card offers you the opportunity to realize that everyone has personal troubles, no matter how perfect their life appears. Nothing can fill the place of what is lost. By expressing grief and making space to mourn, you can honour the loss and seek solace in remembering. At the very least, this card indicates that you've been let down or that you have been isolated from what normally supports you. Waite gives, "The card upright read for a woman signifies the removal or flight of a lover; when reversed, it can signify a nun or devout woman."

Lifestyle: ⬆ Your personal troubles. Sorrow, deep disappointment, or heartache. Brooding upon personal slights.
⬇ Moving on after loss. Denial that anything is wrong. Enjoying your melancholia or letting it feed your creativity.

Interaction: ⬆ Bereavement after the loss of a partner or friend. Jealousy or hurt fills your heart. Separation from dear ones, places, or animals.
⬇ Playing with someone's affections. Acknowledging your own part in inflicting loss, grief, or letting someone down. Reconstructing your life after bereavement.

Impact: ⬆ Normal support structures fail. A period of national mourning or shared loss. Painful truths come to light.
⬇ Hanging on to broken or outworn patterns. Scandalous or painful events are hidden or brooded upon. A loss is narrowly averted.

Environmental: Sorrow. Pollution. Loss of species. Even after a long-ago loss, the heartstrings can still be tender. Focussing on how loss or sorrow is still dictating reaction. Ambiguous grief from ancestral events or unrealised sources. World sorrow at the thought of environmental damage or decline. Honouring the sorrow of all who suffer loss.

Questions:
Whose heart is broken?
What has been lost or separated?
Why has there been a division?

FOUR OF SWORDS

Image: Against a grey background, the effigy of a knight with his hands in prayer lies upon a tomb or catafalque, on which is carved a sword. Three further swords are hung on the wall above him to the right. To the left there is a stained-glass window in which a cleric or saint blesses a kneeling supplicant.

Focus:
"I just need to rest here."
"I cannot yet operate at full strength."
"I seek sanctuary to reposition myself."

Background: Sometimes things are just taken out of your hands, when you are given or have to take an enforced rest or break. This can mean a period of recuperation or a chance to turn within, but it generally means things come to a halt. When you stop running at things, your energies have a chance to refresh, recover, or forget. This card often comes up when you are trying to force the pace or are near burnout. The halo of the saint in the stained glass reads, "Pax." Here, peace remains an ideal, and the reality suggests cessation of activity or fight from necessity. One sword is taken from the fight, but three remain. It is also a card for those who have no agency of their own at present, and whose affairs have to be managed by another.

Waite gives, "A qualified success from the wise administration of affairs, but reversed, actual success following wise administration."

Lifestyle: ⬆ A period of rest or respite. Self-exile, seclusion, or retreat. Convalescence or an enforced rest. Isolation or abandonment.
⬇ Creating a regime that supports your health. Using your energies or resources wisely. Lying low or shamming illness.

Interaction: ⬆ Having to leave activity or work to others. Checking things out before leaping to conclusions. Refreshing your relationship by a temporary absence.
⬇ Being considerate to the needs or rights of others. Taking up a relationship again or becoming available to friends. Filling up your spare moments so that there's no time to relate.

Impact: ⬆ Cessation of activity or halt in the proceedings. An opportunity to consolidate resources and plans. A strike or unexpected event zaps the routine.
⬇ A return to work. Changing the way things are done. Excluding or banning individuals from the group. Reintegrating excluded individuals.

Environmental: Stability of energy and environment is an essential basis to work from. The right to rest and recreation, not to be continually working. Cessation of hostilities. Allowing the ground to remain fallow. Quarantine. Living by natural rhythms. Retirement. Uninhabited places. Economic cutbacks. Caretaking someone or something that cannot act or protect itself. Wise or respectful administration of land management. Honouring the need for rest and respite.

Questions:
Who/what needs rest in the issue?
What blessing is given?
What space is made for health and well-being?

FIVE OF SWORDS

Image: Against a blue, cloudy sky, a su-
percilious-looking man is picking up
swords that have been left on the ground.
Behind him, two men walk away: one
fairly steadily with determination, and
another more distant one who is just
despondent. Behind them is a flat, still
lake, although the clouds overhead look
windblown.

Focus:
"They didn't see that coming."
"They thought I was their friend!"
"I can pick up the pieces."

Background: Things deteriorate and are subject to damage, theft, and
loss. Whatever has been gained is envied by others. You can assuage
envy by offering a share of what you have, but do not leave yourself
open to malice. This card carries with it inevitable losses and has a
sense of dishonourable moves and envious dispositions. It signifies
the one who picks up the pieces afterward or those who salvage what
is not working, also the receivers of a bankruptcy case, and also we
as secret opponents who envy you ill or wish to possess what you
own.

Lifestyle: ⬆ Identity theft, slander, or loss of your good name. Hu-
miliation from treachery or cowardice. Plans are thwarted. Resentful thoughts at being the only one left standing or able to function
after a struggle.

⬇ Revamping your reputation. Not being defeated by past mistakes. Revoking your assets. Being alert to treachery.

Interaction: ⬆ Abuse, assault, or bullying. Unethical behaviour or malicious intentions abound between you. Envy or plagiarism. Lack of consent in sexual encounters or business ventures. An attack upon your fortune. Being unable to join in or engage due to unfair tactics or motivations.
⬇ An advocate or witness supports you. Having regret for envying others or smearing their reputation. Getting to the bottom of a web of envy or malice.

Impact: ⬆ Envious opponents steal business or custom. Divisive means. Groups or individuals feel defeated or suffer defeat. How do words or actions oppress or humiliate others? The impact upon the group or world of a decision or action where one benefits from the loss of many others.
⬇ Rebuilding after a break-in or assault. Making good environmental damage. Laying things honourably to rest.

Environmental: Treachery and betrayal. A night move on the innocent, vulnerable, or unwary. Picking up the pieces. Recovery of the bodies. Salvage. Being drawn into a civil war or divisive enterprise. Refusing to engage with unethical actions or plans. Trolling and sabotage. Overthrow, coup, takeover. Soul fragmentation. Acknowledging that human nature is prone to self-interest and envy.

Questions:
Who or what is gaining the upper hand?
Why are the others walking away?
What needs protection or better boundaries?

SIX OF SWORDS

Image: Against a grey sky, we see a punt, with a ferryman taking a woman and child across water. At the farther end of the punt stand six swords. The waves in the foreground are choppy, but the water beyond is calm. In the distance, two possible landfalls present themselves.

Focus:
"We cannot go back there."
"We will make a new life."
"Hope propels me forward now."

Background: Six of Swords usually offers you ways and means to go forward, rather than a way back. It is a crossing over, especially signifying a trip over water, but it stands for the way ahead, the means you take to achieve something. Whatever lies behind you, it is now being put behind you. The move you need to make is often driven by expedience, changed priorities, or social alterations. Your road may be uniquely waiting under your feet, but you haven't yet noticed it because you're trying to go down another imagined road or someone else's route. When you are clear with yourself about what you want, the road will become visible to you. The people in the boat have dignity and are not hopeless refugees—they are finding the right way for themselves. Finding the means and right approach that works for you brings you into a new place. What loss or sorrow is still shaping your life and dictating your reactions? Waite gives, "A pleasant voyage, but reversed, a legal case with an unfavourable result."

Lifestyle: ⬆ A journey or new perspectives. A means to make a fresh start. A change of occupation. Escaping from the present circumstances. Finding a safer place.
⬇ Taking all your troubles away with you. An inability to move forward or move on. Holding on to your prejudices or views.

Interaction: ⬆ Being an envoy or messenger on behalf of others. A chance to try a different way is given to you both. Putting old relationships or mistakes behind you.
⬇ The progress of a relationship stalemates. Maintaining a dead or dying partnership. Seeking approval. Laying down the law about how a relationship is to be.

Impact: ⬆ Safety and protection are offered to refugees. Expedience drives things. Holidays. Taking the opportunity to jump ship. Finding the right way forward with dignity. Migrations caused by expedience, war, environmental change.
⬇ Moving from place to place to escape troubles. Unwilling to leave the past life behind. Parochial-mindedness. A manifesto or ordinance that creates global movement or a proclamation that results in social unrest.

Environmental: Refugees. Migrant issues. Finding a new habitat. Resettlement of species. Adapting to prevailing conditions. Voluntary, economic forced migration. Displaced people or species. Having to change your position. Honouring the necessity to seek out better conditions.

Questions:
What is being left behind? What lies ahead?
What will not be tolerated again?
What is the right way forward now?

SEVEN OF SWORDS

Image: Against a yellow sky, a man carrying five swords tiptoes stealthily away from an encampment of pavilions. Behind him, two swords remained embedded in the ground. He looks back at them.

Focus:
"I will take care of these."
"I seize the day."
"They thought I was on their side!"

Background: The design of Seven of Swords is probably based upon the character of Maugis d'Aigremont in a thirteenth-century *chanson de geste*, in which he steals the swords of Charlemagne and his paladins, having cast an enchanted sleep upon them. Seven of Swords requires you be alert to what is going on, because it could be daylight robbery of your hopes and values. When there is no right or correct procedure to guide you, you just have to improvise and resort to low cunning or inspired strategy. While such behaviour might be beneath your dignity in normal circumstances, here a small cleverness may be the very thing. When you determine to do something that requires some daring, you can find the courage and make the attempt. The moment may not come again, so do your best! This window of opportunity is wedded to your readiness.

What loss or sorrow is still shaping your life and dictating your reactions? Waite gives, "A country life after a competence has been secured; if reversed, some good advice that is probably not taken."

Lifestyle: ⬆ Fast thinking, decisive action, or improvising on the spur of the moment. Travelling under an alias or incognito. Using your initiative or being ready.

⬇ Fear of being caught. Regretting the lost moment. Fruitlessly waiting for lost opportunities to call again. Impostor syndrome.

Interaction: ⬆ Taking charge of a relationship. Opportunist spontaneity or elopement. Spying on a partner. Scoring points off the other. Stealing from the opposition.

⬇ Getting someone to spy for you. Feeling vulnerable or unready to reveal yourself. Trying to discern the unwritten agenda in a friendship.

Impact: ⬆ Grabbing hold of the controls, a takeover or coup on a country's government, or an attempt on a public institution. Strategy, Dutch courage, or camouflage win the day. Retrieving national secrets or treasures. The subtle erosion of values that everyone holds dear.

⬇ Doing things by the book. Testing a wild scheme before committing to it. Getting expert advice. Resources squandered.

Environmental: Stealth, seizing the chance. Disguising. A spur-of-the-moment window of opportunity. Taking more than the earth can spare. Living off the resources of others. Things being devalued under your very nose. Counting coup. Setting up a rearview mirror to see what is coming behind. Racial or sexual divisiveness. Rebelling against injustice. Eco-activism. Fostering personal grievances. A culture of getting even. Acknowledging that human beings want to get revenge, get even, or do better than their neighbours. Honouring the right of everyone to be valued as they are.

Questions:
What is being taken away?
What is the intention of the thief?
Why does no one notice?

EIGHT OF SWORDS

Image: Against a grey sky, a blindfolded woman, with arms bound to her sides, stands in a marsh hemmed in by eight swords. She stands in a marshy place at the foot of a city on a hill.

Focus:
"I have been brought to this position."
"My beliefs are keeping me safe."
"Is there a surer place to stand?"

Background: Eight of Swords challenges you to notice into what kind of prison you've chained your mind or opinions. This can start as a slow encroachment on your liberty that finally becomes impossible. Doing your bounden duty until your heart wears away is not living, and unless you wake up, you may not be rescued from it. A sense of helplessness or weakness may keep you bound and immobile, unable or unwilling to see how restricted things have become. Being hemmed in. Stuck. Painting yourself into a corner. Taking an entrenched position, circumscribed by the views of others. It is also the card showing someone being gaslit, someone who acts as the fall guy or scapegoat. Waite gives, "When read for a woman, it signifies scandal spread about her. If reversed, it shows the departure of relative."

Lifestyle: ⬆ Being sunk in unprofitable tasks or fruitless occupations. A difficult position. Restriction or lack of perspective. Feeling victimized or overwhelmed. Being in a difficult position.

⬇ Resisting self-sabotage. Seeing things more clearly. Breaking out of limitations or a depression. The unforeseen.

Interaction: ⬆ Fear of what others say. Bigotted opinions or intolerance blights your friendship. Allowing yourself to be convinced. Gaslighting or gaslit by the other. Limited understanding.
⬇ Listening between the lines to understand the relationship's subtext. Accepting help in need. Renegotiating the terms of your relationship.

Impact: ⬆ Affairs are stuck in a mind warp. Public views are in bondage to an ideology or institutional demands. Imprisonment or illness brings things to a halt. Restrictions on free movement. Held ideologically captive by failure of open communication.
⬇ Coming out from the influence of a cult or restrictive ideology. People enjoy freedom of thought and opinion once more. Naming and shaming what binds people. Speaking up to authority.

Environmental: A sense of limitation. Restricted thinking about things. Tethered to outworn modes of doing things. Imprisonment or bondage. Victimization. Restoring species to the wild from captivity. Giving a voice to the voiceless or unheard. Exclusion and marginalization of minorities and their values. Enslavement and trafficking. Honouring the right of all beings to be included and heard.

Questions:
What/who is restricting things?
What is being isolated here?
What would it feel like to be without these limitations?

NINE OF SWORDS

Image: Against a black background, a woman sits up in bed, with head in hands. Behind her, nine swords hang horizontally against the wall. The bedspread on the bed has a checkerboard of alternating roses and lilies.

Focus:
"Nothing can be worse than this."
"This fear is overwhelming."
"Is there no escape?"

Background: Nine of Swords brings disturbing premonitions. Genuine forewarnings often show up below the surface of daily life, in sleep and dreams, begging you to pay attention to what is coming nearer. Dreams clearly show in metaphor what is going on, although we may not have noticed the signs. The sense of waiting for the axe to fall or the phone to ring with bad news can weigh heavily, causing the suffering of painful expectation. This is a card of pitiless realisation and often of suffering. The accidents of life cannot always be diverted or avoided. The Nine of Swords or Spades traditionally was a card of ill omen because the pips looked like a person in a coffin: one spade between two rows of four spades. For Etteilla, this card represents an ecclesiastic or a priest. Waite also gives, "A card of bad omen. Reversed: Good ground for suspicion against a doubtful person."

Lifestyle: ⬆ Premonitions, omens, grave suspicions, or nightmares. A troubled conscience, depression, or ongoing pain. Brooding about fearful things. A sense of desolation. Suffering. Grave doubts. Guilt.

Cruelty. Despair. Depression. The corollary of your thoughtless actions begins to play out. A sense of inevitability.

⬇ Working through recurrent fears or nightmares by the light of day. Finding serenity by facing fears. Coming out of depression. Coming to terms with what has happened.

Interaction: ⬆ Realizing that something has to give between you. A sinking dread that your partner, friend, or work colleague is not who you thought they were. Good ground for suspicion against a doubtful person.

⬇ Seeking out a confidante, confessor, or councillor. Bearing with relationship troubles patiently. Check your suspicions carefully.

Impact: ⬆ Rumour swells and overspills. A feeling of general exposure or vulnerability. Institutions are put under pressure or react with cruelty. A sense of environmental despair that is unassuageable.

⬇ Well-founded mistrust is proven or rumour is exaggerated. Legitimate fears that need investigation. Fear's grip subsides or the danger passes. Tribunals are set up to investigate abuses.

Environmental: Nightmare. Anticipation of bad things. Suffering. The despair of an awful realisation of the extent of environmental destruction or damage. Mental health issues. Events that change the nature of life itself. The foreshadowing of larger movements and changes that are now manifesting. The effects of stalking, domestic violence, etc. upon mental health. Honouring the signs and dreams that forewarn us.

Questions:
What is the nightmare about?
What has miscarried?
What has been gnawing at the edge of your awareness
and is now here?

TEN OF SWORDS

Image: Against a black sky, at the edge of the sea, a figure lies prone upon the earth, with ten swords thrust into his back. Over his body a flood of blood pours forth. Under a black sky, the water is calm, and over the distant mountains the bright light of day shines clear.

Focus:
"I fought and tried; I fought and died."
"Time to clear the battlefield."
"The forces against me were too strong."

Background: The Ten of Swords suggests that troubles have reached their pitch. The aftermath of trauma leaves a sense of emptiness and exhaustion. The overwhelming power of what we fight against proves too strong. In a time of intense tribulation, when things lie in ruins about you, remember that you survive to fight another day. Quiet, even stoical heroism is your support now. It is a card of defeat. Waite gives this card upright meaning, when read for a woman, "spells being stabbed in the back. For a soldier at war, the card reversed signifies victory." Note that though the sky is black, the horizon is golden.

Lifestyle: ⬆ The worst has passed you by. A life-or-death decision leaves you frozen in shock. Troubles reach their height.
⬇ Relief from stress at last. You have survived and things improve. Troubles pass away. A temporary advantage.

Interaction: ⬆ Giving space for a survivor to vent their sorrow. Coming through a narrow pass or dangerous encounter alive. Attending a deathbed or bereavement. Plans come to naught.
⬇ Playing the traumatic scenario over and over to an audience. Constraints between you ease. The emptiness of the heart's well begins to fill up again.

Impact: ⬆ A national catastrophe. Grievances that cannot be answered or assuaged yet. Newsmongers rejoice at the scale of the calamity. Being on the losing side.
⬇ Dealing with the aftermath or war or catastrophe. Quelling rumour and setting the record straight. There is space for something new to arise. Being part of the winning side. Power and authority are restored.

Environmental: Surviving a tsunami of troubles, you have the clearest understanding of where help lies. The emptiness and exhaustion of the aftermath. Last-minute solutions. The immediate aftermath of disaster. Mourning environmental destruction. When reversed, advantageous for those in authority or wielding power. War crimes. Terrorism. Honouring those who have succumbed to war or disaster. Honouring the cessation of troubles.

Questions:
What has been overwhelmed here?
Who defended and lost?
From the depths of necessity, what help do you require?

PAGE OF SWORDS

Image: Against a blue sky, a youth stands attentive and ready to move, holding a sword up to his left shoulder. He faces into the wind and stands upon a green hilltop. Behind him, clouds fill the blue sky.

Focus:
"I will keep watch."
"I seek out what has to be uncovered."
"I move swiftly and unseen."

Background: The Page of Swords makes swift decisions depending on how the wind blows. This a vigilant overseer whose honesty is valued, one who uses reason clearly to understand cause and effect. He researches and investigates with clarity and defends what is right. This is the card of someone serving in the services as a cadet or in the lower ranks or even as a spy or in covert operations, but when reversed, it can signify someone who smokescreens and scams, whipping up trouble and inciting to violence. A newshound or serial blogger or else a scammer who uses words to smear and create trouble.

Person: ⬆ A good companion to see you through trials and challenges, because he doesn't easily give up. He learns things easily because of his eye for detail. He is dexterous and cunning in a tight place. An armed security person.

⬇ Someone in trouble with the law or living under the cloud of shame or disadvantage. He is good at covert operations or investigation but could also be a stalker or snoop.

Process: ⬆ Having fortitude through difficulties. Daring and agility. Determination. Thinking the whole plan through. Solving dilemmas intelligently.
⬇ The effect of a stalker or spy. Sitting on the fence. Delaying through fear of awakening old hurts. Acting unethically.

Event: ⬆ A new skill or idea. Research. Challenges, negotiations, or contracts that need close attention. Examinations, auditions, tests. A mystery to unfold. Intelligent analysis brings clarity.
⬇ Gossip. Anxiety. Confidence is sapped. Tasks are overwhelming. An indiscreet friend.

Environmental: Good air quality, wind power, environmental watchfulness. Rumour. Internet information. Investigative journalism, in-depth surveys into injustice. Listening to the beings in nature. Being attentive to what is being spoken or heard. Honouring the changes that arise in every moment.

Questions:
What needs to be investigated?
Who or what is watching out for you?
How can you engage flexibly with the situation?

KNIGHT OF SWORDS

Image: Against a blue sky with racing clouds, a knight with raised sword charges upon a white horse. His tunic has birds upon it while the horse's caparisons have butterflies upon them. Behind him, a high wind blows the clouds jagged. Beneath him is a sandy terrain with spindly trees.

Focus:
"I ride to the rescue."
"My cause is just."
"I am your champion."

Background: Knight of Swords can be relied upon to champion you or a cause he believes in. He can be outspoken and sometimes critical, but his words have the ring of truth. His assurance and sharp intellect make him a great advocate. He can get easily worked up, and his convinced views might be insisted upon, right or wrong, yet when he appears in a reading, you can be sure that you have the support and self-belief to get through. Waite notes that this card is one of the professional soldier or service person, someone who is armed and dangerous but in the service of the law or country. When reversed, it can show a person who is a rabble-rouser, an agent provocateur who incites to violence.

Person: ⬆ This is a champion who rides to defend and uphold beliefs, for himself and on behalf of others. He has clear views and opinions and makes a good advocate for those who have no voice. He is a friend who is never downhearted but always energetic and spontaneous. A skilled fighter, someone in the military or armed forces, a bodyguard.

⬇ Someone who is tactless, rude, violent, or opinionated, or someone cut off from emotion. The only dissent he tolerates is his own. Trying to deal with a bigoted or violent person. An outlaw, guerrilla, thug, or rebel.

Process: ⬆ Vigilance as you go through the process. Impulsiveness. Heroism and courage. Struggling with ideological compliance or revolt. Environmental activism. Stirring speeches.

⬇ Using subtlety as a way through. Holding a grudge. Festering anger. Exhortations to revolt. In the vicinity of cards of fatality, it can signify a death.

Event: ⬆A cause that you espouse. A speedy turn of events. A decision that needs to be made. A meeting of like-minded people. A revolutionary inspiration. A conference, symposium, or think tank.

⬇ A violent kickback or reaction. An ideological persecution or pernicious notion that adversely influences people, policy, and protection of all. Treating the public as a mere statistic. An attack on the environment.

Environmental: A forthright champion who supports rightful action. Strength of mind and character. Championing good causes, environmental activism. Also, advocating change by protest or activism. Defence of borders, countries, habitats, rights. Sudden attack or assault. Animal experimentation. Honouring the weak and defenceless by defending them.

Questions:
What needs defending or rescuing?
What do you need to stand up for?
Where is discretion necessary?

QUEEN OF SWORDS

Image: Against a blue sky, a queen upon a stone throne with an upright sword in her right hand, raises her gloved hand in salute. Her cloak is covered with clouds, while her crown has butterflies upon it. The throne on which she sits displays butterflies and a winged putto. Behind her, clouds bank up. A single bird is in the sky.

Focus:
"I defend the right."
"No one gets the better of me."
"Underestimate me at your peril!"

Background: The Queen of Swords' sword is not raised in vain. She has the focus and clarity to get things done efficiently, so she leads the attack herself. She has a sense of justice and truth, and when she goes to the heart of the matter, you can be sure it will be very precise. With her beside you, you have the courage to speak the truth, have the strength of your convictions, and see the heart of things. Waite represents this card as signifying the single, independent, or older woman or a widow who controls her affairs without benefit of a partner. It can also, when reversed, carry the connotations of Old Maid, a disapproving older woman or a gossip. In today's values, Queen of Swords is the significator of the independent, self-determining, or career woman.

Person: ⬆ She has honesty, integrity, and pure focus. She is astute and difficult to trick. Direct and sometimes outspoken, her intelligence and independence bring the ability to overcome events and carry on despite stress.

⬇ Someone who is undergoing pain or loss. Someone who speaks out sharply or who has a razor wit. She may lash out if disappointed or frustrated, has a hypercritical tongue, or harbours resentment.

Process: ⬆ Facing unpleasant truths. Not bearing fools gladly. Sorrow from loss. Assessing things astutely. Rational explanation or scientific view. Going to the heart of things. Being independently minded.

⬇ Pride colours everything. Being intellectually prickly. Sadness lingers. Prudishness or bigotry curtails liberty. Female bullying.

Event: ⬆ Truth that needs to be spoken to avoid misunderstanding. Setting the ground rules clearly. Separation, breakup, or absence. Finding freedoms in the midst of restraint.

⬇ Ideals turn sour. Subjection to mind games or lack of care. Self-reliance brings vulnerability.

Environmental: Focussed, daring, intelligent. Dealing with things efficiently. Giving a firm ethical lead. The chair of an environmental association. Raising consciousness of issues that others ignore. Arbitrating on morally difficult issues. Bereaved of a partner. Using good judgment and discretion to bring things to a just outcome. Honouring the independence of all beings.

Questions:
What brings clarity to the situation?
What straightforward approach is needed here?
How do you cut through the tangle?

KING OF SWORDS

Image: Against a pale-blue sky, a King sits upon a throne, with the sword against his right shoulder. Behind him is a cloth of estate with butterflies upon it. The throne is placed on an eminence, while behind him clouds retire. Two birds are in the sky.

Focus:
"I uphold truth and justice for all."
"I perceive the heart of the matter."
"I maintain the standards which are authorized by experience."

Background: The King of Swords has a developed sense of fairness, and all his dealings have an impartiality about them, though never tinged with weakness. His farsighted perspective makes him an excellent strategist who can predict all his moves ahead. He offers the clarity to act with authority without laying down the law, helping you assess a situation precisely. Waite sees this as the card of legality—the lawyer or judge or else the professional person—the doctor, physician, counsellor. When reversed, the advocate becomes a despot, and it is a warning to give up a ruinous lawsuit.

Person: ⬆ Articulate and just, he is a moral leader who upholds standards. His knowledge and research is of the highest quality. His highly-principled discernment brings perspective. Military strategist. Someone who works with mental concepts. A philosopher, advocate, lawyer, doctor.

⬇ He can be an exacting critic, a harsh disciplinarian, or a corrupt official. The godfather or dictator of a family or organization who exacts the cruel justice of an eye for an eye.

Processes: ⬆ Finding a way through chaos by calm clarity. Being watchful and of good counsel. Discerning the truth of a situation. Having the authority of expertise and good judgment. Finding an impartial standpoint.
⬇ Being unfair. An urge to buck the system or bend the rules. Emotional detachment. Inhumane. Male bullying.

Events: ⬆ Advice or counsel. A court case or dispute needing arbitration. Precise information. A disciplined approach.
⬇ An unrelenting situation or harsh treatment. Ultimate forms of authority that cramp your style. Unfair rules or strictures. An atrocity or barbarous happening.

Environmental: Innate good judgment giving the insight to live fairly and justly. A sense of authority and skill, analytical judgment. Discrimination. Government think tank. Environment clarity. Environmental justice, agency, and oversight. Honouring the rights of all beings and standing up for them.

Questions:
Where or on whom is authority brought to bear?
Who has the power of life and death here?
What expertise or good judgement is needed?

ACE OF WANDS

Image: Against a grey background, a right hand appears from a cloud, holding a leafy wand or club. Underneath it is a fertile landscape with a river flowing through it, with a distant castle and purple hills.

Focus:
"I hold the power in my hand."
"The green growth of life waits to be grasped."
"Now I am motivated."

Background: Ace of Wands reveals the beginning of a project, as well as creative or generative impulse. Virility and fertility enable things to grow strong. Under its influence, enthusiasm can flourish and invention gains wings. Once the motivation is generated, this card signals the go-ahead that has been awaited. This card can also represent work or profession, and an established presence in a chosen field. Waite sees it signifying the green growth of the earth, and the vigour of life itself, as well as the power to fulfil something. Reversed, it signifies declining energy or enthusiasm, weakness, or inability to follow the impulse.

Lifestyle: ⬆ Creative excitement and enthusiasm. A sense of eager adventure. You have the courage and personal power to succeed. Place of birth or origin.

⬇ Your plans are challenged. A premature beginning that needs to be rethought. A sudden surge of power that is not sustained. Sitting on the fence rather than following the impulse.

Interaction: ⬆ You have the passion to engage. Bringing a sense of innovation and purpose will kindle or rekindle the affection between you. Your energy is infectious.

⬇ Stepping on the accelerator just stalls the relationship. Be patient and follow through. Not having enthusiasm about a friendship. The project or plan receives intermittent or fluctuating interest.

Impact: ⬆ Abundant energy infuses everything. Opportunity and energy are resonant now. Receiving the go-ahead or approval to start. Something new is coming to birth in the world.

⬇ Be prepared for efforts to be scattered or fragmented. Forcing the issue brings reaction or revolution. The world isn't yet ready for what you offer.

Environmental: The life force in all living things, growth and vigour in plants. Species of plants and animals in one family. The genetic inheritance or DNA of life-forms. Genetic manipulation. A work-force. Creative brainstorming. The decline or threatened extinction of a species. Honouring the right to life in all beings.

Questions:
Where is the power running?
What is growing?
Where does the impulse lead?

TWO OF WANDS

Image: Against a grey background, a man in a brown cloak and red hat stands upon a battlemented roof, looking down onto the sea. He holds a globe in his right hand, while his left grasps the staff that stands before him. On his left is inscribed the rose-and-lily design.

Focus:
"I stand secure in my own place."
"I weigh the results of my actions."
"How might I make things better?"

Background: The Two of Wands reveals the consequences of having authority, showing someone who has already achieved substantially, and who stands in place of power. This card gives you pause about how to proceed: choosing to consolidate your gains, to stay where you are, or looking beyond to new horizons, to expansion or contraction? Personal power, boldness and originality, and assurance are all keywords here. Standing in a place of power gives you certain advantages. The image suggests a consideration of the impact of decisions upon the whole world, as well as the loneliness or isolation of being a leader. The rose-and-lily design set in a cross shape was originally on the first published Waite-Smith Tarot, with the rose representing the Rosicrucian stream and the lily representing the Grail legends from Waite's magical background; the rose signifying passion and purity, and the lily commitment and devotion.

Lifestyle: ⬆ The dynamic drive to achieve your goals. Control and mastery enable to you to take risks and pioneer new things.

Allowing originality to shape your life.

⬇ A sense of unworthiness curbs your power. Loss of faith or failure of confidence. Leaving past successes or losses behind you to think again. A fear or dread of the unknown.

Interaction: ⬆ New partnerships or alliances are possible. You achieve your desire by making good choices. Deciding between responsibility to your dependents and your own plans may create a dilemma. Trendsetting.

⬇ Ensure that your signals are clear so that misunderstandings are avoided. A friend or partner has different objectives from yours. Persuasion. A sense of having to go it alone or lead the way.

Impact: ⬆ Researching opinion and reaction helps your decision-making. Risk-taking has unexpected impact. An opinion or opportunity has a life-changing effect on those around you. Behaving like the Queen/King of the world alienates people.

⬇ Your restraint makes it safer for others. You may be inviting criticism by standing out from the crowd. Lack of a spiritual dimension narrows your horizons and blunts your power. Surprising discovery or unexpected enchantment. Behaving as if you were a person who is equally affected by things plays well.

Environmental: Dominance of a species or mono-culture or the consequences of cultivating one kind of food stuff. Following one ideology. World dominance, life at the top of the food chain. Dead-end politics and power planning without accountability. The weight of responsibility for the world upon leaders and decision makers. Honouring the fact that every being needs support.

Questions: What has been set in motion?
Whom will the plan/enterprise impact?
What are the responsibilities that accompany certainty?

THREE OF WANDS

Image: Against a yellow background, a man with a fillet around his brow stands with his back to us on a promontory, watching ships sail out into the sunlit sea below. He leans forward, while holding onto one of the three staves planted behind him at the cliff top.

Focus:
"All my hopes go with them."
"Cooperative ventures bring strength."
"I venture my all."

Background: The Three of Wands looks for ways to expand horizons of possibility and how to bring a venture or plan into the harbour of success. There is a sense of boldness and enterprise in setting forth. Planned achievements gather momentum where there is foresight and focus. The image shows argosies bearing their freight overseas, suggesting the risk and adventure of any enterprise. Whatever your focus or mission in life, your enterprise is the thrust block to your vocational ambition. This card is one of reciprocal trade and collaborative enterprise.

Lifestyle: ⬆ Your enterprising initiative gets things off the ground. By taking a foresighted overview, you explore all possibilities. Your negotiations pull off a big deal.
⬇ Failure to risk, lack of venture, or creative block circumscribes your plans. Taking your eye off things or daydreaming on the job causes frustrating delays. A sense of being overwhelmed by the overall picture.

Interaction: ⬆ Going into partnership, setting up a commercial venture, or moving in with someone. Agreeing on a strategy. Your shared dream steps into reality. Collaboration is well favoured.

⬇ Ulterior motives can sabotage the contract or agreement. Make sure your certainty isn't abrasive or pigheaded. Squabbling about the best way forward.

Impact: ⬆ Gathering information, interest, or research helps reveal the bigger picture. The leader of a focus group or an influential figurehead or way shower reveals the true nature of things. Setting an example ensures a better way for many.

⬇ Implementing research and results in practical ways. Working to overcome arrogance and over-ambition alienate those around you. Coming to the end of a period of adversity or trouble. Betterment and amelioration.

Environmental: Keeping an eye on trends. Keeping watch over the seas and oceans. A sense of enterprise and leadership. World trade. Risk. Maintaining a collaborative guardianship over the world. Reciprocal enterprises between different groups. Fair-trade investment in local enterprises. Honouring the contribution of all in any plan or enterprise.

Questions:
What is the sincere wish in this matter?
How might the enterprise shape the world?
What will the ships bring back?

FOUR OF WANDS

Image: Against a yellow background, four staves are raised in a public place, connected by leafy garlands. In the background, two figures with garlands raise bunches of greenery, while behind them are the walls of a town.

Focus:
"It is time to be thankful."
"We celebrate the good things of life."
"Peace has brought us prosperity."

Background: Four of Wands sees the completion of one phase of an enterprise and celebrates the enjoyment of the first fruits of your labours. It signals a time of community rejoicing to mark an event. There's a mutual sense of harmony that can make some feel left out of the charmed circle, yet the sense of pride and celebration really reflects upon everyone. It is a card of social events and of communal gatherings when appreciation can irrigate your life with thankfulness. Reversed, it can denote hyperactivity resultant from workaholism. Waite gives, "Unexpected good fortune; when reversed, the children of the family."

Lifestyle: ⬆ The harmonious conclusion of the first phase brings happiness and a sense of achievement. A sense of thankfulness for all that has been achieved. Enjoying the first fruits of your efforts.
⬇ Things remain unfinished or something mars your complete enjoyment. Emotionally disconnected from your achievements. A sense of isolation from the main event. Improving your surroundings, decorating your home.

Interaction: ⬆ Concord, peace, and harmony. Domestic well-being and mutual joy. A time to appreciate the delights of companionship. Going out with your companions or group.

⬇ A lack of appreciation for the joys and benefits of life. Feeling unappreciated or left out. Someone leaves or moves on.

Impact: ⬆ A time of festival and group celebration is coming. A labour of love that has been completed. Consolidating alliances or affirming your belonging. Inclusion in the community or group.

⬇ The end of rest or holiday signals a return to work. A tendency to take things for granted. A lack of focus on those who are left out, or upon their needs. Insecurity or the apprehensions of a minority group or species.

Environmental: Celebration and homecoming. Recreation, enjoying the earth. Ritual convocation. National thanksgiving. Harvest home. Community gathering. A time to sing the old songs and dance the old dances. Being excluded, out of sympathy with the mainstream. Resentful at being unable to celebrate because of personal grief or circumstances. Honouring the appropriate times and seasons.

Questions:
What is being celebrated?
What has prospered or been garnered?
How do you express your thankfulness?

FIVE OF WANDS

Image: Against a blue sky, five youths with staves contend together. Two at the back engage, while three fight in the foreground. The rough ground over which they fight is situated at the edge of a high place.

Focus:
"I will fight and win."
"We contend together for practice."
"We let off steam together."

Background: The Five of Wands offers the thrill of contest and the challenge of obstacles to be overcome. It also heralds power struggles on all levels, from mild debate to heated dissension. Something has to be worked out or through: this might be through mock gladiatorial combat, the bickering of a committee, or just plain, healthy competition. Finding the competitive edge, you may discover just how little of your power you normally use. This card also covers all kinds of sportsmanship, competitive games, and contests. Waite gives, "Success in financial speculation. Reversed: quarrels may be turned to good advantage."

Lifestyle: ⬆ Striving for advantage in a resistant or competitive atmosphere. A sense of salutary struggle in which you make little headway. Becoming agitated or worked up. Competitiveness, power struggle, serious competition!

⬇ Complex details complicate things. Passive aggression manipulates or fans hostility. Exploring ways to make accord. Litigation. Trial.

Interaction: ⬆ Competitiveness and rivalry drive the relationship. Arguments and disagreements are rife between you. Living with the contradictions and paradoxes that fuel a relationship. Rivalry. Quarreling and combativeness. Teamwork and brainstorming.
⬇ Betrayal or cheating on a friendship. Partners abandon the rules of fair play. Long-term disputes drag on and may need arbitration.

Impact: ⬆ Market forces change the face of everything. Dictatorial attitudes obstruct the full picture. Finding mutually respectful ways of negotiation. Discerning whose values win or who benefits eventually.
⬇ Letting others call the shots disempowers things. Harassment or persecution makes associations unstable. Public opinion turns against what it once supported.

Environmental: Internecine struggle. Survival of the fittest. Bordering countries face off in conflict. Territorial contests in a species. Dispute or competitive contention. Sports contests. Horseplay and games as necessary safety valves. Community effort. Taking sides. Honouring the ability to find a level playing field or a consensus through debate.

Questions:
What is the contention about?
What is gained?
What would be gained or lost?

SIX OF WANDS

Image: Against a blue sky, a man with a garland upon his head and garlanded staff in his right hand rides in procession upon a grey horse caparisoned in green. Beside and behind him come men on foot also bearing staves.

Focus:
"I come from winning the fight."
"Rejoice with me as I return."
"A victory for one is not a victory for all."

Background: Six of Wands heralds the recognition or vindication that is richly deserved and gives enhanced power or security to all. Victory comes to those who make headway by steady and continuous effort, or sometimes it just comes as a fortunate gift to the one in the right place at the right time. Honours and promotions can evoke the jealousy of others and make them envious, so modesty in achievement is a better laurel wreath than arrogance and self-importance. And not everyone rejoices when the victor passes, for there will always be those who do not benefit from the victor's achievement and who do not cheer when he passes by. Waite gives, "Servants who lose the confidence of their masters or a woman betrayed by a close friend; reversed, fulfilment of deferred hope."

Lifestyle: ⬆ Advancement realized through steady growth. Pride in achievement or promotion. Self-confidence leads you to success. Praise and recognition are the result of your service.

⬇ Negligible or transitory rewards. Arrogance in success spoils its gleam. Doubting your own self-esteem.

Interaction: ⬆ Winning your partner's admiration. Successfully interesting someone you were pursuing. Knowing yourself to be loved in return. Being appreciated by the other.
⬇ The disloyalty of close friends. Condescending attitudes destabilize things between you. Lack of shared interests leave the other left out of your charmed circle. Betrayal by the other. Watching how other people achieve and how you can duplicate their success.

Impact: ⬆ Recognition or ceremonial honours are granted. Popularity is ensured. Sharing skills and success benefits others. Public service. Serving in the armed services.
⬇ Bathing in the reflected glory of someone else's achievements. Disloyalty of supporters or followers. An unpopular award or victor. Treachery or disloyalty, Trojan horse tactics.

Environmental: Success in environmental endeavours. Making space for a species to recover or survive. A Pyrrhic victory when the losses outweigh the gains. Colonization and colonial legacy. Celebrating or awarding the one who wins out over all the odds Honouring both sides in the peace after conflict.

Questions:
Are these victors on your side?
Were the awards fairly won?
What are the results of the victory?

SEVEN OF WANDS

Image: Against a blue sky, a man with a quarterstaff stands defensively at the top of a cliff as six other staves rise up before him.

Focus:
"I'm taking the higher ground."
"I cannot climb down now."
"I thought I was safe up here."

Background: Seven of Wands holds out against opposition or else is trying to maintain the advantage. Defiant conviction and assertion demonstrate your strong character, so that you can take a stand for yourself or others. Tenacity and perseverance win out with this card in a firm position, and ebullience is fine when the matter is worth fighting for, but ensure that you aren't too focussed on minor points of principle. Sometimes the person taking the higher ground is not vindicated but has to use other skills. This card can also be that of someone who takes the moral high ground but who is nevertheless called to defend what is deeply believed.

Lifestyle: ⬆ You defend your strongly held views or show valour in the face of adversity. Your tenacity and persistence pay off. You assert yourself. Trying to gain the advantage. Having personal courage.
⬇ Having the wind temporarily taken out of your sails. Feeling paranoid or defensive. There's a tendency to seek a fight or to act aggressively. Vacillation.

Interaction: ⬆ Discussion, dialogue, or debate. Check the kind of language you are using in your interaction. Brainstorming to sort things out. Resolving a long-term relationship issue. Bartering and negotiation. Rivals try to knock you off your perch.

⬇ Being pushed to defend your position. Refuting criticism. Feeling inferior or vulnerable to the opposition. Embarrassment or anxiety caused by being at an overwhelming disadvantage.

Impact: ⬆ Persistence pays off. Public opinion is won over by persuasion. Taking a survey about what is really wanted. Resisting authority or speaking up for others.

⬇ Things may have to regroup or reorganise after adversity or criticism. Negotiate reconciliation or different terms. Leaving your defences weak. Inaction or vacillation causes places or institutions to be left undefended.

Environmental: Fighting against deforestation. Hedging to preserve solid ground from being swept away. Standing up for the rights of those who cannot speak or act themselves.
Struggling against policies or enemies to the common-wealth. Creative jealousy. Holding steadfast against encroachments to liberty. Rebelling against injustice. Honouring the moral principle that acts as a boundary of safety for all beings.

Questions:
Who is coming against you?
What do the others want?
What is worth defending here?

EIGHT OF WANDS

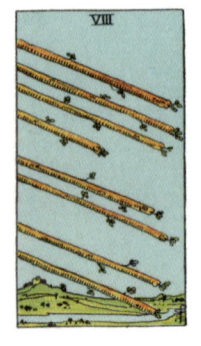

Image: Against a blue sky, eight wands with shoots upon them traverse the space. Behind, a river flows through a green landscape.

Focus:
"I bring things speedily."
"Now is the time to strike."
"Actions speak louder than words."

Background: Eight of Wands brings haste, speed or swiftness, and an acceleration that's hard to keep up with, unless you're able to pace yourself. This is one of the only cards in the Tarot that have no human subject in it. Timely communications, whirlwind romances, or synchronicities confirm that the power is with you. This card deals with short-term time scales or immediate actions rather than long-term ones, so take the opportunity it provides! It often deals with expedient actions or decisions. It tends to predict an escalation of prevailing conditions or of events that move swiftly. Whether desired or not, it might feel like too much of a good or bad thing to deal with in short order. Be sure you are not swept up on a tide of expediency, so that you are serving time, rather than using its opportunities. Speed, expediency, communication, and opportunities come thick and fast. Decisions taken about the environment.

Lifestyle: ⬆ Taking a bold stand. You have the freedom to move forward unimpeded if you strike now. Things move faster than you can control. All the elements are in the air for you. Moving to or visiting the countryside. A welter of events.

⬇ Harassment or delays hamper your style. Energy dissipates due to reversals or interruptions. Your conscience pulls you up short.

Interaction: ⬆ The message you've been longing for is in the post. You become involved together very quickly. Enjoy a last-minute holiday or share spontaneous recreation time together. Plans come together quickly. Plans come together with good collaboration.
⬇ Lack of control makes quarrels flare. Domestic escalation or disputes. Your hasty pursuit frightens off the one you desire or the contact you wish to court. Misunderstanding resultant from moving too quickly.

Impact: ⬆ An incoming influence that sweeps the land. Swiftness of communication. Things have speedy progress and rapid growth. Plunging into a social whirl. Getting behind a movement or action. Having to deal with a lot of things at once, with a consequent feel of speeding.
⬇ Hurtful gossip hits the headlines. Hasty expansion loses its trajectory. Stagnation in decision-making is caused by dealing with too many issues at once. Freeing up whatever has been stuck.

Environmental: This card in world or political readings can reveal either the time to act, or else the imposition of short-term laws or expedient responses when it is reversed. Things coming to fruition speedily. Tending what is growing. Rainfall in drought. Adverse rainfall and flooding. Short-term or expedient decisions damage the country. Honouring the wisdom of the present moment.

Questions:
What is the action to take now?
What impulse is coming online?
How will you seize this opportunity?

NINE OF WANDS

Image: Against a blue sky, a man with bandage binding his brow leans with fatigue upon his staff. Behind him stand eight other staves like a fence, with a green landscape in the background.

Focus:
"Bloody but unbowed, I will fight on."
"Let me just draw on my deep reserves of strength."
"My strength is found in adversity."

Background: Nine of Wands brings things into unknown territory, often against prevailing conditions that cannot easily be judged. Seven of Swords fights the oncoming foe, but Nine of Swords has been in the conflict for a longer time and has his back to the wall. As the fence of staves suggests, you cannot remain safely behind your usual defences. Using a blend of resourcefulness, experience, and whatever deep reserves you can call up, you need to prepare to meet the challenge. Situations with this card involve tapping into the reserve tank to meet the necessity. This card can often flag up a sense of inadequacy and the kind of resources that you need when you are challenged. Venturing into the unknown. Strength in adversity. Vigilance in the face of opposition. Waite also sees this as a difficult card, of being on the wrong side of things, of hindrance and thwarting.

Lifestyle: ⬆ Use your enduring reserves to prepare against adversity. Defining your goals will help map a way through uncertainty. Obstinate endurance and a refusal to be beaten gets you through.

⬇ Recurrent bouts of fatigue or ill health due to overexertion. Expressing or feeling hostility and alienation, whatever the prevailing conditions. Being caught off guard.

Interaction: ⬆ Defending the essentials of health, home, or partnership against all comers. Essentializing and appreciating the relationship in the face of prevailing difficulties.
⬇ Continuous attrition is wearing. Find subtle ways to overcome a strong opponent's challenge rather than wasting your energies. Stepping in and assuming control to disempower someone.

Impact: ⬆ A national or localised struggle. Keeping up a dogged opposition in unfamiliar terrain. Protecting others against attack. Recognizing the enemy or saboteur in your ranks.
⬇ Diminished resources make it hard to hold out. A beleaguered defence that is hopeless. Failure to foresee opponent's intentions. Laying down the fight and allowing others to continue.

Environmental: Perseverance in the face of environmental challenges. Reforestation. Fighting a rear guard action, bringing fresh help into the struggle. Marginalization from dominant culture. Struggling for the wrong aim. Backing someone up or upholding an unsupported cause. Expending more power than you are receiving. Self-sabotage, enabling others at the expense of yourself. Honouring the need to seek more help.

Questions:
What does this challenge mean for you?
What will meet the challenge?
What keeps you going when the chips are down?

TEN OF WANDS

Image: Against a blue sky, a man staggers forward carrying ten staves toward a settlement.

Focus:
"I will see this to the end."
"I am feeling overwhelmed."
"I will do this even though it kills me."

Background: Ten of Wands denotes that things have become oppressive or burdensome. You are carrying everything, doing the major caring or being involved in too many projects. Rather than lose face, you try to do the work of Atlas, continuing to hold up the world. If you find yourself continuously picking up the tab of life's troubles, it's worth considering what you are getting out of this. This is not a card of long-term commitment. There can be success, but if followed by Nine of Swords, things come to grief. There can be a sense of "dining out" on your massive list of commitments or effect, since this is a "staging card" (see p. 238). Waite sees it as signifying difficulties and contradictions, especially when it falls next to a favourable card.

Lifestyle: ⬆ Overwhelmed, oppressed, burdened. Overburdened with possessions. Living up to impossible standards. Misusing or overestimating your own power. Biography becomes biology as life impacts you. Carrying impossible responsibilities.
⬇ Recognizing signs of burnout and breaking free. Walking away from untenable situations. Realizing that you cannot do everything.

Interaction: ⬆ Trying to keep a relationship going against the odds. A sense of victimization or neediness from your partner becomes oppressive. Emotionally overwhelmed by demands. Carrying the other person's burdens for them. Toiling at work.

⬇ A trial separation to lift the tension. Breaking out of an oppressive relationship. Living without ties or contracts for the time being. Breaking off from onerous employment practices.

Impact: ⬆ Carrying the weight of the world on your shoulders. The pressures of responsibility or overcommitment. Delegating responsibility to a team or sharing power. Continuously placating or shoring up an issue that needs community help. Carrying on a difficult or complex task, lawsuit, or long-term struggle.

⬇ Backing out of a group project. Taking time to downsize. Recognizing the weight of the system on your shoulders.

Environmental: Oppressive burdens upon habitat. Unfair burdens upon the backs of those least able to carry them. Abusive terms of employment, zero-hours jobs. This card can also signify a whole community, habitat, or region that is struggling to cope. Obsessive patterns, workaholism. Difficult generational legacies. Honouring the wisdom of laying down excessive burdens.

Questions:
Who or what is oppressing you?
What do you need to lay down?
Can you share or delegate the load?

PAGE OF WANDS

Image: Against a blue sky, a youth stands in a desert landscape regarding a budding staff. He wears a hat, and his tunic is covered with salamanders.

Focus:
"I am ardent in enthusiasm."
"You can rely upon me."
"I bring surprising news."

Background: The Page of Wands is the go-between who accepts the assignment. This is an engaging person with an innovative and playful attitude, who has ardent enthusiasm and an adventurous spirit and who is keen to find opportunities. This resourceful messenger is reliable and loyal, maybe sometimes uninhibited and forthright. He shows the way, often through impossible situations, by daring and dedication. He also prepares the ground by scientific means or by inspiration that reveals a situation's potential. This card was originally associated with heroes, especially Roland from the Charlemagne cycle of the Matter of France or with Hector from the *Iliad*. Traditionally, the Page of Wands was the card of the stranger or a person outside your group or community or of the envoy or messenger; when reversed, bad news, indecision, or instability is signified. When followed by the Page of Cups, this card can reveal a rival.

Person: ⬆ This is a charming and adventurous person who often acts as a messenger or emissary. He may act as a catalyst for change and improvement or represent your interests as a go-between. Someone who brings exciting, surprising, or good news.

⬇ He can be hasty, gullible, or even a copycat. Occasionally over-zealous or bored, he likes to dabble or grab attention. The bringer of bad news.

Process: ⬆ Working your way up the ladder. Having an adventurous spirit. Learning to engage with life. Devotion to an interest or hobby. Jumping into the thick of things. Getting the job done. Reading the instructions or getting deeper into the potential. Opportunities for growth. Doing things playfully.

⬇ Being indiscriminate. Throwing a tantrum. Unable to deal with the details. Ensure that things are not being put at risk. Overwhelmed by bad tidings.

Event: ⬆ Unexpected news. Sudden help out of the blue. Something extraordinary. An opening where you can shine. A dream or vision.

⬇ Strange or unsettling news. An archive or some past history is opened. A disappointing but important piece of intelligence.

Environmental: Replanting trees or plants; cultivating or irrigating barren places. A proclamation or intelligent strategy that takes effect across the land. Making a report about prevailing conditions in a country or habitat. Discovery of a new species. A scientific survey. Supporting the growth and development of emerging cultures. Listening to the needs of minorities. Honouring innovation that supports growth.

Questions:
What details are being considered?
What news is expected?
How would things change if you engaged with this?

KNIGHT OF WANDS

Image: Against a light-blue sky, a knight upon a rearing roan horse is riding with a staff in hand. He has salamanders upon his tunic, while upon his horse's bridle there are trefoils. In the background are three pyramids or conical mountains.

Focus:
"I ride at speed to answer the call."
"My aim is a noble one."
"I am forceful and passionate in all my deeds."

Background: The Knight of Wands is an energetic and impetuous champion who is both exciting and exhilarating, like a hero of old. The pyramids in the background may remind us of crusaders or a man who goes overseas on secondment. His inspired companionship leads into exciting adventures. But he is fearless of the unknown, and his hasty decisions are often risky. He can be forceful and passionate, improvises his way through obstacles to the place appointed, but is also tetchy or choleric. Traditionally, this can be the card of someone who leaves in a huff and walks out, or else a sudden departure of another kind. This could be after a disagreement or division or opinion.

Person: ⬆ He is an impulsive and dynamic person whose flamboyant style others admire. He leaps in boldly where others might fear to tread, and is often the fashion leader or motivator of any group. A dynamic lover who sparkles and charms.

⬇ He can be competitive, a bit of a dabbler, or a show-off. As a rebel without a cause, he can also upset and unsettle others and needs constant stimulus or drama.

Process: ⬆ Being quick witted. Cleverness. Leaving old ways behind. Innovating creatively. Improvising a way forward. Being overcompetitive. Audacity companions opportunity.
⬇ Recklessness endangers others. Unstable circumstances caused by overconfidence. Disruptive temper is less than charming.

Event: ⬆ Travel. Impatience. Hastiness. A chance to change things or move away.
⬇ Plans that quickly flare up only to die back. Separation by distance. Gang violence. Domineering attitudes wreck relationships. A sudden departure or walkout.

Environmental: A critical period in which species and habitat may be irretrievably lost due to failure of a timely intervention. Championing the re-greening of the earth. The courage and daring to envision new ways forward. Political agitation. A sense of adventure and exploration. Respect for Indigenous cultures. Honouring the dynamism and passion of life.

Questions:
Which opportunity is offered in this situation?
What doors will be opened to you?
What degree of dynamism or passion is needed?

QUEEN OF WANDS

Image: Against a light-blue sky, a woman wearing a leafy crown sits upon a throne, holding a staff in her right hand and a sunflower in her left. The throne is supported by stone lions, while behind her is a cloth of estate woven with red heraldic lions. Before her sits a black cat. To the left, there is a suggestion of pyramids or mountains.

Focus:
"I creatively support whatever you want to do."
"Goodwill is my gift to everyone."
"My household is a place of peace and honour."

Background: The Queen of Wands is a strong, active, and energetic woman who enjoys communicating original ideas. She has a shrewd business eye for what works in the popular field, and her common touch lights up the mundane with radiant enthusiasm. She has self-confidence, passion, and radiance, encouraging things to come to fruition.

She accomplishes many things through her resourcefulness, so that her outgoing warmth summons up the strength for you to get things done energetically. A love of life can open up everything with her help. Traditionally, this is the card of a good harvest; reversed, someone who has goodwill toward the querent but who fails to exercise it. When the Queen of Wands appears to the left of another court card, she is interested in that person. This card was associated with Penthesilea, the Amazonian queen, as well as with the beautiful

Rachel, the daughter of Laban, for whom Jacob toiled for seven years. Etteilla saw her as a countrywoman.

Person: ⬆ A popular and dedicated person, someone who has great self-assurance. She has both passion and wholehearted enthusiasm for whatever she does. She is committed and kind, quick to defend or take your side.
⬇ She can be unpredictable and retaliatory if she is crossed. Jealousy, opposition, and rivalry soon arise if the drama queen isn't placated. She may expect high standards.

Process: ⬆ Having sympathy and empathy with the process. Using your ambition creatively. Courteous dealing paves the way to better understanding. A love of life.
⬇ Harbouring slights or insults. Undermining the plans of others. Get an expert opinion before you proceed.

Event: ⬆ A party or social gathering. A business opportunity to consider. A peace offering. Confrontation.
⬇ Sorcery, bitching, or petty spell craft. Burnout begins to bite. Takeovers or makeovers that change everything.

Environmental: The cultural wealth and sacred sites of Indigenous communities. Spreading a sense of social well-being. A good harvest. Good husbandry and land management. Cats. Enriching the soil. Upholding animal rights. Honouring the instinct and insight of our animal nature.

Questions:
What is the effect of your influence upon those around you?
How can these plans best be fostered?
Where do you need to be more courteous, kind, or understanding?

KING OF WANDS

Image: Against a blue sky, the king sits on his throne crowned with a flame-tipped crown, holding a budding staff in his right hand. His cloak is woven with salamanders. Behind him is a cloth of estate woven with lions and salamanders. On the podium of his throne, a salamander is standing.

Focus:
"I rule with tolerance and honesty."
"I honour noble hearts and good intentions."
"I bring a passionate interest to all endeavours."

Background: The King of Wands sets his distinctive and creative stamp on everything, taking charge to mastermind enterprises and get things implemented. His projects and plans inspire others, and many look to his leadership. His certainty and verve make the way plain, though you might find him hard to argue with. His influence enables you to live your life with relish, plunging into new experiences. This card offers benevolence, magnanimity, power, skill. Traditionally, this is the card of a good marriage or partnership; reversed, it can signify someone whose advice you should listen to and take. This card was once associated with Julius Caesar.

Person: ⬆ This is an honourable and magnanimous person, who takes command. He has a strong self-respect and has a flare for establishing a presence, so he is often a market leader or an entrepreneur. A charismatically attractive person. Someone who brings passion and animation into the room.

⬇ Someone who can shirk away from positions of leadership or needs to brand everything with his mark, whether they originated something or not. An autocrat or power-hungry person. Someone whose egotism obliterates the weak or whose work is tainted by a controlling ethic.

Process: ⬆ Being benevolent to those who are needy. Establishing your sovereignty or position. Being assertive or enthusiastic. Maintaining honesty in the face of deceit or attempts at double-dealing.
⬇ Dominating the situation. Bullying others from a place of power. Self-righteousness insulates you. Listening to advice against your own hot-headed impulses or self-persuaded by the convictions of enthusiasm.

Event: ⬆ An opportunity or reachable goal. An enterprise to be developed. Trendsetting business venture. Land management or buying property.
⬇ Copyright or intellectual-property dispute. An aggressive takeover bid. Investments crash. Land or property is mismanaged.

Environmental: An unethical business that is unconcerned with the consequences. Standing up for the rights of the downtrodden. The passion to uphold environmental rights of species or habitats. Living a simple life. Living honestly. Autocracy. Enfranchising species and Indigenous groups to follow their ancestral principles. Reptiles and amphibians. Passionate support of the earth. Honouring the power of leadership.

Questions:
Where do you need to take charge?
How does truth set things free?
Where does benevolence need to be shown here?

ACE OF CUPS

Image: Against a grey sky, a golden chalice rests upon a disembodied palm. Over the cup a dove descends into it, bearing the wafer of the host in its beak. Four streams of water fountain from the cup into the water lily waters below. Drops fall from the cup.

Focus:
"I overflow with love."
"Abundance, healing, and joy can be yours."
"I enable you to return to the heart of your home."

Background: The Ace of Cups brings abundance, healing, and joy. It gives a sense of a new beginning where the belief that things are going to float rather than sink is so strong that you can't help feeling glad. Trusting your intuitions is like allowing the sea to hold you up, so it's possible to indulge your hopes and dreams. Rather than restricting your horizons, see how you can fill them. The emotional limitations fall away as you welcome in the glad day. This card bears the image of the Holy Grail and of the sacramental wafer, brought by the dove of the Holy Spirit. Waite also gives the antithetical meanings of "inflexible will, unalterable law." While reversed, it brings "an unexpected change of position."

Lifestyle: ⬆ Gladness and generosity buoy you up. A sense of nourishment and emotional expansion. Recognition for yourself or for your goals. A glad home.

⬇ A lack of generosity gives little opportunity. A sense of sterility or limited emotional response. Unable to express your feelings. A household where there is little reciprocation.

Interaction: ⬆ Emotional growth brings intimacy between you. Deep feelings engender understanding. Acceptance of each other brings joy and happiness. Giving and receiving are reciprocal.

⬇ Unrequited love. Failure to foster or receive love. Trust is being eroded through limitation or jealousy.

Impact: ⬆ Expansion or receptivity. Restoration or the promise of beauty and fertility after barrenness. Healing a rift within a group, family, or nation. Something new is being born. Expansive emotion, great hopefulness, and gladness.

⬇ Blockage or misunderstanding. Lack of appreciation. Forgiveness and forgetfulness are needed.

Environmental: Water purity, provision of water and sanitation. Health solutions. Allowing the fullness of life to break out of self-imposed or perceived limits. Offering your skills to serve your community. Changes in diversity that have an impact on a habitat. Honouring the power of love to change all things.

Questions:
Where is inspiration needed?
How are you being called to give or receive?
What can bring abundance and expansiveness?

TWO OF CUPS

Image: Against a light-blue sky, a young man and a young woman, each carrying a cup before them, face each other. The young man reaches out his right hand toward her. Over them, a winged lion's head surmounting a caduceus, while in the distance there is a green hill.

Focus:
"We are drawn to each other."
"We give of ourselves to make one completeness."
"We build by reciprocation."

Background: The Two of Cups gives passion wings and immerses differing individuals or viewpoints into a unified vision. The exchanges that arise from this union are mutually supportive because the matchmaking is so exact. Even seemingly oppositional forces can come together with this card, because they complement each other with their unique attraction. This card governs mutual love and affection, reciprocity, romance.

It enables you to find satisfactory agreements on many levels and to make choices that harmonize or bridge divides. Waite also gives, favourable in things of pleasure and business, as well as love, also wealth and honour, but when reversed, it signifies physical passion.

Lifestyle: ⬆ The ability to communicate your hopes and passions. Seeking for reciprocation and partnership in your ventures. Enjoying the give and take of life.

⬇ Trying to go it alone. A period of celibacy or solitude. Realising that lack of balance or sharing hinders your way forward. Consider what it is that you are offering. Physical passion.

Interaction: ⬆ Pledges and promises between the two of you, including engagement or marriage. A contractual partnership is set up. Love, affinity, attraction. Reciprocal interests.
⬇ Divorce, breakdown, or separation due to opposing needs or views. Infatuation abates and leaves you flat. Recent hurts reopen old wounds. Narcissistic motives play on vulnerabilities.

Impact: ⬆ Mutual sympathy helps common goals to be achieved. Cooperative ventures spread concord. Reconciliation of different parties in agreement.
⬇ Disunity or opposition. Group decisions fail through mistrust or division. A sense of betrayal or not being fully met mars any negotiation. Consider the impact of your affinity.

Environmental: Partnership and reciprocation with the earth. The inter-relationship of ecosystems brings balance. Finding the point of exchange is less about compromise than it is about having mutual respect. The sanctity of life. Combatting hunger. Food banks. Plenty/scarcity. Loyalty and friendship. Honouring the power of commitment.

Questions:
What is the basis of trust and respect?
What is attracting you?
How is affinity evoked?

THREE OF CUPS

Image: Against a blue sky, three young women with garlands upon their heads are each holding up a cup, as if toasting one other. Around their feet are piled ripe fruits and vegetables.

Focus:
"We celebrate and give thanks."
"We welcome in the harvest."
"We bring things to a happy conclusion."

Background: Generosity of spirit typifies the Three of Cups, for it has the power to communicate a joy and gladness that embraces all. The bond that you experience under its influence is an irresistible need to come together in peace and concord, for the abolition of differences. Three of Cups is capable of raising generosity in the meanest breast and of building fellow feeling between different parties. When reversed, it can denote a speedy conclusion or timely achievement. Waite also gives, "Unexpected advancement for a military man, and when reversed, consolation, cure, and end of the business."

Personal: ⬆ An opportunity for merriment or a time of solace and refreshment. The satisfaction of joining in with others. Considering things for the benefit of all, rather than from the personal or selfish standpoint.
⬇ Dissipation or doing things to excess. Loss of prestige. Unable to enjoy or join in. Being unaware of an upturn that includes you.

Interaction: ⬆ Having a party or celebration. Friendships you can rely upon. Entering into a fruitful collaboration. Seeking out or meeting up with friends for mutual pleasure.

⬇ Having no time to party or recreate yourselves. Friendships are strained by events. Feeling left out. Rivals undercut cooperative ventures or infiltrate and divide things.

Impact: ⬆ Celebration of alliances. An event where everyone and everything are welcome. Mutual support and appreciation. Including all that is. Appreciating the fruits of the earth. A sense of unity, peace, and concord.

⬇ Support networks are withdrawn. Group gatherings are cancelled or hit delays or obstacles. Mutual support is withdrawn.

Environmental: Community celebration, Earth Day. Being included in the group. Welcoming incomers or newcomers. Gladdening the circle of life. Finding ways of bringing peace. Honouring the first fruits of the earth in celebration.

Questions:
What do you have to be grateful for?
Who or what needs to be included?
How are the earth's resources being renewed?

FOUR OF CUPS

Image: Against a blue sky, a cross-legged youth with his arms folded sits under a tree upon a small mound. Before him stand three cups, while a fourth cup is offered to him by a disembodied hand emerging from a cloud.

Focus:
"I have had too much of a good thing."
"I want to see old things in a new light."
"I am weary of anything you might offer."

Background: Four of Cups reveals stagnation of the spirit or offers an opportunity to be quiet and mundane after too much stimulation. You may be resting on your laurels or feeling bored or complacent about things, but you may start looking for the edge where you can engage with things again. Remaining apathetic or unengaged for too long can lead to depression, or you need to take time out to reconsider how you live and work. Emotional maturity grows through sustained repetition and exercise in all conditions, and this card offers the opportunity to reconsider how we really see things, especially when we seek the novelty of difference. Waite also gives, "Contrarieties, and when reversed, a presentiment."

Lifestyle: ⬆ In the grip of apathy, dissatisfaction, or lethargy. Boredom with mundane life or daily round. Feeling stuck in a rut or a loop.

⬇ Re-examination of your lifestyle. Fresh avenues or new possibilities are considered. A glimpse of change offers a different vista. New things refresh you. Novelty relieves boredom.

Interaction: ⬆ Monotony and familiarity define how you treat each other. A friendship or relationship bores or disgusts you. Not giving time to keep the relationship functional helps it drift apart.
⬇ Refreshing the way you see each other. Working on the bonds that keep you stable. Seeking new friends and acquaintances. New acquaintances freshen your social round.

Impact: ⬆ Dealing with the mundane matters that have to be performed. Dissatisfaction with life. Experience embitters or sours things.
⬇ Reawakening to life's possibilities. Fresh ambitions enliven things. Breaking new soil or sowing new crops for another day.

Environmental: Complacency with the good things of life. A time to reconsider your blessings. Living more simply. Realizing the impact of the human desire for novelty, appeasement, and entertainment upon the earth. Self-loathing. Belonging to yourself again. Honouring life's renewal by a regular spiritual practice.

Questions:
What blessing are you avoiding?
How might you ring the changes?
What stability do you appreciate?

FIVE OF CUPS

Image: Against a grey sky, a cloaked figure stands beside a river with three overturned cups spilling their contents on the ground. Behind him stand two cups. In the distance is a bridge leading to a small castle keep.

Focus:
"This is a mixed blessing."
"Disappointment mars any gain."
"I still have something to pass on."

Background: This card embodies the proverb "A fat sorrow is better than a lean sorrow," typifying a loss that involves an inheritance, albeit one that is not as rich as you expected. It usually reveals what you can salvage from any loss, since three cups are gone but two remain. While you cannot turn back the clock or change things, acknowledging how things are now and finding ways to move forward to the next phase of life. As the water goes under the bridge and cannot come the same way again, this card invites you to notice mistakes but to move on, rather than becoming stuck in the past. It is a card that sometimes marks the anticipatory bereavement of a skill, ability, or resource that is shortly to be withdrawn. Waite gives the card these additional meanings: "generally favourable; a happy marriage; also patrimony, legacies, gifts, success in enterprise; while reversed, the return of some relative who has not been seen for long."

Lifestyle: ⬆ Learning from your own mistakes and losses, assessing your limitations or freedoms. Inheritances, legacies or insurance payouts. Disappointment or regret keeps you in stasis.

⬇ Recovering from loss a bit at a time. Letting bygones be bygones or putting the unalterable past behind you. Hopeful expectations.

Interaction: ⬆ Love, friendship, or alliances in trouble. Mourning the loss of a partner, pet, or friend. Acknowledging the source of your grief or loss to another.
⬇ Reunions or new friends that come into your life. The end of a period of bereavement. Acknowledging what doesn't work and starting afresh. Ties of kinship and alliances that support you.

Impact: ⬆ Something is lost, but something is gained. Descendants can find ways when the legacy of ancestors runs out. Reviewing agreements or promises with the earth. Focussing on failures keeps things depressed.
⬇ Losses that serve to bind communities together. Ancestry or kindred discovered. Realizing how failures pave the way to better strategies. Group grief holds things in stasis. Whatever affects the wider family.

Environmental: A loss for the world is a loss for all. Mistakes that bring loss. Facing the things that we can't change. Ensuring that we can hand over the earth to our descendants in the best way. The milk is spilt; while things cannot be as once they were, it is a time to draw together existing resources wisely. Survivor guilt. Surviving loss. Honouring what has changed through loss.

Questions:
What is lost, what continues?
What is still transmissible?
What can bridge this time and what follows?

SIX OF CUPS

Image: Against a light-blue sky, a pair of children stand in the courtyard of an old house. The older boy is offering one cup to the younger girl. Beside the boy, a cup is raised up on a garden feature with a saltire upon it, while four cups range along the foreground. Each cup has a white starflower within it.

Focus:
"We receive the gifts of the past."
"We transmit our foundational memories to light the future."
"We guide and protect the children."

Background: This card opens up the gifts of the past to be enjoyed in the present, whether on the level of deep, ancestral memories or as loyalties that re-emerge in your life or with the pleasure of remembered links. Such memories may have a tinge of nostalgia or carry the full weight of a trauma that still resounds. These gifts of remembrance have power to shape your life. They also contribute to the gift that you yourself will leave to those yet to be born. Remembrances of what you hold in mind or heart maintain links which continue to feed and gift you. Waite also gives, "Pleasant memories; while reversed, an inheritance to follow quickly."

Lifestyle: ⬆ A stable homelife with simple pleasures. Rediscovering your roots. Nostalgia for simpler or happy times.

⬇ Being stuck in the past or else living on the future's credit. Future opportunities begin to show themselves. Transcending or regenerating your gifts.

Interaction: ⬆ Nostalgic remembrances or past vistas revisited together. Anniversaries return to remind you how you've grown together. An unselfish or romantic gift that expects no return.
⬇ Memory of anniversaries brings pain. Outworn friendships chunter on. Playing on the guilt of your partner. Seeking out future partnerships.

Impact: ⬆ A sense of loyalty or obligation to traditions. The joys of home, birthplace, or homeland. Volunteer or pro-bono service for others. Taking into account the needs and rights of children. Making decisions that will affect future generations.
⬇ The past lays its hand on the future. Steering by traditions that no longer work. Difficult ancestral bequests that affect the living. Institutional child abuse.

Environmental: Remembering. The pull of memory or the past. Children and their rights. The heritage of the past and the impact upon the future. Creating a new environment when old ones have vanished. Cultural heritage as a living way. The gifts and potentials of the past. Anniversarial memories. Past resonances that still resound. Honouring the contribution of ancestors that pave the way to the future.

Questions:
What memories give you life?
How do you transmit your heritage?
How do the gifts of the past sustain the future?

SEVEN OF CUPS

Image: Against a blue sky, a figure stands with back toward the viewer in silhouette. It beholds a vision in which seven cups appear from a cloud. In each cup are different scenarios: a head, a veiled figure, a snake, a mountain, flowers, a laurel wreath, a dragon.

Focus:
"My desires are reflected in my mind's eye."
"I reach out for the vision to be manifested."
"How do I tell truth from illusion?"

Background: The Seven of Cups offers the prospect of many alternatives or a vision so enticing that it is hard not to be drawn into it. It invites you to use your imagination and move your daydreams into reality. Faced with so many choices, it is easy to become enthralled, disorganized, or indolent, forgetting that in order to enjoy your vision, it must be built first. Desire and vision are not the same thing, however. In a reading, this card challenges us to distinguish wish fulfilment and vision from reality and illusion. Waite also offers, "A fair child, idea, design, resolve, movement; when reversed, success, especially if accompanied by the Three of Cups."

Lifestyle: ⬆ Self-deception, daydreaming, or wishful thinking. Indulging in addictive patterns. Rehearsing plans or events to explore the possibilities.

⬇ Getting a clear sense of things by dismissing old daydreams. Implementing plans or manifesting your dreams. Trusting the imagination.

Interaction: ⬆ Caught in the unrealistic attitudes or expectations of another. Role playing and sexual fantasies. Envisioning the perfect partner. Intriguing and entrancing projections cast upon the other. Sharing the same dream.
⬇ Emerging from a phase where you can't read each other easily. Deflating the projections or unrealistic scenarios you've projected upon each other.

Impact: ⬆ Fashionable or influential trends rule the roost. Exploring the possibilities of popular ideas. Building upon or exploiting short-lived trends. Mob delusion, the morass of social-media-fuelled unreality. Entertaining escapist scenarios or misleading, which can influence others.
⬇ The realization of a collective vision. Anticipating what the public needs. Using imaginative solutions to ongoing problems.

Environmental: "Will-o-the-wisp" messages, ideas, and conspiracy theories that can lead astray. "Living in cloud cuckoo land," or building castles in the air. Coming to grips with the reality of things. Unsubstantiated dreams. Living in a haze of conflicting goals. Paranoia. Mental illness. Confusion after long struggle. Environmental daydreaming. Honouring the imagination and clarifying the vision.

Questions:
What is real and what is illusion?
How do you choose from all the possibilities?
Which of these things will last?

EIGHT OF CUPS

Image: Against a dark-blue sky, a lone, cloaked figure treks out of the scene with a walking stick. The terrain is rocky with inlets of water, while the new moon has the old moon in its arms. In the foreground are eight cups.

Focus:
"Things decline, so I move on."
"I cannot build on what I have done here."
"I will seek satisfaction elsewhere."

Background: The Eight of Cups teaches that discretion is the better part of valour. What doesn't work for you should not be endured; dissatisfaction with your current lot often drives you to find a better way or to walk away from what doesn't work. This card signals the kind of dissatisfaction that leads to better ways forward or a change of heart that helps you reassess your options and move on, unless you can stay on and commit to making things better. Disentangling what you've woven may take a little ingenuity, but hold your own deeply felt truths as a beacon before you. The new moon with the old moon in its arms shows that some distance has to be gained before any new beginning will bear fruit. Waite gives, "Marriage with a fair woman. Reversed: perfect satisfaction."

Lifestyle: ↑ Reconsidering your options before it's too late. Discontinuance of your plans after a rethink. A general disenchantment with the run of your life that demands attention.

⬇ Sticking with your plans and seeing them through. Reinstating or re-exploring your original mission or idea. Exploring the alternatives without obligation.

Interaction: ⬆ Emotional ambivalence or failure to commit puts things into stasis. Feelings of abandonment or falling out of love. Being unable to satisfy friends or partners. Inability to work for an employer anymore because of conflicting values or practices.
⬇ Reincluding friends you'd avoided or neglected. Making greater efforts to make things work between you. Refraining from sexual intimacy.

Impact: ⬆ The quest for new values and standards. Alienation with the usual mundane methods. Considering alternatives to the rat race. Making it better for all living.
⬇ Evaluating things from a more universal standpoint. Old debts are paid off. Finding fresh energy in group ventures. Sharing things joyfully in community.

Environmental: Environmental hardships cause changes to come about. Trying to find better ways of living by training elsewhere. Reassessing social policies. Living in small community units. Rehoming species in different habitats. Beginning again by returning to first principles. Radical changes of direction. Honouring the necessity to reframe your aim or vision.

Questions:
Where is retrenchment necessary?
What fresh priorities are coming along?
Where are your energies uselessly committed?

NINE OF CUPS

Image: Against a yellow sky, an older man sits on a bench with arms crossed. Behind him is a semicircular table on which stand nine cups.

Focus:
"I enjoy the best of everything."
"Comfort and contentment are the reward of success."
"I revel in the good things of the earth."

Background: The Nine of Cups signals material security and satisfaction and often appears as the heart's desire card. Additionally, what you wish for comes to pass. Satisfaction of the senses, the mind, and the soul is possible with this card. After the daydreaming of the Seven of Cups or the retrenchments of the Eight of Cups, there is a positive fulfilment at last. This is the wish card, and it will often flag up where you invest your deepest feelings or your heart's desire. There is also a sense of the Irish proverb "Living off the pig's back" or "Having the best of everything." We are more aware today that our ease is often the result of someone's need and toil or a disturbing inequity that comfort for a few carries a high price for the earth at large. Waite gives, "A good augury for military men. Reversed: Good business."

Lifestyle: ⬆ Omens tell you that your wishes are achievable. You enjoy physical well-being and comfort. Difficulties depart or you experience relief at a job well done. Satisfaction, reward, wishes granted.

⬇ Self-satisfaction or complacency robs you of the emotional edge. Wasted opportunities lie in your wake. Finding deeper happiness beyond the material brings you closer to satisfaction.

Interaction: ⬆ Your emotional contentment is perfect. Enjoying a romantic supper or luxurious break together. Having confidence in your friend or partner.
⬇ Unrealistic desires alienate your partner. Projecting "perfect partner" scenarios upon your beloved. Shallow or self-indulgent attitudes alienate others.

Impact: ⬆ Praying for the good of others. Becoming complacent in the face of success. Bathing in reflected celebrity success. The easeful complacence of civilization.
⬇ Misplaced expectations disappoint many. Inability to receive or give blessings. Opportunities for widespread material benefit are lost.

Environmental: Privilege is reassessed. Unless you make space for the changes that you want, they may elude you. Complacency about the duration of abundance and plenty. A period of luxury or expansiveness. Sharing the outcome of your greatest wish. Accustomed to luxury and self-indulgence. Honouring the power of your heart's wish.

Questions:
What is your heart's desire?
Where can your resources and skills benefit others?
How can your success be shared?

TEN OF CUPS

Image: Against a blue sky, a man and woman with their two young children face a rainbow in the sky before them. Arrayed along the rainbow are ten cups. In the distance, a river flows through green countryside in which a homestead is set.

Focus:
"We hold hearth and home lovingly together."
"We count our blessings every day. "
"Let us share the earth harmoniously!"

Background: The Ten of Cups reveals the wholeness and completion that pave the way to contentment. When this card appears in a reading, look for a sense of inclusion in the common joy, whether it be of family, friends, or community. This card builds up and brings together things in a harmonious way, so that you can enjoy the tranquillity of togetherness. This is the card that stands for one's homeland. The sense of indignation at the violation of our globe and the need to restore it to its essence are strong in this card. Etteilla saw this card as representing the city, town, or homeland.

Waite noted that this card in the company of many court cards denotes that one or more people are taking charge of the querent's affairs when they have no or little agency to act for themselves.

Lifestyle: ⬆ Contentment and happiness are enjoyed at last. Repose in the heart. Honour or reputation are recognized and celebrated among your peers. The delight of homecoming and a warm welcome or homecoming.

⬇ A delayed or disappointing homecoming. Exile or a long sojourn away from home. Dishonour or betrayal follows you.

Interaction: ⬆ The blessing of hearth and home warms your heart. Lasting happiness with those you love. Building family values and emotional connections by fostering every member.

⬇ A quarrelsome homelife spoils your contentment. Children leave home or stray delinquently. You experience emotional overload from family expectations or duties.

Impact: ⬆ A sense of belonging to the wider world. Fellowship and family values embrace everyone. The completion of a shared project. Community well-being fosters contentment. Your native land or country.

⬇ Criminal destruction spoils things. The degradation of land or property. Exclusion from the common joy leaves discontent and fosters envy.

Environmental: The inviolate sanctity of hearth and home. Contentment, joyous completion, being included in the family. Kindred beings. Ancestors who look kindly upon you. A sense of recognition that everyone shares the earth. Beauty and harmony. Domestic violence or dissension. Family cohesion. Honouring the family circle.

Questions:
How can you share the commonwealth with others?
What keeps the home inviolate?
Where is emotional satisfaction invested?

PAGE OF CUPS

Image: Against a grey sky, a well-dressed youth in a tunic covered with water lilies stands by the side of the sea. In his right hand is a cup from which a fish peers out. Behind him are the waves of the sea.

Focus:
"I am at the service of love and pleasure."
"What I envisage comes to pass."
"I help you follow your inclinations."

Background: The Page of Cups is a good mediator who can help facilitate resolutions. Imaginative and loving, someone who shows the way to fulfil the deepest desires. With this card there is a willingness to serve and a close affinity with dreams or the unconscious promptings of intuition. You can reach out and touch someone who feels left out, or gladden the heart of one you love. Consideration and service are the fruits of emotional honesty. This card shows how you can best serve and be considerate. In historical Tarots and playing cards, the Page of Cups was based upon both Paris of Troy, who abducted Helen of Sparta, and also the soldier Etienne de Vignoles, the fourteenth-century supporter of Joan of Arc. Waite gives: "For a male Querent, a good marriage and one beyond his expectations. Reversed: sorrow; also a serious quarrel."

Person: ⬆ A good sharer with deep intuition. A romantic go-between or mediator. Someone who is reflective and joyful by turn, making him playful and a delight to be with. A loyal friend who is both cooperative and supportive.

⬇ Someone who can be emotionally vulnerable, easily swayed, or selfishly absorbed in his own troubles. Someone needing reassurance.

Process: ⬆ Contemplating things with a considerate heart. Learning trust. Serving with love. Making a good impression.
⬇ Refusing to listen. Living only in the imagination. Being led or swayed by stronger influences. Sweet-talking persuasion. The beguilement of advertising.

Event: ⬆ Meditation. Forgiveness. Dream messages. Conflict resolution. Fair play.
⬇ Abandonment. Fawning and flattery. Jealousy. Spirit messages. Bringing loving grace out of the depths.

Environmental: Consideration, affection, service, delight. Care of marine life. Overfishing. Bringing all of life together in your heart. Animal distress and exploitation. Extending loving support to different life forms. Giving the voiceless a voice. Honouring the ability to mediate between species.

Questions:
Who/what is getting closer to you?
Where do you need to let beauty into your life?
What deeper trust is being asked of you?

KNIGHT OF CUPS

Image: Against a light-blue sky, a knight in silver armour and a tunic embroidered with red fish and water rides on a grey horse, carrying a cup in his right hand. On his helmet are wings. Behind him, a river flows beside sand and rocks.

Focus:
"I bring you news that will gladden your heart."
"I sing the song that frees the soul."
"I resonate with what is in your heart."

Background: The Knight of Cups is a charming, cultured, and gallant person. Sensitive and imaginative, he takes dreams seriously and can pen a verse or song for any occasion. He runs on a high emotional current and can be unconventional. His fertile dreams invite fellow travellers to unexplored regions. When this card appears in a reading, be prepared to make the grand gesture, be the romantic wooer, or summon up your poetic tongue. Waite gives, "A visit from a friend, who will bring unexpected money to the Querent. Reversed: Irregularity."

Person: ⬆ He is attractive and congenial to be with, exploring the shores of love and friendship imaginatively. He is responsive to others. Someone who is incorruptible and dedicated.
⬇ He can be a seductive smooth talker who plays the field, or an addictive personality who plumbs the very depths in order to be immersed in his own illusory fantasies. Temperamental and touchy.

Process: ⬆ Being emotionally resonant with others. Discovering how to merge with a concept or find accord with a person. Promoting harmony in any situation.
⬇ Exploiting an emotional situation. Cheating on someone. Being unrealistic or fanciful. A fraudulent approach intended to deceive.

Event: ⬆ A reception or welcoming. Compliance or accord. A quest. A union or merger. A romantic gesture. The arrival of an invitation or proposal. A gift or windfall from a friend.
⬇ Introspection. Fantasy. Lack of restraint. An emotional scam. Being led astray by nationalist/patriotic feelings or the influence of social conventions.

Environmental: A romantic idealism of nature. Restoring the waters, defending and cleaning ancient springs. A place of confluence or coming together. Indigenous meeting places. Rites that clarify, clear, and make holy after desacralization. The deepest feelings fuel the flow of life. Addictive tendencies. Honouring the sensibilities of every soul.

Questions:
What is the nature of your contract with life?
What are you getting access to?
What needs to be expressed sensitively?

QUEEN OF CUPS

Image: Against a blue sky, a queen dressed in a white dress and watery cloak, with a high crown on her head, contemplates an elaborate cup. She sits at the seashore on a throne adorned with merchildren.

Focus:
"I keep faith with my dream."
"I am devoted to the beloved."
"I will bring you to your heart's vision."

Background: The Queen of Cups is tenderhearted and kind, with an eye for beauty and nature. She is sensitive and intuitive, with a wide romantic streak. Her natural sympathy compassionately embraces all. This card imparts the gifts of love and empathy, so that you can be in touch with your deepest feelings. Check out the emotional undercurrents when this card emerges in your readings. The promptings of love come unbidden and show you where you truly belong. The cup that the Queen regards is based upon a ciborium—a receptacle in which host is stored—with its twin cherubim supporting it. The Queen of Cups traditionally represented the heroine Judith from the Bible, she who cut off the head of Holofernes. The lovely but dangerous theme is echoed by Waite, who gives, "Sometimes denotes a woman of equivocal character. Reversed: a rich marriage for a man, and a distinguished one for a woman.

Person: ↑ She has a psychic or empathetic ability that can see into your condition, making you feel comfortable or maybe unsettling you with her enchanting vision. She resonates with your emotional condition, for her words are guided by the heart.

⬇ Her cherishing and care can be seen as overprotective or smothering. She can also leave herself open to other people's needs or to abuse. A heartless person given to emotional blackmail. Someone who leads the beloved on a manipulative dance.

Process: ⬆ Proceeding virtuously. Being emotionally mature. Being receptive to others.
⬇ Taking on or beaming out projections. Captivated by illusion or being impressionable. Denying your emotions.

Event: ⬆ Emotional comfort. Psychic perspectives. Dreams or visions. A close study of public feelings and perceptions.
⬇ Unworldliness. Oversensitivity. Self-sacrifice. Security issues. Intrigue. Fixation upon the accomplishment of one's dreams.

Environmental: Having an empathetic view of things, being compassionately insightful. Health of the waters, regeneration. The foreshore of the ocean. The erosion of land by the sea. The innocence of children and young things. Going to the headwaters of inspiration. Honouring the landscape of the soul.

Questions:
Where are you leaving yourself open or unguarded?
What/who is enchanting you?
What have you devoted yourself to?

KING OF CUPS

Image: Against a grey sky, a crowned king sits upon a throne in the middle of the sea. He holds a cup in his right hand and a short sceptre in his left. To his right, a dolphin leaps, while on his left, a ship sails upon the seas.

Focus:
"I open the way to creation."
"Be as expansive as the ocean."
"I bring reconciliation."

Background: The King of Cups is a generous way shower and mentor whose tolerance gives him a peaceful demeanour. Very often he is the catalyst that helps groups and gatherings to gel, for he gives a place to each individual. His creative attitude toward life reveals how you can transform difficult situations by wise counsel. The measure of your acceptance as a mature person is your compassion. This card reveals how to be diplomatic or caring when feelings are running high. This card was historically associated with Charlemagne, the first Holy Roman emperor. Waite gives, "Beware of ill-will on the part of a man of position, and of hypocrisy pretending to help. Reversed: loss."

Person: ↑ He is a generous and caring person. Someone who is calm, wise, and considerate. As a friend, he is respectful of your space, giving you the freedom to explore what your heart teaches. Someone who can arbitrate calmly when the clamour of many needs arises. An older man.

⬇ He can be weak or ineffectual or inclined to milk situations for pity. Someone inclined to melancholy or depression or prone to vice. An exploitative individual.

Processes: ⬆ Using diplomacy. Keeping a broad-minded perspective. Promoting equality. Offering support. Standing as sponsor, godparent, referee.
⬇ Moody or melancholic. Enjoying the unconventional. Impatient of others' needs.

Event: ⬆ An exhibition, art show, or creative display. A support network or help line. Counselling sessions. Cultural events.
⬇ A scandal or cause célèbre. Dependency. A confidence trick. A lack of trust.

Environmental: Calm, caring, generous. Care of the oceans. The interconnectedness of species and habitats. Seagoing vessels and navies. The ocean. Learning how wrongs and abuses may be acknowledged, forgiven, and healed. Commissions for peace and reconciliation. Finding the language or metaphor that enables communication. Honouring the possibility of mediation between different nations and groups.

Questions:
Where is tolerance needed?
What is your loving duty here?
What needs nurturing or fostering?

ACE OF PENTACLES

Image: Against a grey sky, a disembodied hand appears from a cloud, carrying a single pentacle. Beneath it is a garden with a path leading toward a gate in the hedge. In the background is a mountain.

Focus:
"I uphold the intrinsic worth of everything with respect."
"I open the way to vocation."
"I bring good fortune to all enterprises."

Background: The Ace of Pentacles spells security and groundedness, so that you can be sure that everything beneath you is firmly set for success. Satisfaction and contentment bring a sense of security. Trust and confidence in your resources and resourcefulness give you a basis from which to work. You are invited to take up your own space in the world and become established. Magically, the Pentacle is a talisman, often bearing the five-pointed star, a touchstone of good fortune. Since the Pentacles in this suit replaces the Coins of earlier Tarots, we are shown that this card encapsulates all that is to do with worth and value—not just financially, but intrinsically as well. Waite also gives this as "the most favourable of all cards. Reversed: a share in the finding of treasure."

Lifestyle: ⬆ Prosperity and promotion come your way. You consolidate resources and establish your plans. Abundance, attainment, and fulfilment are available.

⬇ You learn the hard way. Money difficulties or responsibilities trouble you. You are overlooked in promotion.

Interaction: ⬆ Valuing your partner or friend. Making a firm commitment brings great rewards. An opportunity to explore your sexual compatibility with someone.

⬇ Greed and jealousy upset friendships. Lack of resources puts partnerships at risk. You pass up an opportunity for intimacy.

Impact: ⬆ Recognition of skills and talents in the marketplace. The inauguration of supportive foundations. An outlay of resources bears fruit.

⬇ Wealth is misused or waywardly administered. The corruption of public interests and resources. Risky investments tempt speculators. The corrupting allure of wealth.

Environmental: Security, trust, groundedness. The sacredness of the earth, valuing the environment. Creating a sanctuary in nature. Conservation. A sense of deeper resourcefulness in all your doings. The natural resources of each land. Honouring the intrinsic worth of everything respectfully, not as a commodity.

Questions:
What natural resourcefulness is needed here?
What is the value of this action?
What do you instinctively understand in this matter?

TWO OF PENTACLES

Image: Against a blue sky, a youth in a tall hat dances upon a jetty, seeming to juggle with two pentacles, which are joined by a green lemniscate or symbol of eternity. Behind him, a high, rolling sea.

Focus:
"I can hold two things in the air at once."
"I network and circulate what needs to be known."
"I can amuse myself for hours."

Background: The Two of Pentacles invites you to be flexible on all fronts, and to find the best balance when confronted with dichotomies where easy decisions are not feasible. Flexibility is easier for some than for others, for whom multiple decisions or multitasking are exhausting or confusing. Having the ability to look ahead and assess how things might play out is fine, but you cannot always discern a final result, so it's important to concentrate on your instinct and keep things playful, then you won't get bogged down. This is the card of the nervous person who is always agitated, fidgeting, or unable to settle, as well as the one who is forever sitting on the fence or the one who can keep several things spinning at once. The lemniscate enclosing the two pentacles is based upon the figure-of-eight band that encloses the two Coins in earlier Tarots. Waite also gives, "Troubles are more imaginary than real. Reversed: a bad omen, ignorance, injustice."

Lifestyle: ⬆ Weighing up your options is advisable. Having the daring to launch audacious new ventures. Coping with two jobs or multiple concerns. Dealing with dichotomy. Playfulness.
⬇ Forced into indecision by too many options. Dithering or sitting on the fence halts projects. Biting off more than you can chew.

Interaction: ⬆ Careful choice of a friend or partner. Entering into banter, debate, or arguments with another. Weighing up big decisions that will affect you both. A dance or entertainment enjoyed in company.
⬇ The ability to keep several relationships in the air may catch you out! Too many commitments alienate your friends. Getting embarrassingly entangled in another's affairs.

Impact: ⬆ Finding flexible ways of budgeting resources. Coping with demands puts pressure on the environment. Gain and loss alternate wildly. Literal-mindedness.
⬇ Fluctuating economies skew everything. Public opinion, advertising, or peer pressure makes its impact known. Resources are spread too thin. Enforced gaiety or simulated enjoyment.

Environmental: Flexibility, adaptation, balancing the books. Rising sea levels, storm, tidal surge, or tsunami. This card also stands for the way in which we are involved with every level of life. Finding a new mandate for living. The key to adaptation and flexibility is to remain playful. Video gaming. Economic fluctuation. Impostor syndrome. Making light of things through skill. Honouring the ability to remain flexible in changing times.

Questions:
What needs to be handled in a more playful way?
How is the dichotomy keeping things suspended?
Where do you need to network?

THREE OF PENTACLES

Image: Against the black background of the interior of a church or monastery, a monk and an architect are observing the work of the journeyman who has been carving a pillar. The journeyman stands on a bench. At the head of the pillar, three pentacles are carved.

Focus:
"My work is rewarded by the esteem of my peers."
"We create beauty together for the good of all."
"The quality of my work is my bond."

Background: The Three of Pentacles is the card of one's profession or career. It shows teamwork and cooperation to a high level of mastery and professionalism. Collaborating creatively with others or calling in an expert means that the results can be excellent. The card is concerned with keeping up high standards on practical, aesthetic, and moral levels at once. The satisfaction of a job well done brings reward to the craftspeople and appreciation from the user of any object. In order to maintain high standards in your life, you need to check on both progress and performance. Waite's background in freemasonry is referenced in this image, with the sense that the entered apprentice has shown his "prentice piece" to his master and can now rise as a journeyman to seek work under his own steam. Waite adds further meanings: "For a man, celebrity for his eldest son. Reversed: depends on neighbouring cards."

Lifestyle: ⬆ Exceptional competence in your chosen field. Professional excellence. Keeping faith with high or professional values. Preparing to give your very best.

⬇ Your efforts are mediocre or barely adequate. Having problems in the job market. Feeling unnoticed. Past mistakes mar your record.

Interaction: ⬆ You bring your best creative instincts to a friendship. Valuing your partner's skill. Planning renovations or improvements together.

⬇ Working too hard at a relationship so that it shows. Feeling inferior or criticized. Diminishing someone's efforts by slight praise.

Impact: ⬇ Rewards, degrees, or certificates are awarded. Things are done with professional dignity or renown. A prototype or new venture gains acceptance. A region or country receives an award for its illustrious service.

⬇ Commonplace views or popular values swamp the field. Undermining public interests by sabotage. Preoccupation with gain rather than serving value brings down a region.

Environmental: Teamwork, masterful cooperation of peers or craftsmen. Restoring the works of the past, maintaining skills of craftsmanship. The renown that arises from the quality of this work is reflected upon all who live in its shadow. Learned institutions. Apprenticeship. The arts and sciences that serve everyone. Honouring professional skills.

Questions:
Are you working to your highest capacity?
What needs more work, practice, or improvement?
What will make the issue perfect?

FOUR OF PENTACLES

Image: Against a grey sky, a crowned man sits cramped upon a throne, holding a pentacle to his chest, while two further pentacles are under each foot, and one above his crown. In the distance, we see an extensive city.

Focus:
"I hold on to that which I already have."
"I look after the good things of the earth."
"I have been appointed as custodian."

Background: The Four of Pentacles is concerned with maintaining the status quo, keeping things unchanged from an innate reserve or caution. This can be highly unattractive when it surfaces as possessiveness or miserly control, but many cling territorially to their resources with a careful eye and hand, as if spending them would diminish them. Talents unpractised soon become inept from want of use, for example, whereas their use makes them flourish. A selfish lack of generosity prevents the sharing of life's good things. This card is also one of gift, legacy, or inheritance, as well as the card of a custodian or warden. Waite adds, "For a bachelor, pleasant news from a lady. Reversed: observation, hindrances."

Lifestyle: ⬆ Clinging cautiously to your resources. Financial security above all things. Being conscientiously careful or canny about your spending. Possessiveness.

⬇ Being careless with money or profligate with your gifts or talents. Living ascetically or more simply. Spring cleaning or stripping things down to basics.

Interaction: ⬆ Saving yourself and your love for a better opportunity, by being parsimonious with affection. Being sparing with compliments or encouragement. Clinging to what belongs to others. A gift that you give to another.
⬇ Emotionally possessive of friends and partners. Failure to share is resented. Time to be generous with others.

Impact: ⬆ Economic control of resources. Hoarding creates scarcity. Collecting or conserving national resources. An inheritance made into the public domain.
⬇ Financial setbacks or a hazard to national resources. Spendthrift institutions risk common resources. Breaking monopolies or institutional blockades.

Environmental: Capitalism. The financial heart of a city, finance systems. The entitlement of "not in my back yard." The material possessions that we cannot hold on to at death. The legacy we leave. Growth enters into things when we allow the use of a resource that we are keeping or when we give away what we no longer need. Custodianship of the commonwealth. The city or metropolis. Financial corruption. Oligarchy. Honouring the need for exchange and reciprocity.

Questions:
What is being hoarded?
What needs to be shared?
What is the inheritance that you will leave?

FIVE OF PENTACLES

Image: Against a black wall of a church, a male and a female beggar pass by in the falling snow. The stained-glass window of the church behind them has five pentacles in it.

Focus:
"We take what we can get."
"We have no home to go to."
"We have lost all that we once had."

Background: The Five of Pentacles reveals how quick the move from security into adversity is, as we pass from Four of Pentacles. Loss of resources or periods of hardship temper any complacence we might experience with salutary humility. A fear of insecurity often lurks behind the struggles of life, but when it arrives it is good to keep focused on possible solutions or to ask for help in a timely way. Whenever hard times threaten, return to your basic resourcefulness and don't be too proud to accept what is given. It is the card of material trouble or destitution. Waite also gives, "Conquest of fortune by reason. Reversed: troubles in love."

Lifestyle: ⬆ Insecurity, financial strain, or barren prospects blight your life. Contending with threat or loss of livelihood or employment. A sense of failure, poor self-worth, or impoverishment.
⬇ Accepting help or part-time work. Rediscovering meaning and self-worth. Persisting through adversity. Disorder or chaos.

Interaction: ⬆ Sharing adversity together brings you closer. Being in bare survival mode creates acrimony. Feeling inadequate. Being impotent. A lover who is not your partner. Being in agreement or on a par with a friend.

⬇ Making new affinities and friendships in adversity. Blaming your misfortunes on others. Illness put strains upon you both. Unfaithfulness, seeking to assuage sexual needs outside your marriage. Discord or lack of agreement.

Impact: ⬆ A prevailing sense of misfortune, wastefulness, or destitution abounds. Scarcity of resources creates general panic. National crisis holds everyone in its grip. Lack of means circumscribes everything, leading to a hand-to-mouth existence.

⬇ Public faith is restored. Adversity and need begin to ebb. Charitable support relieves the need.

Environmental: Loss of resources. Adversity or hardship. Financial crisis. Homelessness. Shortages. Supply-and-demand breakdown. Relieving want after a national emergency. Poverty of imagination or scope. Public housing. Winter. Snow. Anxiety and worry accompany the basic issues of survival. Being outed or excluded. Banned on social media. Codependence. Honouring the right of all beings to have a home and subsistence.

Questions:
What are you grateful for?
What enables you to survive this?
What holds things together at times of adversity?

SIX OF PENTACLES

Image: Against a grey sky, a well-dressed merchant gives alms to two ragged beggars with his right hand while holding a pair of scales in his left. Above their heads, six pentacles shine.

Focus:
"I relieve the immediate need."
"I give proportionately."
"I respond according to my means."

Background: The Six of Pentacles celebrates the sharing of resources and the needs of the present time. It is also the card for "now, or the present moment." Good fortune shared with others gladdens the community because it redistributes resources and creates abundance. Benevolence doesn't have to be patronizing or intrusive, nor does it have to be solely financial. The giving of time, resources, or help is also a blessing to the giver, not just the recipient. This card prompts you to draw upon your own abundance or to receive what you need. Etteilla wrote of this card as "the present time, or instantly," which is how we have to respond to need. Waite unfortunately copied the mistake made by Mathers in translating "the present" from the French as "a gift." The addition of the scales in this image creates a suggestion of judgment, that the merchant gives only to the deserving poor, but we may also see it as giving appropriately or proportionately. Waite offers further, "The gift must not be relied on. Reversed: a block on the querent's ambition."

Lifestyle: ⬆ Generosity, gifts, or redistribution of resources. Acting in a timely way. You receive help, resources, sponsorship, a legacy, or money to take you further. You take training or advice to improve your lot.

⬇ Being unable to receive. Denying your own needs. Payoffs, loans, or inheritances are slow to pay up.

Interaction: ⬆ Acts of kindness that delight another. Pooling resources or "going Dutch." Job sharing, working in harness. Mentoring each other. Someone takes you under their wing.

⬇ Taking things for granted. Envy or ingratitude sours relations. Being treated with scant respect.

Impact: ⬆ The present or acceptable time. Charitable donation or service to the community. Benefits, rewards, and dividends. Patronage, sponsorship, or support.

⬇ Cultural or national jealousy. Acts of selfishness that endanger community. Parsimonious corner cutting that shortchanges everyone. A time of need.

Environmental: Sharing resources, generosity, benevolence. Charitable donation, supportive grants. Benefits for the poor. Emergency response. Fair provision for the disadvantaged. Generous giving and sharing benefits all. Care for others. Meeting the present need responsively. Environmental vigilance and responsiveness. Contemporary concerns. Scarcity and abundance. Honouring and relieving the immediate needs of those who have nothing.

Questions:
What is the most pressing need?
What needs to be given/received?
How must you be responsive?

SEVEN OF PENTACLES

Image: Against a grey sky, a young man in work clothes leans upon his hoe and regards a pile of greenery on his right. Six pentacles shine from this pile, while the seventh is beneath his feet, as if they were vegetables he had harvested. In the background are blue hills.

Focus:
"I enjoy the work that I do."
"I earn my daily bread honestly."
"My work contributes to the circle of life."

Background: The Seven of Pentacles shows the relationship of the worker with the outcome of his work and is a graphic depiction of the worth of work, the wages you earn from it, and the value or return it receives. It is also a card of money, of business transactions, and of a moderate amount of money, roughly equivalent to a wage packet. This is the kind of work that means regular employment or your job—which is not necessarily the deep vocational work that you might wish to have, which is more associated with the Three of Pentacles. The job/work divide is one experienced by many people in our era, where manual or mundane jobs have to be taken up in order to pay the bills, even if you possess higher qualifications or expert skills in a crowded marketplace. Waite adds, "Improved position for a lady's future husband. Reversed: impatience, apprehension, suspicion."

Lifestyle: ⬆ Taking stock of where you are. Doing your job. Fruitlessly speculating on the outcome. Fear of failure or success holds you in its grip. Work satisfaction. Your weekly wage or a moderate amount of money.

⬇ Loans, debts, and financial worries. Poor investments that don't pay out. Overwhelmed by workloads or to-do lists. Poor returns for a lot of work.

Interaction: ⬆ Letting things unfold at their own tempo. Unvoiced suspicions cast a shadow on your friendship. Finding out where the relationship needs pruning or feeding. Transacting business.

⬇ Perceiving someone's potential problems more clearly than they do. Hesitating to cancel a failing relationship. Feeling dissatisfied by the fruits of the partnership.

Impact: ⬆ Dissatisfaction with a body of work, or a long-term project festers. People question public policies. Working toward shared benefits.

⬇ Recurrent problems reveal institutional cracks. Over-development wastes resources or makes a surplus. Institutional policy conflicts with personal values.

Environmental: Taking stock, trusting the process. Harvesting, tending your garden. Enabling resources to grow by steady application or tending. Appreciating the work of your hands, and what it brings to the commonwealth. Cooperatives and unions. Biodiversity. Monocultures. Honouring the resources of the earth.

Questions:
What is working / not working?
What continued effort is needed?
What is being transacted?

EIGHT OF PENTACLES

Image: Against a grey sky, an artisan in overalls is sitting astride a workbench, crafting disks with pentacles upon them, with his hammer and chisel; six are completed and hung up on the wall, one is in his hands on the bench and another lies beneath the bench ready to be worked. In the distance is a cityscape.

Focus:
"I am proud that every one of them is perfect."
"I have the skills to finish this commission in time."
"I have ingenuity of hand and eye."

Background: The Eight of Pentacles shows technical expertise, hard work, and close attention to detail. It demonstrates the discriminating skill and committed service to your craft. Work often entails repetitive actions that must be exact every time, following protocols that have been gained through apprenticeship. This card represents learning a technique or skill that qualifies you to be productive wherever you go. The attitude that you bring to your life and work is also reflected in your lifestyle and what you create, which is why this card stands for pride in your work. You are known by your fruits, which cannot be replicated by any other means than your engagement or application. It is also the card of a mathematician, accountant, or computer programmer. Waite also gives, "A young man in business who has relations with the querent; a dark girl. Reversed: The querent will be compromised in a matter of money-lending."

Lifestyle: ⬆ Keeping your head down for a deadline. Practising a skill until it's perfect. A commission. Pride in your work.
⬇ Repetitive work, manual or menial labour, makes you feel undervalued. Replication, copy, or mere fabrication. Quotidian but essential upkeep of procedures. Frustration over failure to be promoted. Drifting in an idle vacuum. Turning away from your vocation.

Interaction: ⬆ Keeping your promises or dates. Taking care with the details or being careful of a partner's needs. Being totally absorbed in each other. Fulfilling a commission to someone's requirements.
⬇ Living off the skills or productivity of others. Keeping a tab on your partner's performance. Workaholic absences from your household's concerns begin to be noticed.

Impact: ⬆ Productive or profitable undertakings. Assignments, inventories, or productions are assessed. Providing or receiving training to reskill or advance employees.
⬇ Shoddy productions or performances reflect on everyone. Forgery or plagiarism devalues others' work. Large orders or commissions prove hard to meet.

Environmental: Productivity, diligent labour, checking the details. Crafting, doing things by hand. Factory production. Methodical preparation and application make for proficiency. A production line. Pride in work. Using expert skills to aid environmental projects. Ingenuity of mind and hand. Mathematical, computing, or accountancy skills. Technical know-how. Honouring the work of your hands.

Questions:
What is being made?
Who the work for?
What skills will bring benefit?

NINE OF PENTACLES

Image: Against a yellow sky, a richly dressed woman with a hooded hawk upon her gloved wrist is walking in a vineyard. The fabric of her robe is covered with emblematic flowers. Six pentacles are piled to her right, like ripening fruits, and three are piled to her left. There is a dwelling in the distance, while beyond it stand purple hills.

Focus:
"I have all I could ever need here."
"At leisure, at last!"
"I tend my estate well."

Background: The Nine of Pentacles shows how the fruits of great labours can be enjoyed at last. All work and no play make Jack a dull boy, and so recreation is needed. If the pentacles have been about aspects of work or money, then the ninth card reveals the leisure hours that should be part of it also. Delighting in your own achievements also provides personal time and opportunities to pursue those things that fuel your being. There is a sense of being self-sufficient, self-reliant, or well cushioned enough by a wealth of resources to enjoy life with more scope. With this sense of abundance behind you, you can see things through with success and prudence. With this card in a reading, look for where you are maturing your self-image or for the opportunity to breathe out after hard work. Waite also gives, "The prompt fulfilment of what is presaged by neighbouring cards. Reversed: Vain hopes."

Lifestyle: ⬆ Refining your accomplishments or advancing your knowledge. Creative satisfaction. Enjoying your personal pleasures and pastimes. Your projected self-image. Leisure time.
⬇ Feeling trapped or unable to enjoy yourself. Faltering self-reliance brings a sense of guilt or disablement. Having trouble relaxing or being a workaholic. A sense of "not being enough."

Interaction: ⬆ Feeling emotionally secure and materially stable. The enrichment of being with your partner. Enjoying time apart from the other/s.
⬇ Over-indulging in the good things of life. The paranoias that arise from being too solitary. Being undisciplined in your pursuit of pleasure. The relationship feels too leashed in.

Impact: ⬆ Love of nature and beauty is encouraged. A wealth of resources creates abundance for all. A public holiday that everyone can enjoy. Making space to appreciate life.
⬇ The dissipation of gains devalues all achievement. Institutional style or national austerity fails to honour beauty. Leisure facilities or opportunities are inadequate. Self-deception about actual commitment to environmental care.

Environmental: The fruits of your labours. Creative satisfaction. Enjoying the earth's good things. Birdlife. Ripeness. Recreation, leisure time, hobbies. Working or domesticated animals. Witnessing living beings as they really are. Cultural nourishment, hobbies, and recreation. Honouring the ability to recreate yourself.

Questions:
What has been accomplished here?
What happens if you let yourself off the leash?
What/who needs to recreate and refresh?

TEN OF PENTACLES

Image: Against a blue-and-black background, an elder in a grapevine cloak sits with his dogs under his coats of arms. In the street outside, a woman and child speak to a guard. The pentacles are arranged over the scene like the sephiroth of the kabbalistic Tree of Life. This is the only card signed by Pamela Colman Smith with her initials in the numbered box.

Focus:
"What I have is for passing on."
"Family pride is everything."
"I am the caretaker of my heritage."

Background: The Ten of Pentacles honours the wisdom and wealth of ancestral or family tradition. Establishment and permanence are the keynotes of this card. This card reveals how the extended family and household belong to a much larger picture: it shows many inheritances, and how family honour and values shape the next generations. This is the card of big money: from inheritance, winnings, windfalls. Waite also gives, "It represents house or dwelling, and derives its value from other cards. Reversed: an occasion which may be fortunate or otherwise."

Lifestyle: ↑ Enjoying the blessing and security of home and hearth. Your physical house or home. Financial security and support. Making plans to benefit the next generation.

⬇ Gambling away or risking the family inheritance. Ancestral shadows and bequests interfere with your life. Feeling a lack of support from or connection with predecessors.

Interaction: ⬆ Spending time with blood relations, close friends, or professional kindred. Acknowledging your debt to forebears, innovators, and teachers. Ancestral wisdom enriches new generations. Your household or family.
⬇ Burdensome care of elderly relatives or administration of family affairs. Rejecting traditional relationship values. Ancestral expectations and duties hold sway. The family values that you don't share. Playing games of chance.

Impact: ⬆ Archives and national information become available. Valuable incorporation into institutions. Having a sense of belonging to a group. Provision or spending upon the environment.
⬇ Squandering the national heritage, disregarding cultural treasures or denying spiritual wisdom. Feeling cut off from the collective. Traditional skills are lost to the community. Gambling with the future of the world.

Environmental: Belonging to the tribe. The wealth of tradition. Wisdom of the ancestors. Gain. The extended family. Acceptance within / rejection from the bosom of the family or group. Ancestral and cultural heritage. The inheritance of generations. Intergenerational trauma. The values, customs, and traditions of a tribal group or species. The potential and wisdom of elders. Honouring the wisdom of the ancestors.

Questions:
What tradition or family values are being revealed?
Who/what is welcomed to/excluded from the group?
What is the bequest you leave to others?

PAGE OF PENTACLES

Image: Against a yellow sky, a youth dressed in simple earth colours holds up a pentacle in his hands. He stands on greensward, with a clump of trees to his right and cultivated ground and a distant mountain to his left.

Focus:
"I love to learn."
"I dedicate myself to wisdom."
"I value practical ways."

Background: The Page of Pentacles has common sense and dedication and is someone who enjoys learning skills that make him efficient or that lead to prosperity and comfort. This card reveals how you can make things manifest by study, gathering data, or working out the practical coordinates. It brings messages of prosperity or benefit, and it denotes a dependability and trustworthiness. This is the card of the scholar or student and stands for those who are able to manage or organise things in a sensible way. The card was once associated with Sir Lancelot from the Arthurian legends. Waite offers, "A dark youth; a young officer or soldier; a child. Reversed: sometimes degradation and sometimes pillage."

Person: ⬆ A diligent student, researcher, or gofer. Someone who cares for the practical things of life. A friend who values the authentic aspects of your character and sticks to her commitments.

⬇ An idle good-for-nothing sunk into inertia. If his skills are not valued, he can be wild and undisciplined in the face of authority. Someone who is untrustworthy. Self-indulgence.

Process: ⬆ Learning the ropes as a beginner. Keeping things down to earth or actual, rather than virtual. Setting practical goals.
⬇ Vandalizing public property or mocking concepts of authority. Being out of touch with what's real or practical. Immaturity.

Event: ⬆ Apprenticeship or training programmes. Schools, learning, and universities. Concentration or study.
⬇ Theft or pillage. Public disorder. Instability or inertia prevail. Student rag week.

Environmental: Practical common sense. Groundedness arising from life on earth. Understanding the value of the land and honouring it. By noting the physical evidence, you keep track of where you stand. Training programmes. Mapping, geography. Passing on or receiving traditional teachings. Honouring traditional and practical values.

Questions:
What data do you need to gather to make a good decision?
What has to become embodied for things to work?
What needs your dedicated commitment?

KNIGHT OF PENTACLES

Image: Against a yellow sky, a mounted knight sits holding a pentacle before him in his right hand. Under him, his mount is a stolid black horse with red trappings. Behind them is land that has been newly ploughed.

Focus:
"I keep persisting until I complete."
"I will be of service to you."
"I take the responsibility to see this done."

Background: The Knight of Pentacles is hardworking and careful, checking out the details, so that he can be depended upon to get a job done properly. This card shows things proceeding with due care and attention to the terrain, so that there are no careless mistakes to endanger what's in process. Being thorough and realistic, the knight makes better progress than by trying to rattle inspirationally through it. This card denotes the physical application, stamina, and strength to get things done, as well as a sense of usefulness. When you are looking at what would be useful to you, shuffle this card into the deck and see which card the knight is looking at beside him in the cards. Waite gives, "A useful man; useful discoveries. Reversed: A brave man out of employment."

Person: ⬆ This is a reliable and robust person who has stamina and determination. He is naturally adept and has a craftsman's skill. He is a good person to have at your side because he checks all the possibilities before you venture yourself unwarily.

⬇ He can be dogged in pursuit, often pedestrian, plodding, and materialistic, as well as not knowing when enough is enough. He can also take glum melancholia to its extremes or get stuck in a deep rut.

Process: ⬆ Checking the details. Maintaining a steady impetus. Seeing it through. Obliging others. Taking pride in your work. ⬇ Giving up easily. Missing the moment through lethargy and delay. Being negligent. Becoming discouraged.

Events: ⬆ Land management. Industry or employment. Security firm. Persistence. Drawing upon all useful resources. Reliable results. ⬇ Unemployment. Poor self-worth. Lack of humour or compulsion. Stuck in the grip of inertia.

Environmental: Physical stamina, strength, and methodical application. Remaining true to the land, cultivating your garden or land. Tireless application brings things to the finish safely. Having responsibility for your local area or region. A team or workforce dedicated to caretaking or protecting habitat. Soil conservation, land reclamation. Rewilding. Honouring the seasonal round.

Questions:
What needs caretaking to bring it successfully home?
Where do you need to be quietly persistent?
What service is required of you?

QUEEN OF PENTACLES

Image: Against a yellow sky, a crowned queen sits upon a goat-headed throne. In her lap she cradles a pentacle. Above her, there is a flowering tree, while beneath her feet the ground is in autumnal colours. In the distance there are blue hills. In the right foreground is a brown rabbit.

Focus:
"I apportion resources generously."
"I bring security where fear reigns."
"I care for all living beings."

Background: The Queen of Pentacles fosters and nurtures whatever or whoever comes into her orbit. She welcomes prosperity and luxury, so expect a little opulence, though she can also have a natural and wholesome simplicity. She has a natural resourcefulness that nothing can shake, taking all eventualities in her stride. With this card, you may be in the process of caring for something or else finding ways to practically support someone. The card was historically associated with Argine, an anagram of Regina or Queen, which may be a doublet for Argante, the Queen of Faeryland who raised and fostered King Arthur from a child in Layamon's *Brut*. Waite adds, "A dark woman; presents from a rich relative; rich and happy marriage for a young man. Reversed: an illness."

Person: ⬆ A practical woman of deep resourcefulness. A welcoming person whose home is never empty of hospitable good cheer. As a friend, she is loyal, keeping faith with you and being frank about issues needing improvement. She may be a treasurer who manages resources or a curator. Someone who adores beauty and good design. ⬇ She can also be a hoarder or a squanderer or a demanding or timid individual. Someone who defends or vaunts her family against the world.

Process: ⬆ Managing things wisely. Preserving things of value. Making things better. Providing amenities. Dealing with things frankly. Putting money to good uses.
⬇ Wasting resources. Cutting your losses. Finding it hard to function. Pursuing luxury or ease becomes the main criterion of life.

Event: ⬆ Craft and design. Expansive liberality. The commonwealth of a group or community. Security is brought to a difficult situation. ⬇ Familiarity breeds contempt. Refusal to nurture or support. Habits that spin out of control. The breeding of mistrust and suspicion.

Environmental: Resourceful, nurturing, down to earth. The spirit of nature, caring for nature, the Goddess of the Earth. How you respond to the world around you makes you a much deeper part of it. The care of wild creatures. Practical solutions to environmental issues. Pragmatic and intelligent responses. Budgeting wisely with available resources. Making space or giving more generous place to whatever is trapped or hemmed in. Honouring the earth by caring for it.

Questions:
How can well-being best be promoted here?
Where can space be made to ensure security or comfort?
What needs to be preserved or given assurance?

KING OF PENTACLES

Image: Against a yellow sky, a crowned king sits upon a bull-headed throne. He is dressed in dark robes on which vine leaves and grapes are embroidered. In his right hand he holds a golden sceptre with a round top, and in his left, he holds a pentacle. His mailed left foot is raised and rests upon the stone likeness of a bear's head. To his left is a castle.

Focus:
"I foster the growth of all things."
"I use the earth's resources wisely."
"I value the good things of life."

Background: The King of Pentacles is pragmatic and steadfast, offering a secure and comfortable reliability to those around him. He is a natural entrepreneur who understands both value and profit and is often a banker, philanthropist, or merchant. This card represents patience and responsibility upon the path of the life. In a reading it can show you how to work steadily toward a goal. His traditional correlative, the King of Coins, is represented by Alexander the Great, who conquered Egypt, among many of his conquests, which may account for the bear's head in Colman Smith's image. Waite adds, "A rather dark man, a merchant, master, professor. Reversed: an old and vicious man."

Person: ⬆ He is an experienced and mature person, whom everyone naturally leans upon. As a friend, he keeps his promises and is a safe pair of hands. A good financial adviser, businessman, who offers a springboard for likely ventures. Someone who has a strategic overview of things.

⬇ He can also be blunt, stubborn, possessive, or vulgar, given to gluttony or being just plain unimaginative. Someone who is exploit-ative with other people's resources. Someone who preys upon the young.

Process: ⬆ Appreciating the good things of life. Learning to handle money well. Discovering the value of life.

⬇ Cocooning yourself from outside influences. Seeking for protec-tion or stability. Being tempted by financial speculation or scams.

Events: ⬆ Enterprising projects. An estate or land. Conservation of resources or environment. Sponsorship. Good health. Financial support.

⬇ Financial corruption or bribes. Physical insecurity. The misuse of public money.

Environmental: Enterprise, steadiness, pragmatism. Vineyards, the cultivation of fruit. Trade links. Interest rates. Good husbandry. Benefiting from the byproducts of a commodity. Breeding programmes for endangered animals, or the storage of species samples and seeds in conservation banks. Becoming a custodian or steward of the earth. Honouring all that the earth produces.

Questions:
What is the intrinsic value to you or others?
Where do you need to provide support?
Where is life offering you its riches?

FOUR

TIME-CHANGING
SKILLS AND STRATEGIES

Your beliefs become your thoughts,

Your thoughts become your words,

Your words become your actions,

Your actions become your habits,

Your habits become your values,

Your values become your destiny.

—Gandhi

In this chapter we explore some of the basic time-changing skills and strategies that govern good reading practice, drawing upon traditional as well as more innovative ways of using the *Waite-Smith Tarot*. Some of these methods involve direct observation of what is depicted in the cards, as a way of finding clues in the images. This kind of observation began as a reading method only after Waite published his pictorial Tarot: before that time, the Tarot was read more cartomantically, with the reading clues arising from the directionality of the cards and their numeration. With the rise of pictorial Tarots, different ways of reading have continuously arisen. If you choose to read with a Tarot you already work with, then the methods given in this chapter can be adopted or adapted. We start at the beginning of a Tarot consultation with the question and move on to how the querent appears in the reading, to considerations of interpretation, exploring the dynamic potential of the cards, and finishing with concluding procedures.

THE GRAIL QUESTION

Asking questions skilfully is the beginning of how we change things in our era, something that the Grail legends prepare us for. In the many texts of these legends, the perennial theme of the Wasteland recurs, whereby the earth dries up and vegetation dies. It can be healed only by the asking of the Grail question.[7] Sometimes this question is given as "Whom does the Grail serve?"—a question whose underlying motivation is "Why are things like this?" By asking that same question, we may enable the whole universe to focus closely through a narrow aperture that gives us the answer to the question in our hearts, enabling the environmental issues of our time to be brought centre stage.

In times of personal stress and trouble, we ask very necessary questions of the cards, seeking answers that will guide us or help clarify things. But that means the question needs to be composed *very carefully.* We have to remember the cautionary story of King Croesus of Lydia, who wanted to ask an important question concerning whether he should go to war with the Persians or make an alliance (which is an either/or question). He first sought out the most reliable oracle of the many sacred oracles around the Mediterranean, finally settling on the Delphic Oracle, but, unfortunately, he did not focus upon his question for the sibyl with the same care. The question Croesus asked was "Should I go to war with the Persians?" (which is a yes/no question). The answer came back from Delphi, "If Croesus attacks the Persians, he will destroy a mighty empire." Unfortunately, that empire was his own! The Lydians later sent again to the Delphic Oracle, after their king's capture by the Persians, to know what he had done wrong: the sibyl responded, "If he had been wiser, he would have sent again and inquired which empire was meant."

Like King Croesus of Lydia, we sometimes ask careless, open-ended questions so that the resulting reading is unclear—though, I hope, not at so high a cost as the Lydian king had to pay! The first rule of divination is "If you don't want to know the answer, don't ask the question," but the second rule is certainly "Ask the right question."

In divination, your question is the stone that causes ripples to spread in the still pool, until the answer returns to you. The kinds of questions we ask depend on where we stand in relationship to the issue, which will underlie how we ask. For example, someone wanting to ask a question about work stands in a different relationship to it depending on whether they are thinking about changing their job, whether they have been dismissed from one, whether they have been ill for some months and are returning to work, or whether they have been unemployed for years. Whenever our circumstances change, so do our questions, which is why we need to be mindful of the timescale of the question. A reading from a taromancer doesn't stand unchallenged and unaltered for all time, as some querents like to believe. A reading is a direct response to a question that was asked in the present moment: as soon as you start to engage with your life or make changes and decisions, so things will also change. Tarot itself can be time changing.

Like any web search, the universe will bring us a variety of answers, but if we narrow the aperture of the question by focussing more closely upon it, the answer can become more precise. That means close focus upon the topic, upon what you want to know, and noticing carefully which words to use and how they might change the question. For example, "Please show me how best to open up my business in the next few months" is a good question, but when you put "Can you show me . . ." at the beginning of it, you have immediately turned it into a yes/no question. Yes/no questions give very little information. Unfortunately, people want to ask yes/no questions a lot, of course, but I encourage them to think deeper about what they want to know, so that the question can be reframed in a more helpful way for the oracle to answer them. Here are a few forms of questions we need to be clear about:

*Questions in binary formats

Yes/no and either/or questions confuse the oracle and result in unclear answers. When these arise, ask the querent to frame a question that will result in a clearer answer. If it is a matter of choice between two or more options, then either frame each option as a separate question or create a spread that shows the immediate outcome of each option. In most instances, you can reframe a yes/no question by using one of these formats:

What are the consequences of (the action/decision)?
How will (the action/decision) play out?
Please show me how (the question topic) will serve me.

*Questions that use conditional tenses

Apart from the fact that questions beginning in "Should I?" are actually "yes/no" questions, the use of conditional tenses shows that the querent is casting *all* the decision-making upon the oracle, which may not be a healthy thing, especially for very credulous people or those who have little agency in their present position, even if the question is not a grave one. "Should I?" can imply obligation to someone or something, not just on the advisability of an action. I will often briefly explore the basis of the "should" to determine this point, so that the question might be asked in a healthier, less dependent way. So, when Anna asks, "Should I go to Paris with Terry?," I hear another issue underneath her "Should I?" Is Terry being super persuasive or does he trample over Anna's preferences? Is the prospect of just going to a different country where she doesn't speak the language the real issue? Or is Terry a bore or a bully? Reframed, that question might look like, "How will Terry and I get on together in Paris?"

*Questions that include a third party

Third-party questions are unethical in that they are assuming consent on the part of that person. Querents always want to know about family members, partners, or children. Questions like "What is my partner thinking?" or "What is my daughter doing at university?" are really all surveillance questions, and I refuse to ask them, unless it is a matter of someone's safety and whereabouts if they are ill, without agency, temporarily unable to care for themselves, or lost. There are enough surveillance cameras and spyware in the world, in my opinion. I encourage querents to ask a question that will help support themselves, rather than spy on the other. For example, "How can I deal with my partner's anger in a less provoking way?" or "What support can I offer my sister that she will be able to receive from me?"

However, in this book, where you are encouraged to understand the context of the querent's position in the household of the earth, we have to consider the same ethical point. When we read on the wider context, we are also looking wider rather than personally or particularly; the querent's family, group, or friends; the regional or national concerns: or the wider concerns of the world may all come within any of your readings, but the cards do not put words into their mouths. We will see how we gain consent for a reading for a community or for a world issue in chapters 5 and 6.

*Questions about serious matters

Questions that inquire about life-changing issues, such as the outcome of legal issues of cases, the advisability of taking of medications or medical treatment, the investment of large sums of money, or life-and-death issues, are not questions that should be submitted to a taromancer, who is at liberty to refuse to read on such matters. Refer these kinds of issues to those experts better able to advise on the consequences of these decisions. In most countries, Tarot reading is seen as "for entertainment only," and you may leave yourself open to litigation if you read on serious matters of this sort.

*Questions with a sell-by date

Asking how an event will go is clearly a question whose effect will be over when the date of the event is passed. It is a good rule of reading not to take vague, open-ended time questions, but to boundary the question with a reasonable timescale. Questions about someone seeking for a partner or having children in the further-off future are common, but put a timescale on it, so that the question is asked within a context of the near future—by the end of the season, in a few months or by the end of the year. Questions having an expectancy beyond a year's time need to be read upon again the following year, in my estimation, since things will have changed in the interim.

*Questions that have dynamic power to act as a can opener to a blocked or unclear situation include requests such as

> "Please reveal the most helpful way to move on from here."
> "Give me guidance on how to proceed with (topic)."
> "What will result if I (action/decision)?"
> "What needs to change before I can (action/decision)?"

*Questions that the cards ask you

In this book, at the end of each card entry, you will find questions *that each card poses to you*. While being questioned by the cards themselves can be surprising or sometimes confronting, the more honest you or your querent can be when answering these questions brings you both several steps nearer to solution.

HOW SIGNIFICATORS GIVE CONTEXT TO A READING

When, as a time changer, you use the methods of this book, you will want to see where you are in the context of an issue, and that means selecting a card that can stand for you and enter the reading. It is now conventional to choose one of the court cards to represent the querent as a significator, and many taromancers choose one by a variety of criteria based on the querent's colouring, horoscope, and so on. So, which court card might represent you? In an age where official forms ask us not only whether we are male or female, but also whether we are gender neutral, gay or lesbian, or transgender or what race or nation we hail from, as well as a variety of other data-crunching questions, the very medieval theatricality of the *Waite-Smith Tarot* frees us to choose whichever court card best represents the querent. Give the pack to the querent and let them choose a suitable significator from the court cards, so they can find a card they are comfortable with.

If you prefer to work by sun signs, then here is MacGregor Mathers's table that equates the 36 decans (10-degree divisions of the zodiac) to the King, Queen, and Knight of each suit. S. L. MacGregor Mathers was one of the founders of the Hermetic Order of the Golden Dawn, and he was largely responsible for its codification of magic Tarot usage. In this method, the Pages are excluded from the count, but they can be taken to indicate the seasons: Page of Swords for Spring, Page of Wands for Summer, Page of Cups for Autumn, and Page of Pentacles for Winter. However, feel free to use whichever of the 16 court cards that best suits you or your querent.

This chart may also be used for establishing timing by use of the court cards.

TIME OF YEAR	DECANS	COURT CARDS
11 Mar –9 Apr	20°Pisces–20°Aries	Queen of Wands
10 Apr–10 May	20°Aries–20°Taurus	King of Pentacles
11 May–10 June	20°Taurus–20°Gemini	Knight of Swords
11 June–12 July	20°Gemini–20°Cancer	Queen of Cups
13 July–12 Aug	20°Cancer–20°Leo	King of Wands
13 Aug–12 Sept	20°Leo–20°Virgo	Knight of Pentacles
13 Sept–13 Oct	20°Virgo–20°Libra	Queen of Swords
14 Oct–12 Nov	20°Libra–20°Scorpio	King of Cups
13 Nov–11 Dec	20°Scorpio–20°Sagittarius	Knight of Wands
12 Dec–10 Jan	20°Sagittarius–20°Capricorn	Queen of Pentacles
11 Jan–8 Feb	20°Capricorn–20° Aquarius	King of Swords
9 Feb–10 March	20° Aquarius–20°Pisces	Knight of Cups

Throughout most of the last century, the custom was to place the significator card down on the table, where it merely acted as a passive witness for the reading itself. However, a far more skilful way of using the significator is to put it *into the reading*, which is like sending the querent's representative into the array of cards drawn to see how they are responding and reacting to conditions on the ground. This can be done by simply shuffling it into the deck, as on p. 229, where the Page of Pentacles turns up between the 7 of Swords and the Queen of Swords. In this quick "Opening the Book" method, the position where the significator has fallen enables you to select the cards on either side of it to be part of the reading. You can just choose the single card to each side of the Significator or select the two or three cards that lie either side of where it has fallen. *Note:* When the significator falls near the beginning or end of the deck, treat the whole deck as a continuous revolving book and continue to look for the cards at the other end of the deck to find the adjoining card/s.

FIG. 7   *Opening the book: Finding a significator in the deck*

Below, I give two examples where the significator goes into the cards.

Opening the Book Example

Ellis is a student who has just come out as nonbinary between leaving home and going to university and now wants to be known as "they." They ask, how will this decision be received? Above we see how this question is answered with the help of the Significator: the three cards on either side of it have been taken from the deck and laid in a seven-card line, which gives the significator's immediate context. This is how the cards look in a line:

> Kt Swords, 5 Pentacles, 7 Swords, P. Pentacles, Q. Swords,
> Ace Wands, Priestess

This line of cards could be read straight across as a snapshot of the querent in their issue, but on p. 230 I have added parts of the household of the earth as a template on which the cards can be placed. We see Ellis's significator in the middle, with the two cards nearest to it placed in their immediate Personal Zone, while the two cards next to these are laid in their Family/Peer Zone. The two outer cards are laid in the World Zone. The pairs of cards are read together to give us information about how each of the zones respond to their change of life.

FIG. 8 *Opening the book shown as part of the household of the earth*

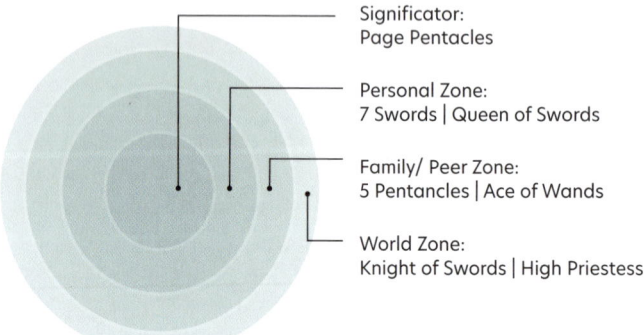

Significator:
Page Pentacles

Personal Zone:
7 Swords | Queen of Swords

Family/ Peer Zone:
5 Pentacles | Ace of Wands

World Zone:
Knight of Swords | High Priestess

Ellis's significator shows them as a student ready to set off in life. In the selection it fell between 7 Swords with Queen Swords, so as representatives of Ellis's Personal Zone, the cards show that they are going to be initially seen like they are in disguise or playacting, but that they have the independence and quick wit to counter this. In Ellis's Family/Peer Zone, 5 Pentacles with Ace of Wands shows that some ostracism is likely among those who have no imagination, but that Ellis's sense of enthusiasm and excitement about this decision will be infectious among those who will welcome them. In the world at large, Knight Swords with High Priestess shows that, while people in the know will champion Ellis, others will see them as enigmatic. Ellis's new identity is not going to be universally received well by those nearest to them at home, but their values will do better in the wider world of university into which they are stepping.

FIG. 9 *Pole of Balance spread*

Pole of Balance Spread

For a more in-depth reading, shuffle the significator into the deck, then, without moving the order of the cards, divide the deck into 7 piles of 11 cards each. (Again, without altering the order of the cards, check in which pile the significator has fallen, discarding all other piles.) With this method, you will have 1 card over, which stands as the theme, gift, or resource of the reading that supports the querent: this will always be the card at the bottom of the pile.

In the following example, each of the three rows of cards is read together in forward narration; that is, read like a story, statement, or sentence, rather than just as separate, individual cards. The central column that is formed by the central cards is read in the same way—as a sequential unfolding story.

Theme: This is the last card of the deck, revealing the theme or mood underlying the question.

Cards 1 and 11 are the beginning and end of the question: what causes the issue and what results from it.

Cards 2–4 show how the issue is manifesting.

Cards 5–7 show how it is affecting people or changing things.

Cards 8–10 show the wider context of the issue.
The central column of cards 1, 4, 6, 8, and 11 represents the path the querent can take, either to balance the issue or how to negotiate a way forward.

Example:
Here, Martin, the newly appointed manager of a manufacturing company, is asking, "How can I resolve the tangle over this contract?" He has to clear up the mess that has resulted from a previous arrangement with a supply company that sends essential parts to his factory, but at a substantially elevated price; it is killing the business and causing production to fall off.

1

FIG. 10
*Example of
Pole of Balance
spread*

Theme

2

3

4

5

6

7

8

9

10

11

The theme of the spread is a reversed 2 Cups, signifying a failure of trust between partners. Martin's company has been honouring a long-term commitment that is not working out well now.

Card 1: 8 Swords shows that this whole issue begins from a sense of institutionalized thinking, which is why his company is stuck in bondage to this old contract.

Cards 2–4: Shows the dynamic at work in the company: Death, 7 Wands and 8 Pentacles. Martin is facing a sense of old arrangements restricting things in such a way that production is being put on the defensive.

Cards 5–7: Shows how that is actually playing out in the company: 9 Swords, reversed Moon, and 6 Swords. There is a sense of dread in which employees are beginning to surmise that changes are coming, and some are already leaving.

Cards 8–10: Shows the wider context of this issue. Knight of Swords, Knight of Pentacles, and 4 Pentacles: a decision needs to be made or the reliable name of the firm and its financial basis for trading will be put at risk.

Card 11: The last card shows Martin himself, as the King of Pentacles, being the solution. He can bring acumen and stability back by handling the financial outlay in a better way.

The column made up of cards 1, 4, 6, 8, and 11 shows the path of least resistance in this matter: 8 Swords, 8 Pentacles, Moon, Knight Swords, King Pentacles. Martin has inherited an arrangement that ties the company's hands. His job is to diffuse the sense of sleepwalking toward disaster, by acting decisively and cutting through the dilemma, by doing some blunt speaking to his bosses. He later learned that the old manager had been under some obligation to the supplier, which is why the contract was framed to benefit the supplier more than the company. We see how the two Major Arcana cards of Death and Moon give the overall sense of dread of the inevitable, while a preponderance of Swords reveals the struggle going on here.

Choosing a significator for the subject you are reading on can also be extended to the rest of the cards. As you start to read on community and world issues, look into the card entries in chapters 2 and 3, which each carry their own criteria. You can then read on the progress of a war (10 Swords), a government's fall from grace (The Tower), a new job (3 Pentacles) or the aftermath of a tsunami (2 Pentacles), for example. Each card has endless possibilities, so it can be the significator of any topic in a reading: you just need the ingenuity to pick the most relevant card for the purpose.

INTERPRETATION:
MOOD AND METAPHOR

There are many arguments within the Tarot community regarding how cards are read and interpreted: intuitively or by the book, which is best? Because we are using the *Waite-Smith Tarot* in this book, you will doubtless be using a little bit of both, so that you can make use of the alternative time-changing approaches to reading given in chapters 2 and 3. Regardless of your personal preference, let us be clear on one thing: the leading criterion of all reading is the question itself, which should always lead the cards to speak about it as eloquently as possible.

All the cards are actors who can assume many different roles, going into our readings to speak the words or demonstrate the actions of our story or drama. A taromancer expertly follows their every stance and gesture, in order to discover meaning.

The mood of each pictorial Tarot card aids and assists us as soon as we try to match what the card presents with the question and the context of the querent. What is the sense, feeling, or metaphor that arises? Let's read for a shy querent who has just joined an environmental organization and is going to its annual social event tonight, who asks, "How will I enjoy the gathering tonight?," and we draw 8 Swords. Consider the card by itself for a moment: you might expect the querent to feel trapped and uncomfortable, at the very least, from the figure's blindfolded and circumscribed circumstances. But, in Tarot, we rarely draw just one card by itself. What changes when we ask the same question with 8 Swords and one additional card? Read each of these pairs for yourself before reading onward, keeping the same question.

FIG. 11 *Gauging the meaning from the metaphor*

a) = 8 Swords + 9 Swords

b) 8 Swords + Knt Swords

c) 8 Swords + 10 Pentacles

d) 8 Swords + 10 Cups.

Your interpretations may vary from the ones that follow; these represent just a few possibilities, drawing upon the metaphor that arises. I have read the pairs predicatively.

a) The gathering is going be rather overwhelming for the querent, who finds large amounts of people a real challenge.

b) The querent will be of one mind with the cause but feel powerless to engage much at this gathering.

c) The querent will feel like she is at a family reunion, though without knowing or recognising anyone yet.

d) The gathering will have a rather self-satisfied agenda, and she will feel left out.

The variables of reading on a question are further modified here by the nature of the querent herself, which deepens its context. Whichever of these pairs we read, being at a public gathering is going to be difficult for her: by its nature, 8 Swords is not a card that speaks of someone participating in a gathering with much engagement—there is an active restraint, a stuckness, powerlessness, or alienation at work in the card already. Eight of Swords with Knight Swords does raise the possibility that she might meet someone at the gathering who might help liberate her from this restraint, however. Eight of Swords with 10 Pentacles can also suggest that being part of a wider family of interest might help her throw off the restraint or restriction that she feels. Eight of Swords with 9 Swords reinforces the restriction with fear of remembered trauma. Eight of Swords with 9 Cups has a sense of people enjoying themselves in the presence of a prisoner, since the cards seem antithetical to each other.

THE STAGING OF THE CARDS: WHAT IS THE BASIS OF EACH CARD?

Because the Waite-Smith deck is wholly pictorial, the images can provide many helpful clues. Successful time changing means picking up on the incremental signs of change, and these lie beneath the feet of the each of the Tarot cards. The artist of the *Waite-Smith Tarot*, Pamela Colman Smith, had a background in theatrical design, which is reflected in a majority of her cards, where the centre figure stands upon a platform or stage. This same platform creates the foundation for many other cards, such as the 4 Swords, where the base of the tomb is included within it, or the stone balustrade of 3 Wands, giving us a sense of the basis for the scene. This format was clearly helpful to her in designing the cards, as it essentially gives each subject a standpoint or landscape that helps anchor it. But it can also be helpful to us and deepen our reading at points where we feel unclear about the interpretation.

We can read these "Staging Cards" as showing the basis against which our question is playing out or as a metaphor, as when Death is seen in a landscape of dead bodies—has it "been a battlefield at work today?" Sometimes, the staging shows that someone or something is grandstanding or "playing for effect," like a persuasive politician or an actor: where the card you drew for a friend shows them as the Page of Cups, persuading you that the cup is really half empty, when you feel it is half full. Or the card may literally show the firm basis of an argument, an intent, or the topic of the reading, as in Five Swords, where someone is literally picking up abandoned swords from the platform: we could say that the story or metaphor is about "picking up the pieces."

Drawing just one card can help show us the story of the reading or can give us clues as to the real basis of a question: as with the Two of Pentacles, where the figure juggling the two coins may be talking about how uncomfortable it is, striving to find balance, uncertain which debt to pay off first; or perhaps just demonstrating financial wizardry at balancing the books. He may be doing a good job in difficult circumstances, if we note the upheaved waves behind him. Whereas in the Ten of Wands, the man carrying all the sticks is actually walking on a nice smooth stage, where we can admire his excessive efforts to best effect, or are the sticks really heavy? Each scrutiny of the card's platform can enable us to pick up the subtext of the reading.

FIG. 12 *Grandstanding or really struggling?*
2 Pentacles and 10 Wands

The Staging Cards are not always trying to deceive, but when you cannot read a card in a particular position, then try looking closer at what the story is really about by investigating the cards in more detail: Is someone really suffering alone or just enjoying the kudos of being "the vulnerable one," around whom everyone else is dancing? These role-playing stances are ones we learn from childhood onward, to get parental attention or peer approbation. The kinds of support we gain from friends and colleagues might range from the "poor me" who needs a little comforting, to "See what wonderful things I am achieving despite my pain," where someone is really suffering heroically but feels unseen, or just someone who wants some appreciation.

In community, world, and environmental terms, the staging of the cards may flag up "newsworthy issues" or a theme that is playing out on a much wider stage, from the theatre of war to the platforms of social media, as well as showing us clearly the scenarios that are playing out all around us that we have been ignoring, because our perspective wasn't wide enough.

In a reading where I was doing a follow-up check upon the situation in Afghanistan in late March 2022, for example, I drew World, Four of Swords, and the Ten of Cups reversed. The Page of Wands was the card I drew to check the story: he stands in a sandy desert with mountains behind him. Apart from the obvious sense of a landscape, it said to me that the situation was now on shifting sand; promises were not going to hold. The World's sense of viewpoint on Afghanistan had become less dominant due to other world events taking priority in the news. Despite all the promises made by the Taliban when the US withdrew, it was clear they would overthrow ordinary family values, relegating women from public life or education. Unfortunately, so it proved just a few weeks later (see pp. 341–345).

A majority of the cards have either a clearly defined stage or a landscape in which they stand, or else they are elevated by a podium, throne, or horse. A very few are anomalous or have a different viewpoint. Here they are for you to see for yourself:

Defined Stage or Platform

These cards have a clearly delineated, empty, rectangular stage or platform. We note that the even-numbered Pentacles have a platform, while the odd-numbered Pentacles have landscape, giving a sense of easy or hard steps. Nine Cups has the largest platform of all the cards.

FIG. 13 *Different platforms*

| Defined Platform: | Landscape stage: | Podium/ Elevation: | Without Platform: |

Swords: Two, Five, Seven
Wands: Four, Nine, Ten
Cups: Two, Five, Eight, Nine, Ten, Page
Pentacles: Two, Four, Six, Eight

Landscape Stage

In these cards, the rectangular foreground / background space is occupied by landscape or natural features of some kind. Here the odd-numbered Pentacles have landscape.

Majors: Fool, Magician, Empress, Lovers, Strength, Death, Temperance, Star, Moon
Swords: Ace, Four, Eight, Nine, Ten, Page, Knight
Wands: Ace, Two, Three, Five, Eight, Page, Knight
Cups: Ace, Three, Four, Six, Eight, Knight
Pentacles: Ace, Three, Five, Seven, Nine, Page, Knight, Queen

Podium or Elevation

These cards show an elevated person on a throne, podium, or horse, except for Judgement which has a descent or opening into the ground. Some podiums are angled, like those in Six Swords or King Cups.

Majors: High Priestess, Emperor, Hierophant, Chariot, Justice, Death, Devil, Sun, Judgement
Swords: Six, Queen, King
Wands: Six, Seven, Queen, King
Cups: Queen, King
Pentacles: Ten, King

Cards without a Platform

These cards are anomalous—mostly because they do not show any ground or are seen from space, such as the Wheel and World, or from the imagination, such as Seven Cups.

Majors: Hermit has just a narrow ridge of ice or rock, Wheel of Fortune is seen from space, Hanged Man is suspended, the Tower has a rock base but no ground in it, the Moon has water and marshy ground, and The World is seen from space.
Swords: Three has no ground.
Cups: Seven has no ground.

To see how we might consider the staging cards of a whole reading, let's look again at Martin's reading on p. 233, and see what kind of basis the cards have from their staging. You already know the story and can quickly pick up the subtext from the cards: three cards have water as their basis (8 Swords, Moon, 6 Swords), revealing the quagmire the company is in. The field of the dead and the bed of nightmare accompanying Death and 9 Swords tell us that not all is well. 7 Wands shows the forces arrayed against Martin. 4 Pentacles and 8 Pentacles have money under their feet, with the company needing to re-establish itself as financially sound. Three elevated subjects sit together in King Pentacles on his throne, with both the Knights of Swords and Pentacles on their horses: the King Pentacles' foot is resting on a bear's head, reminding us that Martin has inherited this problem—while the two knights reveal that the fast pace of production that the company once had is slowing right down. As for the theme of the reading, it is reversed, but the partners represented by 2 Cups reveal that the supposedly equitable relationship between manufacturer and supplier is anything but: the grandstanding going on here is actually an assumption not borne out in truth. This is just a small example of what may be gained from checking the staging.

CHOOSING CARDS AS RESOURCES AND REPRESENTATIVES

We have looked at how we might choose a significator to represent the querent, but in subsequent chapters, I introduce a unique use of the cards whereby they are placed to become either representatives of powers or as resources that can help support the querent or to reveal the help and support available in readings about individuals, groups, or world issues. This method of using the cards as resources, reservoirs of help, or representatives reveals the mythic power and ritual dignity of the cards. It can be a powerful method of reading that supports the querent and their issues, especially in times where people often feel so isolated and disempowered.

A card that is drawn as a resource or a representative of spiritual or ethical power is not read as part of the divination, but rather as a quality that actively supports or mediates its power to the querent's situation (though in Brian's reading, which follows, we see how such cards can be read when purposely chosen). It may witness to the changes that need to come about, or it may provide resources that support an individual or group undergoing those changes. Support cards can be either randomly or consciously chosen. When you want to read the card as a resource, look at all the paragraphs in the meanings section of each card for useful and helpful concepts. If you want to use the card as a representative of a higher power, a spiritual presence, or a quality, look in the "Background" and "Environmental" paragraphs first, to see what this card upholds and celebrates when it appears in a reading. See also pp. 322–326.

A card can represent any power or archetype to represent what is helpful to the querent, group, or topic of the question. A card can be placed to represent people now alive or ancestors who are helpful and supportive to the querent, as well as divinities, animals, places, qualities, or resources that they need now. The selection is limited only by what each card naturally mediates. More about using representatives appears in each subsequent chapter.

Helping the Prisoners

Here is an example of the simple placement of cards as resources as part of a reading: Brian is training as a prison chaplain to pagan prisoners. His job will be to offer the comfort of familiar rituals and to be the nonjudgmental, listening ear of those whom he serves. His question concerns how he may best serve these prisoners; while his training has fully prepared him, he nevertheless feels a little anxious about his own abilities. I created this reading so we could look at the situation in a wider way: lines 1–3 represent the actual reading. Lines 4 and 5 represent the cards that support the prisoners and Brian, respectively. These cards were randomly chosen by Brian, pulled unseen from the fanned deck.

1. What Brian brings to the job: Tower, Chariot, 6 Wands

FIG. 14 *Helping the prisoners*

2. What the prisoners need from him: Devil, rev. 8 Swords,
   Kt. Pentacles

3. What underlies that need: rev. 4 Swords, 3 Swords, Hanged Man

4. What best supports the prisoners: rev. 5 Cups, Kt. Swords,
   4 Wands

5. What will support Brian's work: 6 Cups, K. Pentacles, Q. Wands

1. Tower, Chariot, and 6 Wands: Brian brings that rare asset—the
ability to pick yourself up after a terrible experience, and to go forward
with the will to share his process in a way that benefits others. He
already revealed that he had been a wild youth and had once spent
his own time in a young offender's unit for a few months. His own
story could so easily have been that of one of the prisoners.

2. Devil, reversed 8 Swords, Knight Pentacles: The prisoners need him
to help them resist the patterns of violence and coercion to which
they had been exposed, and be shown how to break out of their
limitations to become reliable members of their community.

3. Reversed 4 Swords, 3 Swords, Hanged Man: Underlying these needs
is the desire to return to the world after incarceration, and to leave
behind the sorrow and frustration of being out of the world.

4. Reversed 5 Cups, Kt. Swords,4 Wands: The prisoners' support cards
show resources that enable them to put the past behind them, giving
them the sense of having an advocate and being championed, and a
return to a more harmonious life in which they could play their part.

5. 6 Cups, K. Pentacles, Q. Wands: Brian's support cards show the
potential of the past working with the ability to foster growth in a

patient way, as well as an unfailing kindness and empathy for the prisoners.

While Brian will always need to understand the individual context of each prisoner to best help those in his spiritual care, he appreciated the support cards for himself and for the prisoners. Considering the two lines of support cards, he said that this combination of cards together gave him hope that he could bring out the good memories and potentials of his charges and help them celebrate their life on Earth once again.

TIME AND ETERNITY: READING FROM THE PRESENT MOMENT

This book is both about the changes wrought by time, as well as about changing the times with the help of Tarot, and so we need to look at time itself before going further. It was Einstein who proposed that time is an illusion that moves relative to an observer. "Time" is what we call the measuring of duration while we live on Earth, on this side of reality, but "eternity" is what we call the condition of life on its other, unseen, side—which we will be exploring further in chapter 7.

The two Tarot cards that concisely represent time and eternity, respectively, are the Wheel of Fortune and the World. The Wheel of Fortune gives us the sequence of time, but the World gives us the spaciousness of eternity. Even the images on the cards show us this: on the Wheel of Fortune, the regnal sphinx at its top is just as much fixed to the revolving wheel as the dog-headed man hanging from its base. They swirl round and round sequentially. The hermaphrodite within the green garland of the World is no longer troubled by sequence because they have entered into eternity or timelessness. Even the two sets of holy creatures—the winged man, eagle, bull, and lion—are seen from different perspectives: in the Wheel, we see them at distance, but in the World, we are face to face with them—the mythic concepts we glimpsed as time-bound beings become mythic realities when we move out of time. This accords with what we know of reality's two sides: they are complementary understandings about our being in the universe, both as manifest beings and as unseen souls. The five senses of our bodies give us experience of everyday life, but our instinct, intuition, imagination, and insight give us experience of the unseen life we are also living. Both sets of observational faculties are as important as the other. We don't need to die to work in eternity: we just observe with our souls.

FIG. 15   *The wheel of time and the world of eternity*

As taromancers, we do a lot of moving in and out of time in our reading. As you can see from Brian's reading on p. 245, I have read the cards largely from the perspective of the present moment. A card reading always shows us a snapshot of a situation from the standpoint of the present: it is not a fateful or immovable prediction, though, because it will ripple out through time and place, meeting other kinds of ripples and being modified by them. A reading shows the potential of someone's choices from the moment we address the querent's question. We sometimes also look back at the roots of things, to their point of origination or epicentre of emanation. We sometimes look ahead to anticipate where or how the issue will play out, so that the querent can make better informed choices.

So much of our lives are lived in fearful or hopeful anticipation of the future, or in yearning or regret for what lies in the past, that I believe the potentialities of the present moment are very precious to us. When we stand in the future or past, we often make poor decisions. So how do we read in the present moment in ways that are helpful to clients?

Those of you with a satellite navigation system in your car may well understand that it can plan a route for you, but that is singularly useless when a flood, snow, escaped animals, or the traffic caused by a local rock concert changes the ground conditions, and you need to find an alternative route. The satellite navigation is working by global positioning via satellite information: it can boost our human vision from its perspective, but it cannot tell us about ground conditions. The cards, on the other hand, can both give us an overview or a mirroring of what we need to know about these ground conditions, and also be like the bird that overflies the roads to see connections where we cannot. Card consultation takes us "out of time" to perceive these possibilities, as well as showing us things in the sequencing of time.

Laying cards and entering into their pictures to see the story of the querent is a way of suspending disbelief, just as we do when we become absorbed in a play or film. But the images before you are not passively presented to you, as in a film, because here you have a living story, the play whose main protagonist is sitting right beside you: they've just stepped out of it briefly to look at the time sequence or the greater overview with you. As a taromancer, you cannot be anywhere else but involved in the present unfolding, but you also have to move skilfully between time and eternity a good deal. The querent may get to look into the rearview mirror to see their past or sideways to view their blind side or to receive a bird's-eye overview of what their story holds, but it will always be from the standpoint of the precious present moment.

In the next chapters we will step out of the expedience and weight of time into the way the Tarot can work in timelessness.

THE MOVERS AND SHAPERS:
FATE, CHANCE, DESTINY

In the rest of this book, we will be looking at the unfolding of many issues: personal, communal, and world impacting, both in time and out of it. But before we embark on reading for community and the world, let us consider the factors that run through every life: the life-shaping factors of fate, chance, and destiny.

Fate is that which we cannot alter, such as our parents or the nature of our basic physiology. Some inevitably fateful things will indeed be part of a client's picture: the seeds of a latent illness, the onset of age and death, the effect of actions they have set in train that were caused by their reaction to earlier events or by the influence of upbringing and environment. Fate is like the factory settings we came into life with.

Chance is the randomness of things that happen, whether lucky or unlucky, fortunate or unfortunate. It may present wonderful opportunities that come along because you were in the right time and place, or it might be the luck of the draw that it was your bus that ran off the road into a ditch that day. The randomness of things happens to everyone, although we sometimes correctly read the signs that enable us to take those opportunities or to avoid misfortunes.

Destiny is that which lies potentially within each of us. This can be an aptitude, gift, or art that can be developed, with practice, until we attain expertise, or the skill might simply remain a pleasant hobby. Whichever potentialities are seeded within us, they will equip us to serve the household of the earth in some unique way. Those who live attentive to these seeds of destiny and cultivate them still have to tend and maintain them: while they are given, they will not tend themselves. Destiny is the blessing that we came to deliver, but only you can bring it to fruition.

The choices we make for ourselves are not so much about free will but usually involve us in how we play the best game with what we have been given—which means how we manage the drawbacks of our Fate, the opportunities of Chance, and the potentialities of our Destiny and where we centre ourselves in any issue as a result of it.

In this Shapers and Movers spread, you can explore any issue with an eye upon the factors that will change the question's ripples. Shuffle your issue into the cards. Lay out one or more cards on each of these positions.

Siobhán is an artist who has been invited to expertly paint an old community hall while keeping to a tight design brief. How will the project be received by the community? Here we lay two cards for each question.

1. 3 Wands + King Wands: Siobhán stands ready to begin the venture, where collaboration looks well favoured. It is something she will enjoy setting her creative stamp upon. The community expects a creative masterpiece.

FIG. 16 *The Movers and Shapers spread*

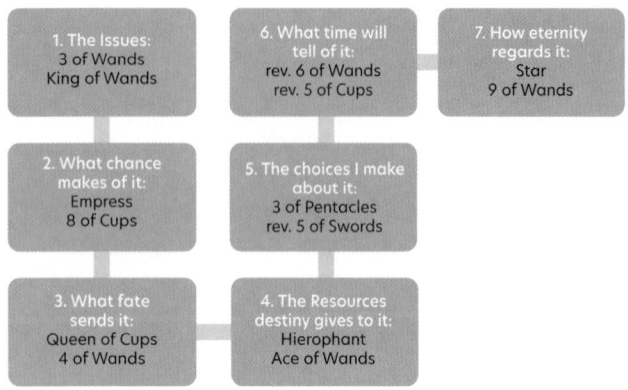

1. The Issues:
3 of Wands
King of Wands

6. What time will
tell of it:
rev. 6 of Wands
rev. 5 of Cups

7. How eternity
regards it:
Star
9 of Wands

2. What chance
makes of it:
Empress
8 of Cups

5. The choices I make
about it:
3 of Pentacles
rev. 5 of Swords

3. What fate
sends it:
Queen of Cups
4 of Wands

4. The Resources
destiny gives to it:
Hierophant
Ace of Wands

2. Empress + 8 Cups: Creatively renovating a well-loved centre to such a tight design brief still gives her a chance to artistically consider her options as she goes along, but it is these small diversions from the brief that will bring it alive.

3. Queen Cups + 4 Wands: Siobhán's vision is one that people will literally celebrate within, since the rebeautified hall is used for all manner of the community's functions, parties, and events.

4. Hierophant + Ace Wands: She has been given the skill to inspire others with her paintbrush, which others will appreciate.

5. 3 Pentacles + reversed 5 Swords: The choices she makes are dictated by her professional artistic skill, enabling her to renovate this hall in a way that suits its character best. This sensitivity to design will be appreciated by all who use the hall.

6. Reversed 6 Wands + reversed 5 Cups: Time will speak of this endeavour in terms of a place where people can recover after a loss.

7. Star + 9 Wands: The beauty of the hall endures as a testimony to the community's journey.

Siobhán was as mystified as myself about "what time would tell," at least until just before the hall's reopening, when its first use was to serve as a temporary shelter for a small local settlement whose homes were overwhelmed by the ocean.

CONCLUDING A SESSION

We started with the framing of the querent's question, but we rarely consider what happens at the end of a reading. Nowadays, the querent will often take a picture of the reading on their phone prior to leaving or might record the session on their phone's recording app, but there are a few other considerations before they go through the door.

    *Whether reading for someone, a group, or a community, never leave the reading without hope. Look internally at the cards or read around to find the hope. C.f. pp. 345–349

    *We need to sow seeds that can enable the querent to effect the changes that are arising. What will bring harmony sometimes first involves a change that is disruptive, rather than a simple, peaceful process. Change is usually not seen by the querent as a happy thing, because it may be painful or involve toil or inconvenience. This is when you can read one of the questions from the end of the card entries in chapters 2 and 3 and ask it of your querent, within the context of their question, or read the Focus statement from the front of each entry. If the wording of the question is not exact, please change it to be appropriate.

Here's an example from Martin's spread on p. 233. Since the last card of the reading was his own significator card, I chose to look at the King of Pentacles, whose questions are:

What is the intrinsic value to you or others?
Where do you need to provide support?
Where is life offering you its riches?

I chose the middle question as the most appropriate one, but also including the topic of his question "Where do you need to provide support to your company?" His response was immediate: "I need the whole board to understand the seriousness of this contract's outcome so that I can continue to be its manager."

*Becoming aware of everyone who is in our group, family, or community as a collective support and strength can help give the querent a sense of not being alone when they are on a narrow path or in a challenging position. This may include ancestors who have stood where you stand now, but who overcame the challenges, or it might be resources that are needed to enable us to continue living (see p. 326). To give the querent a gift from the collective wisdom of our world, you can ask them to draw a chosen card as a representative to stand beside them, especially if the way forward looks very narrow or bleak. Using the previous example with Ellis, I encouraged them to choose a card from the deck for this purpose, since their choice to come out as nonbinary was clearly not going be entirely uncontested. Ellis chose King of Cups and was delighted to find that one of the sentences from the "Focus" section of this card was "Be as expansive as the ocean." Ellis laughed, saying in response, "Then I will be like water that just flows around opposition and prejudice."

*Reducing the cards. Many people like to discover an additional resource or help for the querent by adding up the card values of a reading to obtain a Major Arcana card. This is done by reducing the card values to a number between 1 and 22. In this method, the Major Arcana cards take their own number, but the Fool is numbered 22 for this purpose. In the Minor Arcana cards, each Ace–10 takes its own number, with the Page being 11, the Knight 12, the Queen 13, and the King 14. So, if the cards in a reading are XV The Devil, 8 Swords, 4 Cups, Knight Pentacles, and VII The Chariot, they equal 46 in total. We now add 4 + 6 = 10, which gives us X The Wheel of Fortune. This could give a final resource or representative card with the message "Honour the cycles of life."

Now we turn to putting these skills into practice, and learning how to read for groups, institutions, and our community.

STEPS AND DANCES:
READING FOR OURSELVES AND
OUR COMMUNITY

Alone we are lost; together,
we shall bring the morning.

—Alan Garner,
Elidor

This powerful quotation invites us to consider what changes can result when we include the wider world in our readings. The evolution of human consciousness in the last century has been rapid, but it has also happened during a time of intense societal change, whereby individuals have tended to become more isolated from their communities and may often have less support when things go wrong. Many of the problems we have as a group or community are not solvable by single individuals, but by bringing more resources to bear, more support to hand, we create a wider basis to help us with situations that may be beyond our personal power to alter. Just as when you have a load that is too heavy, you cannot just transport it in the back of your car but need a bigger vehicle that has more sets of wheels on it, to spread the load. And that is what we are going to do in this chapter: engage the Tarot to provide us with a great capacity, as well as a universal set of qualities that will focus the changes that need to come.

Because community and group kinds of readings are of a different nature, we also need to understand a few things first before we proceed, because they are critical to reading with responsibility on community issues. These understandings will enable us to spread the reading cloth wider.

CONSIDERING GROUPS, INSTITUTIONS, AND COLLECTIVES

If you have ever been a part of any group, you will already know that it comes with its own dynamics, tendencies, and complexities. The group will support you and help you feel you belong. But if you try to make it do something different from its aims and objectives or attempt to wrangle a personal way of doing things, you may meet stony-faced resistance. Group members, like family members, can help you feel like one of the "in" crowd or can eject you just as easily. Groups can also implode if agreement cannot hold its members together. Whether you look at a book club, a meditation group, or a collective of people who share similar hobbies, conditions, and lifestyle choices, you are experiencing the umbrella sense of belonging to that group.

Since time began, we have banded together in groups to strengthen the larger community, to be the custodians of skills and knowledge that serve the community, being involved in handing on those skills to suitable people with vocational aptitudes. From these groupings have arisen first guilds and professions and then much larger collectives and institutions that still serve us. A whole society is based upon these institutions. The societies of all nations together make up the human world. Our ability to understand groups, collectives, and institutions is critical to how we might divine on the issues that they raise.

Some years ago, a student asked me about the institution that she worked for, feeling that maybe something was wrong with the land on which it was built. Hearing her story of misplaced trust, the bosses' failure to support the staff or bring better ways of working, I rapidly concluded that it was not a question of the land, but about the institution itself. With the help of this same student and other friends, we set up a Spirits of Institutions group to explore the nature of groups and institutions, which was just one step on the road toward this book.

What we learned was that we ourselves had many muddled ideas about institutions, which tend to be misunderstood or pilloried when things go wrong. An institution is a collective that strives to deal with the purpose for which it is formed. So, a football club is created to deal with those playing football, a church is formed to surround those who worship a divinity, and a post office receives, sorts, and delivers mail. We all need institutions to manage the essential servicing of our lives, and any anarchic requirement to cast them down would just create a whole set of other problems, as many revolutionaries have discovered: if the infrastructures of society don't work, society itself begins to break down. Institutions are the servants of society.

What we also found was that all institutions, groups, nations, families, countries, other collectives, etc. are governed by their own unifying power or spirit: we each experience this because we are part of the group soul of these systems. So, a family will have a set of ancestral values, a bank will have a founding principle, a philanthropic society will have a high ethical aim to assist, a football club will be founded on the values of the "beautiful game." The spirit of an institution, its founding principles, and its essential values are what we all wish would govern the institution, because they serve us when they remain the central motivation of the institution. Unfortunately, things can go wrong because institutions are run by people who will modify the systems to benefit themselves, so the organization becomes muddled; rather than serving us, institutions that have been subverted can begin to imprison us.

When the football club becomes more interested in multi-million-dollar transfers of players and the sale of merchandise, it literally takes its eye off the ball and alienates the fans. When the bank starts to invest in unethical enterprises, the investors get richer while those with bank accounts get angry at being implicated. When the children's charity starts to have cases where children are bullied or abused by the charity, everyone is appalled. What is happening here?

In the words of Walter Wink, a theologian who has discerned what institutions really are and how they work, "If we want to change those systems we will have to address not only their outer forms, but their inner spirit as well."[8] When things go wrong, when the institution stops working well, it means that the power or spirit of the institution has been usurped by other interests: these usurpers need to be unmasked, and the originating power or spirit needs to be restored, so that the institution or group can work once more and be of service.

It is important to remember that it's not that the foundational powers or originating spirits of institutions are evil: it is the *uses to which the institution's powers are put* that we experience as good or evil. When those running an institution become corrupt, we all feel bullied, messed with, and impatient for liberation.

In our Spirits of Institutions group, we discovered that because we are often part of the institution in question, it is very hard to also perceive it. It is like regarding your own body—you feel you know it, that you can guess its workings or understand what it is doing, but you still need a mirror or more witnesses to help it come into clear focus. And there is another drawback: when an institution deviates from its prime directive, we have to be on alert that we aren't also being collusive or complicit with practices that humiliate us, or we merely dishonour ourselves. In other words, we can become not just inmates within the institution but also become those who aid the superintendent to enforce the system. This is how institutions that have become corrupted traditionally control their members. So, in our group, we learned quickly that we had to avoid polarizing ourselves and any institution or collective in question by seeing ourselves as "good" and the institution as "bad"; we ourselves—by virtue of being part of a group—were just as likely to be enmeshed with its values and might be acting collusively, by reflecting and enhancing the conflict within it.

In order to heal and restore something that has been wounded, the Grail Question is really useful here: "Why are things like this?" or "What is actually going on here?" By gaining context and perspective, we can realize not only the scale of our own entanglement in any system, but we can express our feelings of anger or sorrow about how that entanglement has enmeshed us. Only then can we begin the process of unmasking the usurpers of the system, not by being "holier than thou" but by noting that we all are wounded by the system. This is how models of peace and reconciliation have worked in such places as South Africa and Northern Ireland: whereby *all* participants in the conflict recognized—whether they were victims or perpetrators—that all were wounded by the usurpation of their country by coercive, ancestral, or ideological issues that warped its whole society.

To summarize, a group, collective, or institution is an entity made up of three main parts:

1. At its core is the spirit, essential value, or founding principle, which is inviolate and essential to the service that the group provides. It provides the character and values of the group.

2. Surrounding that core are the powers of the group that are massed around the spirit: these provide the focus and agency for the group to work.

3. At its outer edge are its activities; these are how the core value/spirit and its powers manifest in our world, providing their unique service to the community.

For example, a book club might have "the spirit of literature" as the spirit at its heart, a set of focalizers who, with its members, embody the powers of the book club to explore literature in a motivated way; the meetings or events are the activities of the book club, where the reading, study, and enjoyment of literature are shared.

FIG. 17 *The anatomy of a group, collective or institution*

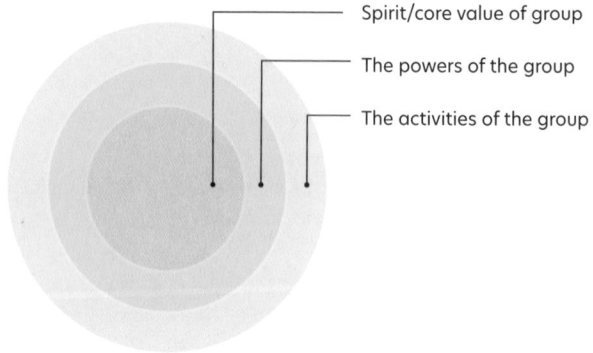

- Spirit/core value of group
- The powers of the group
- The activities of the group

BUILDING COMMUNITY SPREADS

While you may already have some useful spreads in your repertoire for individual readings, when it comes to reading on a group or for your aspects of your community, you need to customize spreads so that the issues and factors are included. When we begin to read for our community, we need to understand the dynamics of its groups and institutions in order to read with clearer focus, particularly if we ourselves are a part of that community, so that our own entanglements with it do not drag the reading off-centre because of our own existing prejudices and judgments. Here are guidelines for reading on group and community issues, which will enable us to keep our own thoughts and feelings out of the way, so that the whole picture can be seen:

◆ Every group, collective, or institution has its founding principle, essential value, or spirit that coordinates and embodies the group's activities. We need to acknowledge that spirit or principle when we divine by seeking its consent to read on any issues concerning it; then the subsequent reading is ethical. It is a matter of respect, just like having the permission of a person when you read for them. Choose a representative card for that spirit/principle, holding the card, focusing upon that spirit quietly, making your intention clear: "I am seeking to explore/help/clarify (the situation/issue) of the group/community that you serve, with your help. Please open the way for me/us to look at this in a respectful way."

◆ If the core values or spirit of that group have been usurped by other practices or are being manipulated by an individual or a board of self-interested leaders, then the group is becoming unable to serve society. We need to invite and include the spirit/founding principle back into the institution within our reading.

◆ When a group is struggling, lay cards whose qualities will help support and witness it: these cards can be chosen or randomly selected, to act as representatives. Here, you are calling upon the honorable powers and resources of each card, and so you should place these supporting cards upright, unless the card's reversed meaning is more helpful—as in the reversed Devil card. Check the "Environmental" paragraph of each card's meanings or select from any of the other paragraphs to find suitable and holistic qualities that will support the group. These support cards are to be read as qualities in their own right that will witness to the situation and help rectify it, as well as to act as resources or support for the group (see also pp. 322–336).

◆ Whatever the group or institution serves—whether it be people with the same hobbies, animal welfare, children, the land, or world peace—the subject of that service has to be included. This is especially important where the group's founding principles have been usurped, because leaving out the ones served by the group is often what results in reality, as when a pharmaceutical company begins to focus more on the investors' profits than on the actual healthcare of sick people.

◆ The querent who brings the community issue to be read upon will also be included as part of the reading in some way, although the reading is not all about them personally.

To maintain good focus while doing this work, you will find further ways on p. 285 in this chapter.

In readings of this kind, it is helpful to ask a few questions to enable how we approach the group's question, and how we customize a reading.

◆ For what purpose was the group formed?
◆ Who/what does the group serve? What results from its activities?
◆ How can we receive the blessing of the spirit of the group and not usurp it to become its curse?
◆ From whom/what does this group need to reclaim its founding principle?
◆ What will help support this institution to resume its mission?
◆ What does the spirit of the community need from us to return to its original position again?

In order to put all these principles into context, here are two examples: the first is for a small meditation group, while the second is an example of an institutional reading for a hospital trust, showing how we can do this kind of reading.

WIDENING THE CIRCLE

Kali helps run a small fortnightly meditation circle that has been in existence for several decades now. The majority of its members are gradually aging, and, despite occasional newcomers dropping in, no new core members have joined for a few years. One or two acrimonious issues have also arisen recently, and there is a sense of the centre falling apart. So, she wants to look at what might need to change to reinvigorate the circle.

Cutting the cards to get an initial sense of the issue, she draws reversed Knight Wands, 5 Wands, and Hanged Man, which speaks of a few dominating personalities becoming combative in an atmosphere of stalemate. She then shuffles in the High Priestess, which she chooses to represent the group's spirit, asking her to help reveal what is going on in the group. These are the cards that come out of Opening the Book (see p. 229):

(see p. 229)

FIG. 18a   *Widening the circle, stage 1*

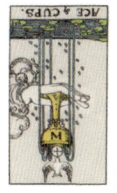    

| rev. Ace Cups | Ace Pentacles | High Priestess | 4 Pentacles | rev. Magician |

A reversed Ace Cups and Ace Pentacles show a sense of sterility and lack of emotional nurture despite a wealth of experience among its members. To the other side of the Significator are 4 Pentacles and reversed Magician: a clinging to the values of how things have been done in the past is sapping the self-assurance of the circle's members.

This is all rather dismaying, and so Kali's question now is about what future mileage the circle might have, and what kind of service it needs to be offering. She draws two cards for each question, placing them above the first line.

FIG. 18b *Widening the circle, stage 2*

| Queen Pentacles | 10 Swords | 10 Cups | Queen Swords |

Queen Pentacles with 10 Swords answers her forthrightly: the circle has upheld the meditations wisely, but its time, as presently constituted, is coming to an end. The service it needs to offer now is one that embraces community values and is not afraid to bring more honesty and better focus, perhaps dealing with issues that the original circle didn't encompass. Kali also notices that these four cards are mirroring each other, with a pair of tens and a pair of Queens. She cannot help but understand the first set as "the circle that was" and the second set as "the circle that could be." The relaxed, slightly folksy group that began in the 1980s needs to sharpen up to appeal to any others.

Kali then randomly selects some cards to help support the group in its present crisis, since things cannot go on like this. These cards are 8 Wands, Page Pentacles, 2 Cups, and Knight Cups, which she lays beneath the first line. These will enable the circle to honour the wisdom of the present moment by passing on their knowledge and experience of meditation to younger people; by being reciprocal, they honour their commitment to meditation by offering it generously. Finally, she selects two Major Arcana cards taken from nearest the top and bottom of the deck: Strength for the top line, to lend support for the group's current struggle, and Hierophant to acknowledge the circle's respect for what was held in everyone's soul. This showed a group that had held true to its principles but was clearly needing to change to appeal to younger people now. Given the members' ages, it might just fold, but not before handing on its wealth of experience.

First Row

Second Row

Third Row

SUPPORTING THE HOSPITAL TRUST

Margery works for a National Health Service Foundation Trust for a hospital, as a community and nonprofessional member of the trust. The hospital itself is underperforming according to not only a recent inspection, but also the copious testimony of patients. She came to me to explore the situation. The many changes to the organization and funding of the National Health Service over the last decades in the UK had left a few gaps in the system, she felt. She wanted to know if there was anything she and the trust might do differently to bring improvements. After discussing the complexities of the issue, I composed this customized reading.

FIG. 19a *Shuffling the spirit of the hospital trust into the deck*

4	Page	The
Cups	Pentacles	World

Please note that this reading is not a personal one, and although Margery is a part of this institution, she is asking for help on behalf of it. In the event of reading for a group, we first seek the consent of the founding principle of the institution, so I first of all asked her to select a card to represent that principle or foundational spirit of the hospital trust. She chose Page of Pentacles, because she felt it depicted what the trust was originally founded to do: to care for the sick and to support the study and research of ways to bring better health impartially. Focussing first upon the spirit of the trust and seeking permission, I then shuffled the representative into the deck, inviting the spirit of the trust to come and help support it, and to show us the basis of the problem and some solutions and resources. The trust's significator landed between these two cards. 4 Cups showed that a stagnation of spirit was afflicting the trust, possibly even as strong as a self-disgust, as if it knew its activities were not bringing much blessing. The World showed the great potential and care that was able to bring concord and health to its work.

The first nine cards were drawn to observe the hospital trust itself, the patient's experience of the hospital, and where things need to improve. I then invited Margery to draw random cards for positions 10–21 to support the patient's experience on arrival and at discharge, as well as to set up support cards both for the trust and the improvements it hoped to bring.

As you can see, cards 1–9 show the situation as it is currently, while the surrounding cards are placed to support improvements for the patient's experience and present resources that support the trust as well as the improvements that Margery hoped could be brought into place. She knew that she couldn't bring these improvements alone or without a good deal of help, and she found the concept of resources or supporters for the trust's taxing role very helpful. The following is the shape of the spread:

FIG. 19b
Reading for the hospital trust

10   11   12

13   1   2   3   19

14   4   5   6   20

15   7   8   9   21

16   17   18

Cards 1–3 The hospital trust itself:
rev. Hermit, rev. Moon, Ace Pentacles

Here, the cards spoke of the hospital trust operating without guidance, making them procrastinate through uncertainty. They also had little sense of the rhythm of their work, and there was a prevailing mental confusion and illusion, though they all were committed to providing every resource to the hospital, and to upholding the healing process with respect and care. Margery nodded, recognizing this: "Only a few of us nonprofessionals feel we know what we are doing with any authority; since things changed in the National Health Service, it feels as if we are struggling to achieve targets and trying to hold things together."

Cards 4–6 The patient's current experience:
rev. 10 Wands, 8 Pentacles, Strength

Most people attending the hospital acknowledged that they were unable to get help anywhere else. They generally experienced the staff as hardworking and capable, doing all that they could to help them return to fitness and health, but the staff was staggering under heavy workloads.

Cards 7–9 How things in the trust need to improve:
9 Cups, rev. 3 Swords, 9 Pentacles

The trust could improve things by ceasing to be complacent about their provision of resources, and the sense of their own accomplishments. They could look closer at the exigencies of those they served. Margery added, "Quite a few in the trust come from privileged backgrounds. They've never known a day's want in their lives, and I think they cannot fully see where things are failing. If they could stop pontificating for a moment, they might see it."

Margery was invited to choose or randomly select Tarot cards whose qualities would support the following (these cards were chosen to witness to what was required in this situation):

Cards 10–12 What supports the hospital trust:
3 Cups, Hierophant, 9 Wands

Here, we have generosity of spirit, a deep understanding that can coordinate things for the health of all, and a realisation that more help was needed by the trust.

Cards 13–15 What factors need to be in place to receive a
patient: Ace Cups, 6 Wands, Star

Here we have the power of healing itself, a trusting that things could steadily improve, and the need of a regenerative environment of recovery provided for the patient.

Cards 16–18 What supports the trust's improvements:
6 Cups, 5 Swords, Queen Pentacles

Here, we see the remembrance that keeps the vulnerable in mind; also, a clear reminder that self-interest has no part in the trust's work, but rather that the trust must be the advocate for the provision of the hospital, and that a resourceful care for its users is needed.

Cards 19–21 What factors need to be in place to discharge
a patient: 4 Wands, Lovers, Sun

Here, a sense of harmonious conclusion and a return to health is clearly shown, along with an ongoing commitment to the return of good health.

The central nine cards had 3 Majors; one each of Swords, Wands, and Cups; and 3 Pentacles, showing that this reading was largely underpinned by money or its lack. The last process was to take the spirit of the trust, the Page of Pentacles, and place the card in the centre of the reading, over the 8 Pentacles. Margery placed it there herself and then took a picture of the cards. It was clear that some members had put themselves at the centre of the trust, rather than the spirit/founding principle, so that restoring it to its central place was critically important.

This reading reveals some of the complexities of reading for a group, as well as how resources can be mustered to help it. On pp. 285-287, you will find a wider series of questions to help you focus more closely upon any community, group, country, or institution, so that you can discern its dynamics and your relationship to them more precisely in times of great change. We also have to sadly acknowledge that some institutions themselves need very radical change or dynamic reform as their accountability becomes impoverished. Indeed, some institutions have now become so broken or corrupted that they need the creation of a parallel but ethical institution that really serves the community.

The spread and layout suggestions in chapters 4–7 can be adapted to read on community issues as well as for the wider household of the earth in many different ways. But on p. 285, we consider ways of dealing with how systemic issues have an impact on us: where the individual, group, or community is affected by what is happening around them. I give a few methods of approaching these issues.

FROM HERE TO THERE SPREAD

Sometimes, events move faster than we are prepared for or we are part of a much larger event that railroads us. Trying to orient ourselves at such times can be confusing. This spread enables us to find the major stepping stones to help us track how we get from where we are to where we are going. This spread makes a cell of cards that help you discern those tracks in matters where our way forward or continued movement is unclear or very difficult. It can reveal a radical personal change to be made, such as in the journey of a relationship separation or a bereavement, which is a process, or it can follow a plan that is developing. The number of stepping stones or cards you add into this is up to you: about 3–5 cards is generally sufficient. But the number of cards chosen should be the same number in the top as in the bottom line. In the top line you read how your own path or plan is going to have to deal with things appearing in your community, your country, or the world at large; the lower line will reveal resources that you will be needing for the journey as you live through the issue, especially in hard times, as we see in the following example.

FIG. 20a *Shape of the From Here to There spread*

1. Shuffle your cards thoroughly while considering your question.
2. Cut the pack into 2 piles.
3. Drawing from the first pile, lay one card on each position 1–4 (or add more steps if needed).
4. Drawing from the second pile, lay one card on each position 5–8. Or add more steps, if needed.
5. Take the bottom card from the first pile and lay on A: this is how the story starts.
6. Take the bottom card from the second pile and lay on B: this is where the story reaches its conclusion.
7. Read A with 1–4 as the progression of the story.
8. Read 5–8 as what can modify, shape, or support the story. Then read B.
9. If you need go deeper, then pair the top and bottom line of cards together, allowing the lower-line card to describe the topmost card. So, 5 describes 1, 6 describes 2, and so on. This is optional.
10. Read A and B together as the title of the story as a summation.

Example:

In this example, Arlene and Rob are members of a conservation group for an ancient woodland with a unique biodiversity of trees, wildlife, and plants. To their dismay, this irreplaceable habitat lies in the path of a proposed new train line that has been given the go-ahead by the government. Corporate interest is going to override their work and destroy this precious habitat, and there is little more they can do about it, despite vigorous opposition and activism. While they were not alone—because many such groups had fought and lost the same fight along this rail line—they felt at their wits' ends, wanting insight about the coming month, now that the axe was poised to fall. I suggested that we looked at things by using the From Here to There spread:

FIG. 20b *A reading of the From Beginning to End spread*

A. Arlene and Rob were currently caught in the prospect of the many alternative scenarios they had entertained to save the woodland: dreams that led them to hope.

1–4 These cards told the unfolding story of the road ahead: the first step is moving on from their long struggle. The Chariot could literally stand for the coming of the new rail line itself, since it represents transport, but also signifies their loyalty and commitment to their goal. The arrival of the train line inevitably brings deep grief at the destruction of the woodland, and the anticipation of its coming overshadows everything else.

5–8 The cards that support them in this sad journey lie below: The Star offers them its sanctuary as they begin to move away from their position as campaigners, offering them an ability to refresh themselves. The reversed 4 Cups offers them the possibility of working for a different habitat to conserve. The High Priestess honours and witnesses their grief, offering them a sanctuary to see the bigger picture and keep faith with it, while 9 Pentacles reasserts the sense of the power of nature to renew itself.

B. The arrival point on their journey from loss is 10 Pentacles, the card that honours the wisdom of the ancestors and the inheritance of this rare woodland habitat that they have tended this long time. While the living trees and plants have been removed, the wildlife driven away from that woodland, their descendants endure. Arlene and Rob would not cease doing their work, since they regarded themselves and their conservation work as service to the earth itself. They both have joined a more radical environmental group, whose activism has included dramatic acts of public mourning for the wildlife lost as a result of this rail line.

On one level, this is a story of dreams being overturned by corporate values. At another, timeless level, it is a story of much-loved woodland entering the ancestral realms. This reading was likely to have little hope in it, because the destructive clear-cut line through the countryside is now a stark reality across the land, which is why I chose to lay the lower line as resource cards to support them.

UNDER THE PREVAILING CONDITIONS READING

In this section, we establish how the household of the earth is affected by what is going on locally, socially, or in the world at large. Sometimes whatever we attempt to do labours under the disadvantage of some prevailing condition that, like an unchanging weather pattern or irritating backdrop to our lives, becomes a factor in our reading. This might be the aftermath of a pandemic, a protracted family crisis, an idea that is socially divisive, a political campaign, a disruptive development in your area, or a national anguish/catastrophe that is setting up its own interference. These subtle influences can be merely irritating or escalate into a war of attrition.

Few people take these sorts of prevailing conditions into account, discounting their influence, but they are part of the context of your life, so it is sensible to consider how they change things and how you might best mitigate or work through them. This reading also helps us push beyond the kinds of superstition or conspiracy-mindedness that many people entertain at some low and unsupported point in their lives, to reach a more discerning and balanced perspective. It can also help you look at the truth of factors that are prevailing upon a family or group.

Method for Reading on the Prevailing Conditions
Choose one or more cards for all or some of the following questions, which will become positions in your reading. Since you may have other questions to add to these or may change the ones given here, I am not providing a set spread, since your own will be different. You can choose to focus small on you and your family or go wider if you are looking at a national or global situation. Here, your "purpose or intention" can represent your personal code of honour or what you are trying to achieve at this time, or the central mainspring of your life that is being prevailed upon by the conditions around you.

- ✦ What guides your purpose/intention?
- ✦ What is the nature of the prevailing condition/s?
- ✦ From whence do these influences arise?
- ✦ What fears/anxieties/concerns do these conditions arouse?
- ✦ How is my purpose being influenced by these conditions?
- ✦ How are my circle of family/friends being affected by these conditions?
- ✦ How is society / my country being agitated/ divided/ disempowered by prevailing conditions?
- ✦ What resources are needed to mitigate the influence of these conditions?
- ✦ How can I/we best avoid being pulled into the vector of this influence?
- ✦ What radical changes need to come about as a result of these conditions?
- ✦ What are the resources we can all draw upon to steer a course through these influences?
- ✦ What gift/truth arises from holding to my purpose?

Select one or more cards for each of the questions you use in your layout. Finally, select the Major Arcana card from nearest the bottom of the deck as the wisdom you need to guide you through this period.

Example:

Catherine asks for some clarity in her personal, family, and social life as the world moves out of lockdown for the first few months. She has been disturbed by shifting and conflicting influences that seem to be dividing those people dear to her; they have become subject to fears and suspicions and are repeating or being spooked by wildly inaccurate information, over which they argue. She creates her questions and arranges them like this:

FIG. 21 *Prevailing Conditions spread*

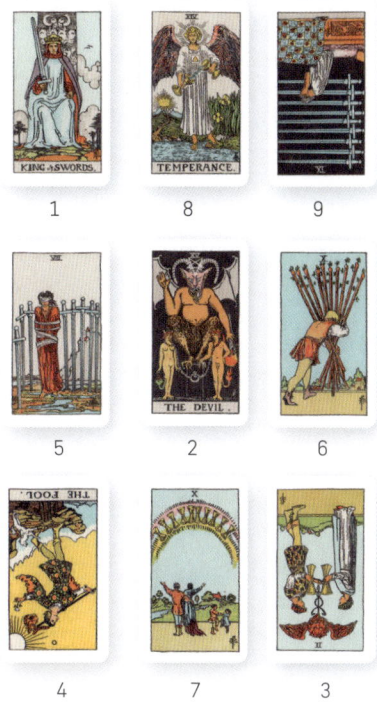

1. *My core purpose*: King Swords. Catherine is a principled woman with a strong sense of truth and fairness, which gives her perspective on life.

2. *The prevailing conditions*: Devil. A pervasive sense of fear is abroad, which is manipulating opinion and reinforcing attitudes that enslave and bind.

3. *What is it about these conditions that makes me feel shaky?* Reversed 2 Cups. The divisions that have arisen between social interchange are alarming, cutting across close friendships.

4. *How are my family and friends being affected by them?* Reversed Fool. The scariest thing is that their behaviour has become over-reactive or stupidly naïve.

5. *How are these conditions dividing myself and my loved ones?* 8 Swords. Everyone has been in a state of physical restriction, feeling victimized and held to ransom by the unsubstantiated views of social media.

6. *Whence have these conditions arisen?* 9 Wands. A refusal to be beaten by lockdown has undoubtedly been instrumental; continual attrition has worn down everyone's stamina, as they each fought on alone.

7. *What mitigates the influence of these conditions?* 10 Cups. The long-lasting affection between her family and friends lies inviolate beneath these prevailing influences. Bonds of family love and friendly loyalty are more cohesive.

8. *What resources help keep me true to myself?* Temperance will give her the harmony and balance to stop merging with these influences. It can also help reconcile the conflict at work among her loved ones.

9. *How can we avoid being submerged by these conditions?* Reversed 9 Swords. By checking suspicions carefully and not being overwhelmed by them, her dear ones can stop being led by exaggerated mistrust and fear.

Catherine found the bottom Major Arcana card to support herself, her family, and her friends: Lovers. She covered the Devil with Lovers, visualizing the angel watching over them all, reminding them of the love that bound them together. Interestingly, in this 10-card layout, three of the angelic cards were present; the only angel absent was that of Judgement—the card that might signal the regeneration of society was not quite ready to appear at this early point after lockdown!

TERO GOLDENHILL'S HAZMAT SUIT SPREAD

In changing times, it can feel as if by even considering community issues, you are being overwhelmed by the welter of events. This Hazmat Suit spread is by Finnish author and skilled taromancer Tero Goldenhill. A hazmat suit is, of course, the protective clothing and equipment worn by those who have to go into emergency situations of volatile chemical spillage or other toxic environments. This spread gives you guidance when things have hit crisis or breakdown point: it pinpoints where the situation started and what will be the fallout, as well as giving you the help and resources to get through it.

1. Lay down the Tower card: this signifies the sense of fallout or crisis.

2. Shuffle the deck and count through it to remove every 16th card, laying them *face down* under the Tower as cards 1–4. This foundational line shows the effect of the crisis.

3. Now turn your deck face up. Count through the deck and remove every 16th card and place them as cards 5–8 *face up* between Tower and cards 1–4. This upper line shows you the protection, help, and resources that are available for whatever shows up in the foundational line.

FIG. 22 *The Hazmat Suit spread*

4. Turn over cards 1–4 and read about the hazard. Read the hazmat suit or protection lines 5–8, and then read the upper and lower lines together: card 5 with 1, 6 with 2, 7 with 3, and 8 with 4. What is the sense of the protection or resource that you are given?

5. Now, place the Tower upright into the remaining cards of the deck, shuffle it thoroughly, and turn the deck face up to find where the Tower has fallen in the deck (see p. 229). Count 16 cards to the left of where the Tower fell and lay that card at position 9: this is where the crisis was born or where and when it originated. Then, count 16 cards to the right of where the Tower fell, and lay it on position 10: this is where or how the crisis comes to an end. Treat the deck as a continuous book for this purpose, if the Tower has fallen at either end.

SEVEN WAYS OF ENGAGING WITH THE SPIRITS OF COMMUNITY

We can prepare ourselves to engage with the spirits of groups, our community, and our world by observing seven principles. The questions underneath each principle may also act as prompts to self-clarify how we interact with them, as well as providing questions for reading on issues involving group, community, or world issues. Each of these points of engagement can become a reading in its own right: use some of these questions as well as ones of your own.

1.   TRUTH: *Recognizing what is going on and not being bound by illusions, delusions, veils, and persuasions.*

What is happening here? How am I part of it? What has clouded my vision? How have I been fooling myself? Where is truth not being served?

2.   JUSTICE: *Witnessing and restoring honour and dignity.*

Who is being oppressed? Where is power and soul lost/dishonoured? What do I need to witness and understand here? What restores honour and dignity? What is my part in the restoration?

3.   PEACE: *Not continuing the conflict by engaging in it, using non-retributive and nondual methods, realizing how we too can be enmeshed in the conflict.*

With whom am I at war / in conflict? How am I passing on my anger/frustration etc. about it in other places? Who is being affected by my conflict? What do I project upon the group/institution? How would my truce change things?

4.   KEEPING FAITH: *Honouring spirit and ethical principles wherever they are revealed, and refusing to be blind to the intrinsic potential of all beings.*

Where is spirit revealed in the institution? How am I refusing to allow that spirit/principle to shine/bless? How does the spirit/founding principle of a group/system uniquely serve? How am I served by this spirit/principle? What are the characteristics of the group's spirit and how do I relate with it?

5. ACKNOWLEDGING VOCATIONAL GIFTS: *Honouring any special gifts, following, educating, developing, and using them to serve our fellow beings. Not prostituting our gifts or allowing them to be dishonourably or misleadingly used.*

What is the contract between myself and my gifts? What is the contract among me, my gifts, and the group/institution? What drew me and my gifts to the service of this group/institution? How are these gifts being diverted from their prime directive? Where do my gifts and the world's need meet?

6. SPIRITUAL/ETHICAL SERVICE: *Finding a spiritual/ethical way by which to live, and practicing these principles. Being part of a larger context than any problem that arises so that we are not overwhelmed.*

What is my spiritual/ethical way? What aspects of childhood/earlier pathways have shaped that way? What religious/cultural factors litter my path or hobble me? What spiritual/ethical truths do I live by? What does my spiritual/ethical way teach me? Where am I not implementing these teachings? Whom do I serve?

7. PRAYER/COMMUNION/MEDITATION: *Keeping in strong communion with our ethical principles or the spirit of the group. Seeking the balance of prayer/ communion/ meditation keeps our hearts focussed and serviceable.*

How do I regularly connect with ethical principles/spirit? What aperture opens when I pray/meditate? How does my vision keep open the door? What flows toward me as I pray/meditate? How does my prayer/communion awaken spirit to awareness around me? What happens when I concentrate on my weakness or inability? What happens when I focus only upon my self-sufficiency? What happens when I invite the archetypal powers?

Now we turn to considering ourselves and our lives in the light of the world, and how we gauge the impact of one upon the other.

READING FOR OUR WORLD

The earth is the centre of the universe

The house is the centre of the earth

The family is the centre of the house

The person is the centre of the family.

—Basque song

RIPPLES IN THE KNOWING FIELD

This Basque song takes us back to Hierocles's idea of the household of the earth, and the nesting viewpoints that make up our continuous and interconnected experience of life on earth. We may think of ourselves as just individuals, yet we are also members of a family, a part of many groups and communities, a citizen of our country or members of a worldwide group or spirituality, and so on.

The questions we pose to the Tarot ripple much wider than just the personal zone. As soon as we ask a question, we open a knowing field whose ripples pass through every part of the universe.[9] A knowing field is like the mysterious intercommunication that enables flocks of birds to navigate and understand the right times and places for them: made up of every zone, it is a field of shared understanding that is responsive. Even when we pose questions whose answers we cannot guess at, the universe knows: because we are each a part of its all-encompassing knowing field, the ripples of our question will keep running through the field until they bring the answer home to us. This concept gives us one of the largest spread cloths for our question, since it can include the whole household of the earth.

In chapter one we explored the household of the earth as a series of nesting, concentric circles, but here is a different model where I have located each zone around the edge of the vast knowing field of life. Four main zones interconnect here to create one big knowing field: we can imagine them all overlapping further than they do in this diagram, so that they lie over each other. We each stand in direct relationship to these zones, and whatever our question, they will affect or be affected by it. Here are its four zones:

The Family/Ancestral Zone: Represents the family and background from which every individual takes their initial foundation. It will include the family values we grew up with, and the formation of our upbringing and beginnings. In a deeper way it also connects us to all our ancestors and the potentialities of that vast field of forebears.

The Group/Community Zone: Represents the society and groups in which we spend our adult life. It will include the community value of our chosen social groupings, our friends and peers at work and at play, as well as our interactions with them; it will host our sense of belonging to our region and the nation of which we are a citizen.

The Personal Zone represents each person's individual focus, which matures and reshapes itself as we grow older as we gain more experience of life. It will include our personal values and our dreams, aptitudes, vocational skills, and understandings. All that inspires and nourishes us is found here, connecting us to deepest levels of cultural inheritance and understanding.

FIG. 23 *The Knowing Field of the question*

The Universal Zone represents the wider life and the wise experience, both seen and unseen, of all the inhabitants of the earth and beyond. It will include ethical and universal values, the life of nature and the environment, our spiritual understanding, and the affiliations we make, as well as our spiritual allies, sacred beings, and soul guides. This field connects us to the world of nature and to an all-inclusive understanding.

In this model, we can understand how we are each born into a family whose ancestral values we inherit. As a child, we accept those values very naturally because they are normal to our household, but as young adults, we gravitate toward the world at large, where we enter society to become part of different kinds of groups. We cultivate our own personal views and understandings as we age. We are simultaneously part of the wider, universal world of time and place, as well as being included in the timelessness and spaciousness of the unseen world.

In truth, each of these zones overlaps, with our lives lived within the knowing field of them all.

It is important to realise that we cannot step out of any of these zones: we will always be the child of our parents, the descendant of our ancestors; we will share the aspirations as well as the prejudices of groups to which we belong; we continue to adhere to the personal understandings that life's experiences have given us and to our dreams and visions; we cannot cease to belong to the household of the earth in any way. We live within a network of zones that have an impact on us, and on which we have an impact, all the time. We are a part of all that is.

When including the knowing field within our readings with querents, we need to hold in mind the following points, since not everyone engages with each zone in as complete or balanced a way:

*People may be estranged from or alienated by their birth family and may not know anything of their ancestral roots, especially if they were adopted. While we do not need to know our ancestors, they will still know us. If immediate family members have been abusive or difficult, then invite the querent to consider the Family/Ancestral Zone as extending much further back in time: somewhere in that field there will be one or more ancestors who look kindly upon them in a good and healthy way to support and encourage them.

*In the Group/Community Zone, some people may be very reclusive and unsocialized for a variety of reasons, but they are nonetheless part of its various groups—by virtue of their work or avocations. Those alienated by human society or bothered by the passing of time are often more drawn to the Universal Field, where a general distrust of human beings may show itself in a love of nature, animals, and being solitary, and also a sense of being outside the stream of time.

*In terms of the Personal Zone, some individuals may not have a strong self-awareness or a good knowledge of themselves. You can help them discern what motivates them, what dreams they foster for the future, and where their lives are tending, helping the querent take up their own space in the bigger picture. Alternatively, the querent may be so self-focused that it is hard for them to include the other fields within their focus.

*The Universal Zone is large, consisting as it does of the whole world, seen and unseen: this zone invites us to step out of time so that everything can be considered. If the spaciousness of this field is too vast or the querent has no sense of spiritual belonging, invite them to think of the world of nature in their locality, and of specific witnesses of universal movements that have brought betterment to all beings.

By including the knowing field in our readings, we access the whole context of someone's life and are able to note the influences that prevail upon the querent, which means we need both consent and respect. We seek consent for our reading by making a prayer or request of the knowing field, asking it to please answer the querent simply and honestly. In whatever spread you make to look at these things, you can give each zone of the knowing field a place in the reading. We can ask what each of its zones needs from the querent, as well as looking also at the help that each zone may provide. You can draw one card or a pair of cards or more for each position, as appropriate. On pp. 294–295 is just one possible shape your Knowing Field reading might take: be guided by the context, factors, and dynamics of the issue.

WORKING WITHIN THE KNOWING FIELD

In this example, Evan has recently left university and is entering a career in the world of politics, but he knows it is difficult to remain impartial and also uphold social justice. His question is "How can I best serve my country as a politician?" After he had shuffled, I asked Evan to cut the deck into four piles, one for each of the fields. From the top of each pile, I laid three cards for each field. For positions 13–16, I took the nearest Major Arcana card from the bottom of each cut pile as the help that each field provided to him. I then added the values of cards 13–16 together to get the 17th card.

Cards 1–3 What does the family field need from me?
The Family/Ancestral Zone needs Evan to be just in all his dealings, to ensure that adequate healthcare is in place for families, and to introduce flexible ways of budgeting resources so that family finances are upheld.

Cards 4–6 What does the community field of society need from me?

The Community/Group Zone requires him to bridge the divides in society, especially to rethink failing security and social policies.

Cards 7–9 What does my dedication to social justice require of me?

The Personal Zone of his dedication requires Evan to be creative and generous, not to try to be a perfectionist, but to consider that any decisions he makes will include not only for himself but for everyone in generations to come.

Cards 10–12 What does the field of the universe need from me?

The Universal Zone needs Evan to acknowledge that the so-far-rather-plodding attempts to deal with the environmental crisis require a more imaginative approach, to help mitigate the waste of the world's resources.

Cards 13–16 The help that each of the fields provides to help me.

The resources and gifts that each field provides to him are inspiration (The Star) from the Family Zone, Justice from the Community/Group Zone, ingenuity (The Magician) from the Personal Zone, and a sense of committed oversight (The Emperor) from the Universal Zone.

Card 17 How will my career in politics change things?

By adding the values of cards 13–16 together: 17 (The Star) + 11 (Justice) + 1 (The Magician) + 4 (The Emperor) = 33. Then, 3 + 3 = 6, so we find The Lovers. This answers Evan's question about how his work might change things—he has the ability to relate to and care about people, to bring out the best gifts within them.

Working with the knowing field offers a Tarot template for people who stand at a threshold or turning point in their life, where we are actively asking each zone for help, insight, or clarification. It gives perspective to questions where change is desired, where new

FIG. 24
The Knowing Field arranged as a spread

DEATH.

10

11

TEMPERANCE.

12

9

THE EMPEROR.

16

KING of SWORDS.

1

THE WORLD.

8

THE MAGICIAN.

15

THE LOVERS.

17

THE STAR.

13

2

THE EMPRESS.

7

JUSTICE.

14

3

THE HIEROPHANT.

4

5

6

directions are needed, inviting the whole universe to speak to us and tell us what it expects of us.

ASSESSING THE AFFINITY SPREAD

Every thought we have, every action we make, and every word we utter has an effect somewhere: both for ourselves and for those around us. Use this spread when you want to assess the impact upon your own life, your community, and the world, in any question you are reading on. It also enables you to gauge the affinity or cooperation between your question and the household of the earth.

In this spread, the way each zone is associated with your question is read horizontally in rows 1–3, while the cooperative relationship between the querent and their world can be read vertically in columns C, D, and E. Where the rows and columns interconnect is precisely where the Knowing Field springs up to answer the question. The remaining cards in our assessment are read as a final insight. Reading the cards in two different ways is an older, cartomantic method that enables the spread to work much harder, to reveal not only the meanings but also the dynamic of the question. I have adapted this spread from Etteilla's Three Wishes spread. The shape and method are outlined here:

Row 1 looks at the personal or immediate vicinity of the question—about your own involvement with the question or if it is about a work issue or a local issue.

Row 2 is for your family/group/community/region.

Row 3 is for your country/world/environment.

1. First, read each of these three rows across with forward narration, as a story or statement.

2. Then read columns C, D, and E as the Nine Witnesses who speak with one voice about the matter.

3. As a final process, you can pair together the end cards, to find a closing message for the querent: reading cards 1 + 15, 2 +14, 6 + 10. These pairings often make short descriptions or statements, as you can see below.

Example:

Alex has created an education project that he hopes can be adopted in many zones of conflict worldwide, where traumatized children who've been exposed to conflict can be assisted: he wants to see what effect this project will have among his own colleagues, among the teaching community, and throughout the world.

FIG. 25b *Alex's assessing the Affinity reading*

| A | B | C | D | E | F | G |

Row 1: Alex's project brings real hope and consolidation to those helping to reintegrate children who've been excluded from education by their vulnerability, giving them space to appreciate life again after terrible or shocking events.

Row 2: The project brings a sense of optimism and adventure to those who are teaching vulnerable and traumatized children, giving them compassionate ways for a community to mentally adapt or step beyond unhelpful ideologies.

Row 3: The project offers a sanctuary for all who have been overwhelmed by heavy news or who are in the grip of unfounded rumours; it provides a stable method for young students everywhere to bloom.

Column C: The children's return to normal life after trauma first requires a sanctuary.

Column D: A compassionate space helps calm down those who expect only the worst.

Column E: The impact of shocking events needs to be cleared so that children can stop feeling insecure.

The paired end cards speak to Alex of what his project does: Star + Knight Cups: bringer of hope. 4 Wands + Page Pentacles: celebrating education. Fool + reversed Hermit: bringing freedom to the downcast.

While the project is currently being trialled in just two places in Europe and the Middle East, it seems likely from initial results that a review will find improvements in the lives of children who have survived conflict.

READING ON WORLD EVENTS
AND THEIR EFFECT

The temptation with reading on world events is to keep casting cards every week to see how things are playing out, which is why it is wise to read sparingly and to ask a question with a timescale on it: for the next 3 months or the next year. However, it must be said that time-based readings have a way of running out or being fulfilled a lot earlier these days, in my experience, as time speeds things up. At the elapse of a time-based spread, then we can read again, as we must when we have no chart for the unknown waters ahead.

Over the last few years with the effects of the pandemic lockdown, planning anything to an exact time and place has been nearly impossible: most people have had to do more work online than in person, and to be prepared to be flexible or ingenious. The effect of one thing upon another has set up adverse ripples that are hard to fathom or factor into our plans across the world, because the original causation of those ripples is still playing out. Our flexibility and preparedness can be helped by a skilful use of the Tarot.

For those who work in international networks and associations, looking ahead or guessing trends is an art that keeps their work ahead of the game; potential areas of danger or developing trouble are usually known to them, but we can all be caught out by unknown factors that will impact our world, as we have all seen. The World through Time is a simple time-based spread that puts the querent or group at the centre of an ongoing situation. It includes both the past and the future, since understanding the past is as much a guide to the present and future as in any predictive reading. The origination of an event or situation is included here, as is the recent past, while the querent's row shows the present time, then the near future and further future—the timing will vary according to the period of time being read for.

1. Shuffle the chosen significator into the deck and discover where it falls: take the significator and the two cards on either side of it to make the middle line, which is laid first.

2. Take the five bottom cards of the deck and lay them beneath the first five.

3. Take the five top cards of the deck and lay them above the first five.

Row 1 shows the prevailing situation.
Row 2 shows the querent's own position within the situation.
Row 3 shows the factors that are likely to develop and also world reaction to the prevailing situation.

Read the rows across and the columns down for a full picture.

Cards can be added to extend the timescale, giving new columns. It is possible also to add representatives to each side of the picture as resources, witnesses, or supporters.

Example:
Carey works for an international cultural association and asks, "'How will the Russian-Ukrainian war affect our work in the next 6 months?" The war started on 24th February 2022 and it is now June: already countries have dropped Russia from scheduled international arts and sporting events, but Carey still has to keep the channels open because, in a war, the cultural identity and heritage of a people are as much at risk as their physical well-being, their land's economic health, and its environmental integrity.

FIG. 26 *Carey's the World through Time spread*

| Origin: | Recent Past: | Now: | Near future 3 months:: | Future 6 months: |

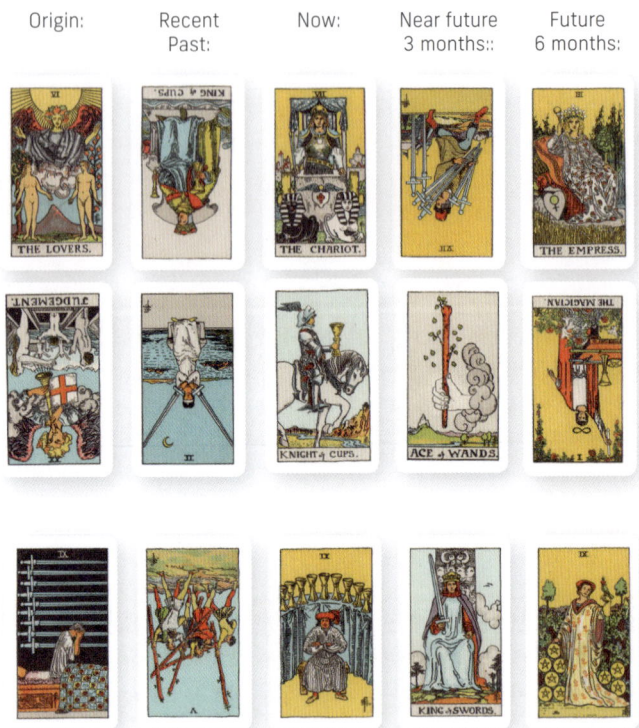

We see in row 1 that the situation of the war starts like an unwanted proposal of marriage or a coercive relationship, and where the arts themselves are subverted or filtered in an exploitative way. The current situation rides like a juggernaut across Ukraine. In the months ahead, there is a sense of Russia flinging its resources into the breach, in its attempt to reunify Ukraine into Mother Russia.

Carey's significator is Knight of Cups: in row 2, we see the kind of apocalyptic scenarios that she and her association were running in their minds when the war started, and the sense of sealing themselves off. Looking into the coming months, it is clear that they need to take the creative initiative once more by promoting performers and presentations whose integrity and vigour can uphold the truth in the face of growing propaganda that is diffusing world harmony.

In row 3, we see the world waking up to the coming of war, and the way it deplores the betrayal of international agreements on the autonomy of sovereign nations. In the present, there is a measure of self-satisfaction in international response to the war. In the coming months, international courts of justice and world leaders will be trying to negotiate an impartial way through the chaos. Performers and presentations will be badly needed to nourish those affected by the war.

Columns 1 and 2 have been largely read above. For Carey, column 3 is saying that it is imperative to keep the arts centre stage at a time when a certain complacency is setting in around the world. Column 4 shows her trying to discern the unspoken agenda of those in the conflict zone on both sides, so that performers, poets, and singers might address combatants and civilians in clear and impartial ways. This combination of reversed 7 Swords, Ace Wands, and King Swords also speaks of the Russian attempt to subvert Ukrainian culture. Column 5 shows how important beauty and creativity are, especially when shared appreciation of such things is being subject to propaganda. The arts are desperately needed to bring refreshment to war-weary countries.

Carey's time-changing responsibility is clear. War cannot stop the arts, which traditionally unite people everywhere, despite the petty cancelling of certain nationalities' music or artists that has already been happening with her association's programming of concerts. Carey is determined to put the arts first as essential food for the soul. This will practically mean also supporting Russian

artists, whose skills are being marginalized because of their nation-
ality, as well as bringing the arts to Ukrainians still in war zones and
as refugees abroad. I invited her to pull the first Major Arcana card
from the bottom of the deck to act as a supporter for her endeavours;
she produced Strength, saying, "I see I will need some help to be
persuasive!" For Carey, this resource would be about "strengthening
the weak and calming the anger," that the arts might flourish.

INVITING THE ANIMALS INTO
THE KNOWING FIELD

When we look at world issues, the sense of being overwhelmed or
powerless can be strong, particularly when we look at matters such
as environmental destruction, as we saw in the last chapter. It is
common for people to experience despair and hopelessness about
these kinds of issues. In the next chapter we will look at other methods for addressing this sense of being overwhelmed, but here is a
way of bringing perspective and clearer focus upon the larger issues
that are developing throughout the world.

The contribution of every living being to the household of the
world is essential, and species loss is a loss of knowledge and wisdom
for the whole world. When we read on matters that concern an
environmental issue, we can step out of our human point of view
and invite in the animals, the plants, or a whole habitat to speak from
their point of view. There are many ways to spread the cards for this
purpose, but here a simple knowing field provides the basis. Inviting
in the world of nature to be the questioner is a very powerful method of working: it can become the basis of discussion and more action,
as here. Use this method too when you need to see the other side of
an issue or gain some perspective about what changes are needed.

In this example, honeybees were themselves invited to be the querent, with each card drawn enabling *them* to pose their questions of the person who had brought the issue. These questions can be found in the "Questions'"section at the end of each card in chapters 2 and 3. You can adapt the questions to the issue, as necessary.

Example:

As a member of Friends of the Earth, Judy is concerned about a banned pesticide that has been recently approved for use on farms by the government; it will strongly impact honeybees and other pollinators, to the detriment of all life. She initially wanted to ask what could be done on behalf of the bees, apart from the protests and petitions she has participated in. After discussion, we created a spread where we invited the bees to be part of the reading and speak for themselves, so Judy amended her question to "I am inviting the bees to question me about what this pesticide means to them." The Empress—both as the provider of safe space and as an allusion to the queen bee—was chosen as the bees' significator and shuffled into the deck. From the Opening of the Book (see p. 229), the two cards on either side of the Empress were set on the Knowing Field positions: (from left to right) the left one goes on the Universal Zone, the next card on the Personal Zone, the significator in the middle, the next card on the Family/Ancestral Zone, and the last card on the Community/Group Zone.

FIG. 27 *Inviting the animals into the Knowing Field*
(the headed cards ask the questions the accompanying cards, marked
*with an * under them, represent the answers)*

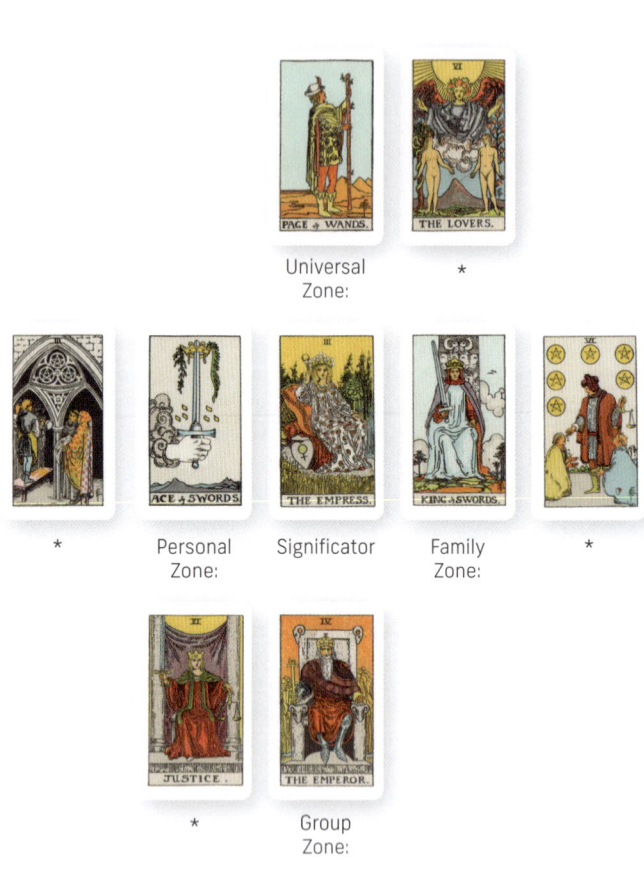

Universal
Zone:

*

* Personal Significator Family *
Zone: Zone:

* Group
Zone:

Judy selected questions from the individual entries of the cards from
chapters 2 and 3 to set the bees' questions.

In the Family/Ancestral Zone, the King of Swords asked, "Who has the power of life and death here?"

In the Community/Group Zone, the Emperor asked, "Who needs to take the authority?"

In the Personal Zone, the Ace of Swords asked, "Why has power turned to excessive force?"

In the Universal Zone, the Page of Wands asked, "How would things change if you engaged with this?"

Judy found this set of extremely consistent questions very powerful to be on the receiving end of, like a catechism or inquisition, so she drew one further card at each position to help her answer the bees. I invited her to look at the "Focus" section of each of the cards as guidance, if she needed it. These are the randomly selected cards that helped answer these searching questions, drawn from the "Focus" section of each card in Chapters 2 and 3:

In the Family/Ancestral Zone was 6 Pentacles. Judy answered, "Those who see only the immediate needs of themselves have decreed life and death for you."

In the Community/Group Zone was Justice. Judy answered, "Justice and truth need to step into authority."

In the Personal Zone was 3 Pentacles. She answered, "Preoccupation with gain has set the agenda on this decision."

In the Universal Zone was the Lovers. Judy answered, "If we engaged with this issue, things would change because love of nature and the whole universe would dictate the agenda."

After the reading, Judy told me she had taken this method of questions and answers to her Friends of the Earth group and that they had prepared from it a piece of street theatre with a local school to raise awareness of the problem.

HOW THE DREAM CHANGES: REVIEWING THE CONTRACT

The way we live matters, yet, in the tides of time, we seldom make time to consider how we are doing it, what is motivating us or why. Throughout our lives, we wish for many things, some idle, some serious. But how do our wiser dreams, visions, and desires change things: what impact do they have? As world citizens, we need to consider these things, because when a personal wish becomes a community desire or when a group desire becomes a world aspiration, then life begins to change in extraordinary ways. Some people talk about these things as "the contract we have with the universe." However, we should not think of this contract as some passive or fated one: it needs tending, engagement, and keeping in mind for it to have momentum. Part of the upkeep of our contract is the way in which we rescind old wishes whose time has gone, as well as reshaping or refining our vision. We may also need, when conditions change, to renegotiate some of the agreements. By revisioning and sharpening our focus of the whole knowing field, we actively belong to the earth once more.

We may not always have a strong sense of belonging to the earth; indeed, some people do not feel as if they belong to or are cared about by anyone. We all know someone who has become marginalized or started to excerpt themselves from family, social life, and their usual pursuits. Sometimes our contract can become onerous or unwieldy because we have just forgotten to renegotiate its clauses for a period or for our remaining time of life: becoming ill, growing older, changing our educational pathway or work, learning how to live without a loved one—all these things can require a change to the contract, so that we can feel part of things once again. When you feel left out, lonely, or unconnected, you can also strengthen your belonging to life by including yourself once again in the knowing field through this means.

There are many ways of using this method of reviewing your contract:

1. Use a classic Tarot approach of laying one or more cards for each question. Read and consider.

2. Invite representatives of the different zones of the knowing field to pose questions to you, as in the Inviting the Animals method above. Answer their questions personally to examine the small print on your own contract; see where changes need to be made or where agreements can be strengthened.

3. Adapt or simplify these questions to dream together with a group, when you want to envision a new direction or re-envision your purpose. Group members can stand for each Zone, each with a Tarot, and draw cards at random that selected members answer or everyone considers. Use the questions and focus parts of each card meaning to make a well-focussed Tarot ritual.

4. Read on a world issue, rather than personally, to understand how it can be revisioned.

The following set of questions is not exhaustive, nor do you need to use them all: they are for guidance only. Use the general questions alone or, if you wish, use the additional questions in their Zone as well. Adapt or create your own questions, according to your needs. Use the questions from the central part of the Knowing Field at the end, as a summation.

General questions:
What is my part in the life of this zone?
What old, outworn dreams from this zone need to be cleared
  or refocused?
Which new visions wait to be called forth?
What does this zone require of me?
What do I need from this zone?

In the Family/Ancestral Zone:
What beliefs about my life contract stem from this zone?
What ancestral gifts flow through me too?
Where does the ancestral vision still resonate today?

In the Community/Group Zone:
What values about my life contract stem from this zone?
What group visions do I share?
How does the community share or appreciate them?

In the Personal Zone:
What are the responsibilities that accompany my gifts and aptitudes?
How do they serve the other zones?
What are the dreams I foster for myself?

In the Universal Zone:
What wisdom do I gain from this zone?
What aspirations do I have for this zone?
How do these aspirations support this zone?

In the centre of the Knowing Field:
What needs to be refreshed for the good of all?
What is waiting to come into being for the good of all?
How can we bring that dream into being together?

WHEN THE SPIRITS OF NATURE SPEAK: MAKING THE FRITH

Some of the oldest forms of divination in the world are based on consulting the spirits of the natural world, and by being attentive to its signs. Today, that same guidance still stands about us all the time, ready to council us, if only we would notice. Here I invite you to take your question out into nature and see how it answers you. As a secondary layer of reading, you return inside and compare your *frith* to what the cards also say. This is a method where the whole Knowing Field universe itself shows you the answers.

Over the last forty years, I have been teaching the Gaelic art of divining from the omens in nature, called the *Frith* (pronounced "free"), an ancient divination method that used to guide rural communities before electricity connected us.[10] Every land and climate zone has its own natural habitat, and so the criteria of the omens you encounter will vary greatly from place to place: every person reveals their own connections to what is observed, heard, or felt, rather than reading them from a book.

To understand the messages of nature, you need to attend to the interfused senses of your body, and the impressions that arise, from observing or hearing what the senses show you. You consult your own deep and immediate understandings, your own mainframe of symbolism, not someone else's. It is not about discursive thinking or consulting standardized symbols, such as seeing a white feather as a symbol of cowardice or understanding a tree as the Norse world tree Yggdrasil. Nor is it about psychological or rationalised meanings or about following after every sign and wonder randomly at any time of the day. The *Frith* is a purposeful opening of the space to ask a question, setting an aperture for the universe to speak to you, and for you to be in direct contact with the spirits of nature. An individual can make the *Frith,* or you can work with a group and find answers together. This form of divination can be done literally anywhere, though I recommend you go outside to do the first part, taking your questions about the issue, and a small notepad and pen or a phone, though please turn off the sound. Read through the following method before you try it.

1. Consider what issue you want to divine upon. This method works for personal, community, or world questions.

2. Go outside into nature or into a garden or park with the intention of asking about the issue; find a place with a space around it where you would like to ask the question.

   Close your eyes and enter into the timelessness and spaciousness of your true abiding and consider your issue.

3. Now, with eyes closed, turn on the spot a few times until you come to a place of rest, just like when you shuffle the cards, stopping when they feel "done." The direction ahead where you come to rest is "ahead," making the opposite direction "behind"; the directions on either side of you will be right and left relative to where you first came to rest, as well as "above" and "below."

4. You are going to be asking a series of questions (see p. 313) about your issue, one in each direction, as you turn to each in sequence. Then, at each point, you will open your eyes and observe, hear, and feel whatever lies in that direction, paying attention to what faces you in relation to the question. In this method, be aware not only of what your eyes or ears first experience, but also of what happens in your body, which you are using as a resonator and receptacle of understanding. For example, on opening your eyes, you see a bird on a branch: in stillness, open a line of communication between yourself and the bird on the swaying branch and allow the sense of it to arise in you, even though it may not seem very tangible. Briefly note down your impressions.

Remember that omens can also be sounds, as well as sights; they might include the song of a bird, the rattle of trucks on a distant road, or the laughter of children. In an urban setting, your sights might include people passing by, the smell of exhaust fumes, a piece of rubbish lifted by the wind. These are also part of the oracle. You might also be aware of memories or patterns that come to your mind—note these down also, because these are all part of your understanding, triggered by the omen.

5. Now, you turn to face in each of the directions, with eyes closed, coming back into your true abiding once again before you turn to each direction, one at a time. Remembering which direction was "ahead" for you, ask what wisdom comes from that direction, as follows. Note that each question may need to be adapted according to the nature of your issue:

Ahead: What opportunity does this issue bring?
Right: What help is available for this issue?
Behind: What memories/understandings does this issue bring?
Left: What challenges/fears does this issue raise?
Below: What empowerment does this issue offer?
Above: What inspiration can clarify this issue?
Within: What would the resolution of this issue entail / feel like?

When you have completed "above and below," you turn within and just experience what arises in you as a result of asking the last question about your issue.

6. After making brief notes, return to everyday consciousness, thank the bringers of the omens, go back inside, and take up your

cards. Now you lay cards for each position and read them, comparing them with what the spirits of nature showed you.

Example:
As I was finishing this book, I had some frustrating news from another publisher concerning a major book of mine that is used as a course book by most of my students: the publishing board had decided not to reprint it, just to put it up as an e-book. It had also taken them two years to make this disappointing decision, so I took this issue out into the garden to make my *frith* and explore the possibilities about this book.

The Frith:
   Ahead: After I had finished spinning, I opened my eyes on my hornbeam hedge, where one single dead leaf showed among many green leaves: this has been a standout book in my writing and teaching career, so there is an opportunity to refresh it where it can stand with the rest of my work.
   Right: Turning right, I heard the scolding sound of a magpie chattering. Immediately, I knew this told me to keep on hassling about this, and not to passively let it go.
   Behind: Turning behind, my eyes lighted upon one bent bough in among many upright ones. It reminded me that this same disappointment has happened before, many times, where publishing houses that print my books have been replaced by less careful ones.
   Left: Turning left, I was aware of one bare bough on a tree that has stopped bearing fruit: yes, I could just let the income of this book pass away naturally, but I'm challenged by the notion that the way this one book has been treated may be the kind of way the publisher is going to handle my other titles that are still with them.
   Below: Looking down, among the many plants growing in my lawn, there was one unique leaf of a different kind. Again, my sense of the book as standing out from the others was confirmed. It has

FIG. 28 *Spirits of Nature layout*

Ahead:

Left:

Above:

Right:

Below:

Within:

Behind:

had a life of its own over 25 years.

Above: Squinting up, the whole sky was cloudy except for a hole in the clouds, shaped like a cow sitting down, through which the sun shone. "There is milk in the cow yet," I felt.

Within: Going within, I considered how it would be to have resolution, and had the sense of water rippling freely, unimpeded, like the vibrations of a song. This was immediately reminiscent of the book's title.

Thanking the spirits of nature for their advice, I went in feeling I had received a clear consistency in these answers of my frith, but I further checked the picture. You can see the cards I drew on p. 315.

The Reading supporting the Frith:

Ahead: Reversed 5 Cups. The sense of mixed blessing was strong in me, as something was lost and something gained, but since the card was reversed, my sense is one of salvaging what I can.

Right: Wheel of Fortune. While I can be flexible and adapt to this situation, I can also start afresh with another publisher.

Behind: Page Pentacles. This card speaks of my many students who use this as a course book in their studies and practice, whom I don't want to let down.

Left: Queen Cups. The challenge to me is about defending and regenerating the vision which this book conveys.

Below: Reversed 10 Wands. This card confirmed that the empowerment for this issue might come from walking away from the publisher and breaking off the rather onerous relationship we have had.

Above: Hierophant. The inspiration given is to find better ways for my book to serve the community.

Within: Devil. I laughed on seeing this card, which speaks about being indentured in a coercive bond, and took it to stand as a witness for my book, in its sense of "liberating the prisoner."

It was clear that the publisher was seeing the book as "half dead," or not much profit to them, so I accordingly determined to ask for the rights back on my book and try to reprint it elsewhere, rather than have it available only as an e-book, which would not be very useful for students who would need the book beside them as they practised. My astonishment came just a few days later, when the publisher seemed to have had a rethink and was now offering to keep it going as a limited reprint. As of the present, I am still awaiting copies of that reprint, since the publishing house has been taken over by another firm.

The more often you engage with the spirits of nature in this way, the wider your criteria of omens will spread: like any Tarot card, an omen can reveal many meanings, according to the parameters of the question. While you will certainly gain an increasing repertoire of signs and omens that are usual to your surroundings or place on the earth, the most valuable thing is that you learn to ask the universe your questions and how to understand the signs in relation to aspects of your issue, which is the central foundation of all divination.

SEVEN

ENGAGING THE POWERS
BEYOND TIME

We have to make the imaginative leap
into the ancient mind and the likelihood
of a different world now.

—Alan Garner,
Boneland

REACHING BEYOND UNCERTAINTY:
ESSENTIAL MENDING

The twenty-first century has only been going for over two decades, at the time of writing, and already we have had to deal with the rise of world terrorism, mass migrations to avoid oppressive regimes and ideological policies, a world pandemic, and a European war. It is clear that the cosy, parochial, pre-war world that Waite and Colman Smith inhabited has gone forever. We no longer have assurances that the world is a safe place in which to live.

As I was in the final stages of this book, the Russia-Ukraine war began. Many people worldwide, living well outside the immediate conflict zone, seemed to enter into a kind of mental paralysis, being no longer able to commit to doing even ordinary activities such as evening classes, going to the theatre or visiting relatives, because they had become so anxious. Fear began to cloak everything in uncertainty, especially when threats of nuclear deployment were mooted. Many young adults who had never had to cope with the prospect of war in Europe during their lifetimes were particularly affected. For everyone, this was also the first war where reports from the front were widely viewable on social media: even for those who usually ignored the TV news, there was no avoiding the shocking images of carnage, destruction, and grief on social media platforms, as we all randomly scrolled down.

When our times change as much as this, our anxiety about ourselves and our concern for those undergoing such dangers challenge us to come into a place of truth and compassion. The security that we all yearn after may not be a given in a changing world, so it is for us to consider how we keep balanced and functional so that we do not plunge into fearfulness. The frustration we experience about world changes and their impact can be tempered by the level at which we engage with them, which is how we are changing focus in this chapter to go deeper in order to find skilful ways beyond uncertainty.

Within the mystical tradition of Judaism is the notion of *Tikkun Olam* or "the repairing of the world" or "repairing the whole of time," a concept particularly associated with the kabbalistic writings of the sixteenth-century mystic Isaac Luria. Luria's vision for this repair was based upon the idea that the vessels of divine light shattered after the world was created; when these same sparks of life come together again, the world will no longer be a broken place. What enables the raising up of these sparks of light is the fulfilment of our ethical obligations, prayers, and good deeds, based upon Psalm 89:3: "With kindness shall the world be built." In more recent times, the obligation to enable *Tikkun Olam* has shown itself in terms of social action, responsibility, and justice, as well as charity and acts of kindness, because this concept did not just stay within Judaism but spread into European esotericism and philosophy through Leibnitz, Newton, and Henry More.[11] Different world religions see this understanding in various ways. In Buddhism, it is the Boddhisattva who reincarnates over and over, never entering nirvana, until all living beings are realised. In the world of the Celtic peoples, it is seen as a *tuirgin,* or "a circuit of births," into every splendid shape, until time becomes timelessness in a great spiral of life. Whatever your own understanding or myth for why the world is not perfect, the concept of "repairing the world" is one that we can all work with.

We also need to understand that *Tikkun Olam* is not just for the end of the world—*it is always happening* as we remake and mend the world. While those who live outside the possibilities of this mythic vision may see themselves as sealed into an inevitable timeline that requires an apocalyptic end of time, followed by the eternal punishment of those who are blamed for its demise, but I invite you here, as a time changer, to comprehend this necessary mending as part of the eternal spiral of life into life, where service and gratitude are the essential tools in the mending basket.

Hierocles's idea of the household of the earth—the relationship that we have with all living things—is a major step toward the mending of the world. This concept includes relearning our connections that keep us in life, seeing clearly how we help or don't help each other, and the ways we communicate or fail to do so, by extending our view to include all living things. The old sense of alienation, of feeling stuck inside an eternally solitary place where individuality and self is everything, just relegates everything else in the household of the world to an afterthought. By rekindling our connections to community and spirit, we can heal the loneliness and sense of abandonment that come from living in an increasingly unconnected way. Some of that sense of abandonment is a direct reflection of how we envision and treat others in the universe.

We all have grown up with a sense that the world we live in is regulated mostly by personal politeness, by courtesy and respect to all, by international agreements, where we have an agreed-on consensus of behaviour toward each other. So, the sense of outrage and violation that the worldwide community felt about the recent unprovoked shelling of Ukrainian citizens, the complete disregard for international treaties, may stand as a small token of what the rest of the living household of the earth must feel about our own unthought-through lifestyle and disregard of other life-forms.

The human world has become, in the words of the South African Bushman, "far-hearted." In seeing other life-forms and beings as convenient resources or "as containers for our own uses," we have ceased to notice that they have their own intrinsic holiness or wholeness.[12] As we adjust our views, so our hearts can grow more generous and expansive.

In chapter 1, we considered how it would be to read for querents by considering them as part of the widest circle of reality, where they can be witnessed as they essentially are—at the fullest potential of their soul, not just as the sum of their body or their physical circumstances at the time of the consultation. This witnessing provides a hospitality of spirit enabling the querent to settle down and attend to the question that is concerning them in the widest context, where both change and possibility can be seen. In this chapter, we are going to consider the resources of the mythic, of the timelessness of spiritual reality, where past, present, and future can come into one place by rituals and readings that take a timeless perspective. By stretching the reading cloth even wider, we are able to invite the deeper range of possibilities and pathways into our work. By calling upon the mythic levels of our stories and upon the help of the collective ancestors and lineages, we reinclude ourselves and begin to feel less abandoned.

TAKING THINGS OUT OF TIME: THE AMBASSADORS OF MYTH

We are not just people who passively live through changing times; we can also be people who change our times too. By skilful, intelligent, and inclusive reading, you can become a time changer for those who are sunk hopelessly in time-bound issues, by opening to them the possibilities that are available *outside time*. This way of working calls upon the deepest level of help that Tarot cards can bring, by enabling them to represent mythic beings, loving ancestors, or dynamic powers. Indeed, anything and everything that is of personal help to the querent can be invited to be present within the reading or be represented by the cards. By reading out of time, you can help a querent re-vision their predicament or help them bridge anxious or fearful periods of their lives with powerful support, illuminating their dark places with myths and archetypes who can hold high the lantern to shine upon their path.

But what is myth? Back in the fifth century, the philosopher Sallustius observed that myth was "something that has never happened and that is continually happening."[13] In modern parlance, a myth is more often taken to mean "a fictive or untrue story." But in reality, myth is the truest thing that ever was, because it holds essential truths and spiritual and ethical teaching models, passing them down to generations of descendants unborn.[14]

Myth is also paradoxical: It looks at both sides of life—time and dream—simultaneously. It breaks down closed doors and shuffles meanings until they become clear. It collapses past, present, and future into the precious present moment, enabling the rediscovery of a lost wisdom that can illuminate our lives.

The numinous terrain of myth helps us clarify the things we know or don't quite know, what we can see or can't quite see. Myth is both apparent and not manifest at the same time, enabling us—as in The Moon card—to grasp something with our imagination. Since imagination is nothing less than the faculty of the soul, it engages our understanding: without its guidance we would steer blindly through the world. By stepping out of time and standing briefly in timelessness, we enter the landscape of myth where our own story is playing out.[15]

All the cards illustrated by Pamela Colman Smith speak eloquently of so many situations that, no matter how many times we use them, its images and metaphors come straight into our understanding. For example, when we have been called upon to do something we can't easily contemplate because it frightens or upset us, and we draw 2 Swords, we cannot help seeing the blindfold of the sword-carrying woman on the card as a direct expression of our own inability to look at the thing (see the example on p. 332). This could be a situation where we might send in an ambassador card to look for us at whatever it is, or to give us a timeless perspective that liberates our way of thinking about it.

When we are feeling low in energy or with the beginning of an illness or infection, we may appreciate the stillness of the Knight's effigy in 4 Swords as a statement of a need to rest, or we can experience the blessing of the stained-glass saint, or even imagine our infection being absorbed and neutralized by the saint.

Things that are broken in time can begin to heal in timelessness. By using the cards as representatives and resources, we are enabled to read "out of time" for those things that are being experienced "in time," giving us an extraordinary perspective.

We have seen how cards can stand as resources that uphold someone or a group within an issue, where we bring another influence into the mix to remind the whole situation that particular qualities or resources are there as supports and witnesses. But we can also invite one or more cards to go into the situation for us and look for us, like an ambassador who takes the temperature of a situation, so that we have a better sense of things. Choosing a representative card to stand beside someone who is feeling vulnerable, or sending a representative into the cards as an ambassador, are methods that are useful when the issue is too big, when the querent is overcome by its enormity, or when the issue is one that afflicts everyone alive.

This method of working actively draws upon the mythic and archetypal powers that are represented in each Tarot card, whereby we consciously select one of the Major or Minor Arcana to bring their powers to bear on the situation; as liberators of events that are beyond our power to remedy they can lend us their resources. Here are some of the abilities of the powers represented in the Major Arcana: these can be brought into play as active powers, not just as representatives, supporters, or witnesses, in your readings.

Those who are fearful of cards as "the devil's picture book" often impute malign powers to cards, which are merely scraps of pasteboard, feeling that they are deceivers that will pollute them. But here, I invite you instead to discern the healing archetypal powers that stand behind what is depicted in your Tarot cards. These archetypal ambassadors stand ready to be invoked, to reach beyond our insecurity and fear, and convey us into the timeless zone of mythic reality where their healing powers are the salve to remind us of all that is true and alive.

The abilities listed here are not the only powers that these archetypes possess: you will find others as you work. You can also create your own personal list for each card of the Minor Arcana as you discern each of their powers.

Ambassadors and Their Powers

The Fool: opening the way, freeing the heart
Magician: freeing the gifts, mediating skill
High Priestess: rediscovering wisdom, honouring the vision
Empress: maintaining a safe space to grow, recognising beauty
Emperor: restoring protection, honouring boundaries
Hierophant: bestowing a blessing, honouring the soul
Lovers: healing the heart, freeing the choices
Chariot: navigating courageously, witnessing to the dignity
    and essence
Strength: strengthening the weak, calming the anger
Hermit: refreshing the path, illumining the darkness
Wheel of Fortune: untangling the muddle, restoring the rhythm
Justice: dissolving illusion, upholding truth
Hanged Man: cleansing pollution, granting forgiveness
Death: shifting shape, granting rest
Temperance: abiding in balance, reconciling the conflicted
The Devil: binding the uncontrolled, freeing the prisoners
Tower: separating the irreconcilable, dispersing the outworn
Star: upholding hope, inspiring the soul
Moon: unfolding the dream, honouring the changes
Sun: restoring happiness and health
Judgement: freeing the ancestors, cleansing memory
World: bestowing compassion, rejoining the dance

Ways of engaging these active, dynamic powers in a practical way are given below. So let us discover the ancestral zones whose denizens can bring help to the querent.

LINEAGES OF CONTINUITY: THE PRAYERS OF THE ANCESTORS

We think of our own time, place, and life as supremely important, but we are actually part of vast interconnecting lineages of continuity. These lineages are made up not only of human ancestors, but also of cultural ideas, spiritual traditions, and the whole world of nature, which have seeded and shaped the social organization of civilizations over time. We are part of them, and so will our descendants be. Every single person has benefited from being part of this continuity. By reconnecting with our different lineages, we stand stronger. As we saw from the zones within the knowing field, just as we can simultaneously be a part of the world, our nation, our community, and our family, so too can we be connected to the universe in spiritual, not just physical, ways, out of time.

The human soul is both one and many and supplies us with understandings that make sense of the universe through our imagination, whereby we are enabled to use our inner senses to comprehend the things that we experience. It helps us look beyond time and place into timelessness and spaciousness, as well as validating our own inheritance from these groups.[16]

These lineages provide collective wisdom, support, and nourishment, as well as perspectives showing us ways we had not imagined. They are the ancestors of us all:

Ancestral Lineage: The ancestors of our bloodline who have shaped us, those ancestors who look kindly upon us and who actively continue to support us by their wisdom from every age

FIG. 29 *The ancestral Knowing Field*

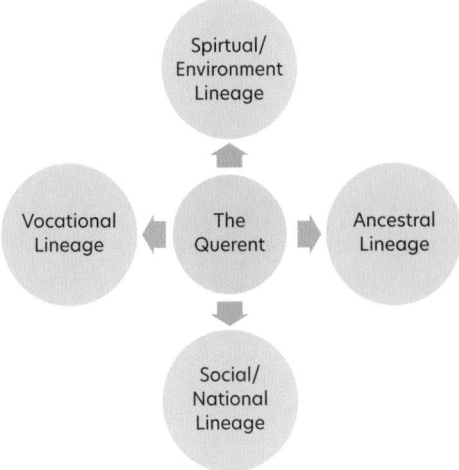

Social/National Lineage: Those culture heroes, time changers, and clear-sighted leaders of every age whose civilizing and restorative influence changes our society and country, and whose examples and ideas guide us still

Vocational Lineage: The ancestors of our spirit, who have engaged in the same work and pursuits as ourselves from every age, the inspired practitioners of the arts, sciences, and crafts who have beautified and nourished the world by their skill

Spiritual/Environmental Lineage: The soul shepherds who have opened spiritual pathways and continue to guide us; spirits of place and sacred places; the animals, plants, and trees who witness to us; the spirits of all ages who have inspired and shaped us

Each of these lineages can be placed upon our template of the knowing field, where the help of generations can be called upon to clarify things and reshape or heal the story.

Inviting the lineage ancestors into our reading is an act of loving witness, whereby they reach through to us, even down to the depths of the entangled places where we become enmeshed. We can claim and call upon the ancestors of our different lineages, even though we do not know their names or any of their stories, because the timeless continuity connects us. Just as these ancestors have been drawing on the prayers of their ancestors and lineages, so too, can we pray through and beyond time and space and reach for the markers and handholds that they have left for us to find in those times when we need help most.

Be aware that not all ancestors within the fields are helpful to us. Those who veered off course, whose deeds muddled or impeded the progress of others, those who are stuck in time or enmeshed in difficulties and entanglements that obscure the way still—these all need compassionate clarification and spiritual mediation, so it is not upon these that we call into this work. It is good to specify whom you mean when you work this way, saying, "I call upon those ancestors who look kindly upon us," to signal that you are calling upon the collective wisdom of the lineages.

By inviting in those in the company of our lineages of continuity, we not only gain greater support and solidarity, but a wider wisdom, where the seeds that were sown in times past for the aid of times to come can blossom in our lives. In our time, we too leave caches of help, strength, and encouragement to those who follow us.

The Chinese have a concept called *yuánfèn,* which has the sense of "destined affinity." It can be best summed up by the Chinese proverb "It takes hundreds of rebirths to bring two persons to ride in the same boat, but it takes a thousand aeons to bring two persons to share the same pillow."[17] While *yuánfèn* is often translated as "karmic or fateful coincidence" or is seen as near to Jung's sense of "synchronity," it is also about the innate recognition that we experience when we are with someone or in a place or situation that has resonance in our own epigenetic, ancestral, or reincarnational memory. These key points of recognition of destined affinity have been experienced by everyone: they are often precious bridges into our lineages of continuity where the wisdom lies to help us, as well as enabling us to come into a more resonant accord with our own living myth. Our collective ancestors stand close to us at such moments, especially when we are hovering on the thresholds of change.

Let us see how this can be brought into practice in the Ancestral Council.

THE ANCESTRAL COUNCIL

The timeless, archaic movements of myth surround us all the time, and so we don't need to call upon known or traditional myths in order to work this way: all we need is a Tarot and to be able to assess the situation going on, so we can bring in the ambassadors of myth to support the querent. By calling upon the active imagery and metaphor of the cards, we step out of time into a place where the myth depicted in the cards can heal and change things.

These questions are helpful to understand the querent's context:

✦ What is going on or what keeps recurring?—Here we see what is held in time, where repeating patterns are often based on old assumptions, on previous instructions that have been embedded by upbringing values, or on peer or social pressure to conform.

✦ How is the querent experiencing the situation?

✦ Who are the actors or what are the factors in the situation?—
the various aspects of the issue and those who affect it for good
or ill.

✦ What needs to change?—This becomes the myth that enables
life to flourish.

✦ What resources does the querent need in this situation?—This
is the help the querent needs to make the changes.

✦ Who needs to be invited into the arena to support the querent?—Here we can invite the ambassadors of myth to speak
timelessly.

The Ancestral Council uses the lineage template on p. 327 as a format
or layout. This needs to be done slowly, at the pace of the querent,
because it goes a lot deeper than mere surface reading. We choose a
soul guide from the Major Arcana, then look in each of the lineage
zones to give us information about the roots of what is happening,
laying a pair of cards in each zone: this part of the process usually
shows the old story or pattern that keeps recurring or where things
are time bound. We then choose / randomly select a single ances-
tral-lineage representative card from each zone to give advice, help,
or support. At the end of the reading, we can invite the querent to
choose one or more of the Major Arcana cards and place them
wherever they are most needed in the reading, although sometimes
the Majors may have already landed in the reading to bring their
help. Cards can be chosen throughout for the Ancestral Council,
though you may find that random selection is more powerful. It is
also possible to change or incorporate the added cards into a final
pattern that brings resolution to the situation.

Example:

Jane has humiliatingly returned to the parental home after leaving her second acrimonious marriage. She still feels rage and frustration with herself for picking yet another unsuitable man. She wants to look at what is going on so she can start again, with a better sense of what is good for herself, because she still wants to have children. I gave Jane the choice of consciously selecting cards, but she wanted them to be randomly discovered, so we created an Ancestral Knowing Field, drawing upon cards that all came out of a four-way cut, drawing cards from each pile for each zone. We took the first Major Arcana from the bottom of the deck to act as Guide. Then, we drew cards for the roots of what was happening in each of the zones: Cards 1–8. Next, we drew a representative from each Ancestral Zone: Cards 9–12. Finally, we looked at the timeless myth that the cards created.

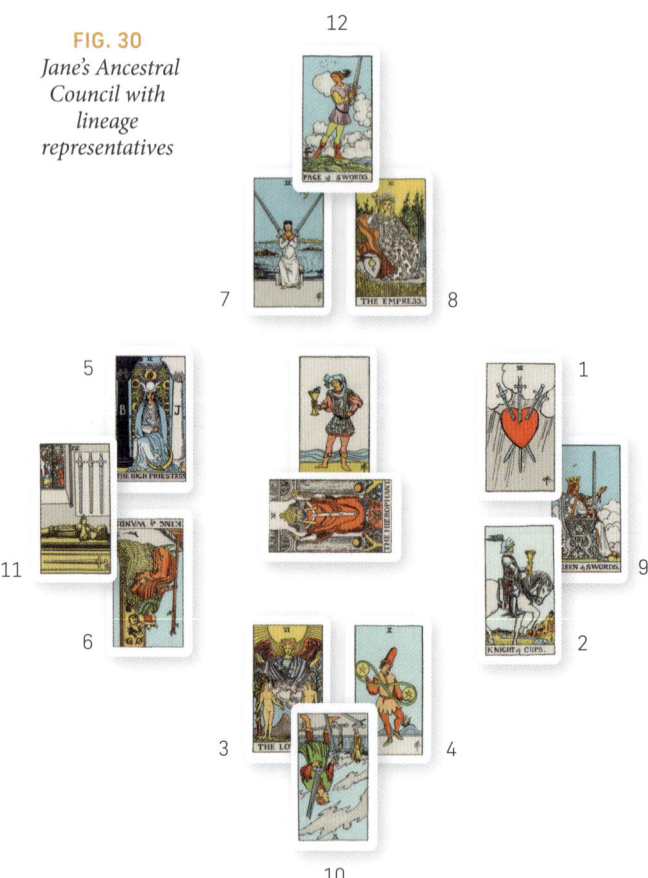

FIG. 30

Jane's Ancestral Council with lineage representatives

The Hierophant as the guide seemed to be acting as the marriage guidance counsellor in this reading, which is a traditional role for this card since he is the one who brokers and blesses the marriage. I reminded Jane that his job was to bestow a blessing and help her honour her soul's choices. Throughout the reading, I asked her to think of him supportively beside her as we looked at the roots of what had been happening.

Ancestral Lineage: 3 Swords and Knight Cups showed us the sorrow and separation at parting from what seemed the perfect partner. When I asked how Jane generally thought of any potential partner, she said she usually chose someone who resembled her ideal man, although she was beginning to realize how that was not working well for her.

Social Lineage: Lovers and 2 Pentacles showed that there was ambivalence around trusting love. This was the area that Jane felt unsure about, since she didn't handle the ups and downs of a relationship well, she felt.

Vocational Lineage: High Priestess and reversed King Wands show a deep woman who chooses dominant, even aggressive men. "I like a man to be manly," Jane said.

Spiritual Lineage: 2 Swords and Empress spoke of a hesitation about stepping fully into her womanhood. Jane admitted that she felt little sense of self-esteem as a woman. We both noted how the blindfolded 2 Swords couldn't look at the Empress.

We noted that all of Jane's ancestral representatives were drawn from the Swords suit, showing that order and discrimination were the main focus of this council. I explained how these cards were speaking as witnesses or ambassadors from each ancestral lineage. I spoke for each of these cards, drawing upon the "Questions" section under each card entry in chapters 2 and 3.

The ancestral lineage representative, Queen Swords, said, "I can bring you clarity about your partner."

The social lineage representative was the rev. 5 Swords and said, "I can help you pick up the pieces and be a part of things again."

The vocational lineage representative, 4 Swords said, "I can give you sanctuary so you can regain your health and well-being."

The spiritual lineage representative, Page Swords, said, "I will watch out for you."

Looking at the Major Arcana that came into this reading, I flagged up the help that was already potentially available: the High Priestess could help Jane rediscover her own wisdom and honour her vision, while the Empress could give her a safe space to recognize her own intrinsic womanhood. The Lovers could help with healing her heart, as well as freeing up her choices.

I then invited Jane to rearrange her reading by what she had learned here, to remove or reselect cards or include the ones that worked for her. She turned the King of Wands upright, removed the 5 Swords, and placed her own significator, Page Cups, next to the Lovers instead, as well as removing the 3 Swords and substituting Queen Swords next to Knight of Cups. Her new alignment reveals a timeless, living myth that can replace the old repetitive patterns, one that has a strong sense of self-determination running through it. I then spoke aloud as these card pairs and how they might support her:

Page Swords + Empress: "We will enable you to manifest the woman you really are."

High Priestess + King Wands: "We will plumb the depths of love together."

Queen Swords + Knight Cups: "We will help you choose the right partner."

Lovers + Page Cups: "We will help you explore and appreciate the romance."

Jane emerged from this council with some good help and powerful realizations: the power over her was an old story of seeking out unsuitable partners. This new myth included her and gave her space to be herself, so that she would not succumb to the first man who came along through lack of self-worth. She did not immediately jump into yet another relationship but has begun to be more discriminating in her choices.

There are many different ways to work with the mythic aspect of someone's story, to show new pathways and perspectives. Sometimes, as you lay the cards or speak as them, you may be aware of a specific sense of the card's representative from different parts of the Ancestral Lineage. A sense of resolution may be experienced from laying the Ancestral Council, or a sense of an old part of the story finishing and a new stage of the journey continuing. The work of the Ancestral Council is part of the essential mending that we all need. It works, too, for community and world issues and can be done as a group reading where the querent meets and talks with the human representatives of each cardholder in the timelessness of an interactive ritual.

CULTIVATING THE VIRTUES

Taromancy has not enjoyed the best of reputations. Tarot use has been frequently inveighed against by the Church, while taromancers themselves have been widely regarded as dubious people of low morals. But I would like to change the times on such suppositions and rather see Tarot as one of the divinatory arts that is found at the edge of society, for the simple reason that when the people in the marketplace are stampeded to the edges by the disorders in life, they will hopefully find us before they go over that edge. It requires an ethical practice, a warm welcome, a compassionate attitude, and a groundedness of soul to be a taromancer.

I would also like to point out to Tarot's detractors that in every Tarot deck, there are four cards that represent the keepers of the ethical code of the ancient world: the cardinal virtues of Temperance, Fortitude, Justice, and Wisdom. These virtues are called "cardinal" because they are the hinges upon which all life turns, be it in the life of a human being or that of a group or nation. In the ancient world, these virtues were considered essential for the formation of every person, so that people might know themselves and become balanced human beings:

Temperance governs self-control and self-discipline and is found in the way we moderate our habits, emotions, and actions.

Fortitude governs perseverance and courage and is found in our enduring ability to meet change and challenge.

Justice governs truth and equity and is found in our sense of fairness.

Wisdom governs prudence and foresight and is found in our common sense, values, and beliefs.

In historic Italian Tarots, the cardinal virtue cards were usually positioned next to each other in sequence, but the modern Milanese-style order that the *Waite-Smith Tarot* follows has split them up now. The cards on which they are depicted are XIV Temperance, VIII Strength, and XI Justice (transposed from their respective original positions at XI and VIII by Waite, for astrological and kabbalistic reasons). But which card now represents Wisdom or Prudence? Opinion is split: some say that it is the World card, while others say it is the Hermit, who inherits Cronos's hourglass, now transposed into a lantern.[18] Either card can represent Wisdom: you make the choice.

We can demonstrate that the cardinal virtues govern the whole deck, since each of them carries an emblem of the four suits and holds all 78 cards in one united bond.[19]

These four active virtues can guide us on the path of Tarot in many ways, not only as virtues we might all cultivate in our personal lives, but also as part of our reading skills. People most often come for a reading when one of these virtues is out of balance, as you can see in the following example. In this method we can call upon the cardinal virtues to show us what needs amending or rebalancing: here, the first two cards speak mostly of things as they currently are, and the last two cards of what action is needed.

Ensure the cardinal virtues are upright in your deck and shuffle well, while asking for their guidance. Using the Opening the Book method (p. 229), see where each of the four cardinal virtue cards has fallen, and select one or more cards from either side of that position. *Note*: in this method, some cardinal virtue cards may share adjoining cards with another virtue, or a virtue card itself may be included as the adjoining card; note which cards you have drawn for each line, and read them respective to each virtue. Alternatively, you can shuffle each cardinal virtue card separately.

Read the cards from left to right and then add up each virtue's line of card numbers to obtain a total of 22 or under (p. 229). The concluding Major Arcana card discovered by this reduction and its pairing with the cardinal virtue are what will be helpful to the querent.

Example:

After the death of her parents, Nia was both upheaved as well as bereaved: her solution was to seek solitariness in rural Wales, but as lockdown ended, she was finding it difficult to come back to a more normal life. She had no friends, was moving from place to place in various unsuitable lodgings, and was doing cleaning work to keep alive. She acknowledged she was not managing things well and needed some radical help. I chose the Hermit for Wisdom in this reading. I drew these cards:

FIG. 31 *Cultivating the Vitues layout*

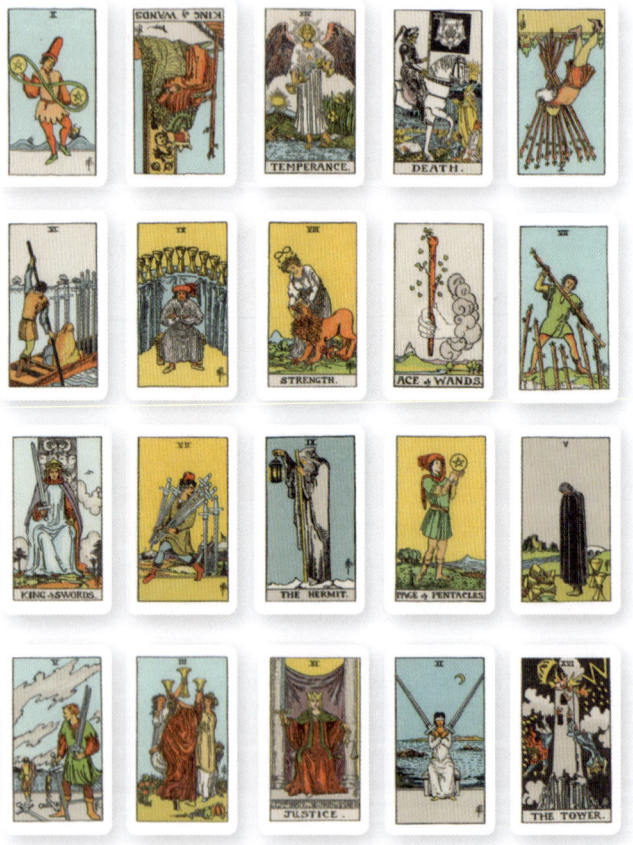

In the Temperance line, it looks as if Nia is having to be endlessly flexible about her finances—possibly to the extent of ruining her health—and that she largely moderates her life by a kind of self-per-suaded, almost bullying, conviction. Temperance urges her to stop resisting change and to lay down the impossible burdens she is carrying.

Adding up the number values of the top line, we get 53; 5 + 3 = 8, or Strength (see the secion on Reducing the Cards, p. 255).

Pairing Temperance with Strength, I spoke what they had to say to her: "Together we can bring help to temper your self-control and strengthen you to make changes in your life."

In the Fortitude line, Nia is struggling to arrive at a position of physical and emotional comfort. Fortitude urges her to have the courage to reassert herself, but we note that reversed Ace Wands with 7 Wands shows a tendency to withstand things without any growth or profit, and this combination can be the sign of someone "doing things the hard way."

Adding up the number values of the second line, we get 31; 3 + 1 = 4, or Emperor.

Fortitude with the Emperor says, "Together we can bring mer-cy to your heart and strengthen you to make changes in your life."

In the Wisdom line, we see Nia defending the boundaries of her beliefs by seizing whatever will assist her. Wisdom urges her to learn something or take a course so that she can substitute something nourishing to her soul in the place of the losses she has suffered.

Adding up the number values of the third line, we get 44; 4 + 4 = 8, or Strength.

Wisdom with Strength say, "We hold you gently so you can be nurtured and illumined on your path."

In the Justice line, 5 Swords and 3 Cups showed Nia's resentment at the unfairness of being the only one left in the family to pick up the pieces, and wanting to be included in the round of friendship. Justice sees the requirement of seeking out help and mediation before Nia has a breakdown.

Adding up the number values of the last line, we get 37; 3 + 7 = 10, or Wheel of Fortune.

Justice with Wheel says, "We can dissolve the fearful shadows and untangle the muddle."

We can see that Temperance is one of Nia's strongest virtues, but that she is possibly being too temperate, even ascetic in her lifestyle. Her predicament was alarming to me, as the cards show; she needed to cultivate the virtue of Fortitude in order to come out of the passivity of her current friendless and unsupported position. The appearance of 5 Cups in the Wisdom line showed that Nia was still very badly bereaved, so I encouraged her to seek out local bereavement services. To begin to attend to things in her life, she will need more than Tarot, so I also referred her to a therapist who could help Nia rebuild her life.

It is always wise to refer vulnerable clients to expert help, rather than leave them to tackle their issues by Tarot alone. Tarot can be a signpost to need, but it cannot supply all the help.

RECONCILING HEAVEN AND EARTH TOGETHER

"The Great Work" is the name given in alchemy and hermetic magic to the bringing together of heaven and earth: this means nothing less than the bringing closer together of the seen and unseen worlds in harmony and in concord. The whole purpose of a spiritual life is to contribute to this coming together. We acknowledge that this is a long-term aim and that things that are disordered or broken cannot conveniently restore themselves and come into harmony instantly by the wave of a magic wand. It is something we have to live through, contribute to, and pray with. The Great Work cannot arrive by pleading or persuasion, nor will it come through any coercive means. Nevertheless, we can all bring the Great Work into our hearts, and our meditations, as a focus. The example below reveals a method of using our cards in a contemplative way, to help reconcile things, to bring balance, peace, or harmony again.

Example:
Khadija's family is going through a particularly traumatic time: she has been forced to flee back to Britain, since she gained her higher education and was married in the UK, but she has also been an outspoken journalist in her own country. Apart from two brothers in the United States, most of her family still live in Afghanistan, where things are becoming increasingly difficult, especially for the womenfolk, where their rights to education, social interaction, and personal agency have been completely circumscribed once again. The menfolk are likewise having to toe the very narrow line of the Taliban's strict social and spiritual expectations. No one is having it easy: food and money are short, no music or dancing is allowed, and conditions are worsening. Their suffering weighs on her heart. Ironically, the beliefs of the Taliban arose in an attempt to unify Afghanistan in one spiritual bond against corrupt leaders; unfortunately, their fundamentalist method of imposing that aim comes with both puritanical zeal and ultimate, coercive force, as well as an extremely restrictive view of all women.

Khadija focuses upon bringing balance and peace, both to her country and to her family. She consciously chooses these cards to represent the qualities that she sees as essential for Afghanistan:

Ace of Swords for clear thinking and education

Ace of Cups for compassionate care and the return of joy

Ace of Wands for good governance and a return of trust

Ace of Pentacles for the good order of the country and restored economics

She chooses the Sun for good health and freedom, Judgment for the good sense of her ancestors, and the Magician for dynamic connection and good communication,

She chooses the 2 of Cups for the restoration of ordinary society where women and men can be together in one place—which is not currently possible, in most situations.

At the centre she places 10 Cups for her family, and for the last position, the Star for the return of peace and harmony again.

Khadija can contemplate these cards at any time; praying with them, holding the idea as an earnest wish and vision for her people. She can also use these purposely chosen cards as the positions upon which she lays her other, smaller Tarot deck—both to assess the current situation and as a means of maintaining her focus when things change.

But when, in late May 2022, the Taliban decreed that women should cover their whole body, including their faces, leaving only their eyes visible—something that is not mandatory under Islamic law—Khadija laid some cards to understand the effect of this upon her family, since, if women do not cover their faces, it is their male guardians who would be fined or imprisoned.

As you can see, there is a defiant reaction against this latest injunction, as if the cards chosen to represent betterment for both family and country are protesting too. The Fool is speaking of the absurdity of this ban, while the Star pours her waters upon Ace of Wands for the return of a balanced government. The two Pages of Cups and Pentacles with the 3 Pentacles speak loudly for education. The only reversed card, 10 Swords, continues to speak of the possibility of something new arising. Temperance is urging caution in everyday matters. At the centre, the cards speak specifically of the necessity of her family to leave their country and find a place of sanctuary elsewhere.

This method of contemplation and reading shows the ideal or aim of Khadija in the chosen cards she first laid out: these are the cards out of time, representing heaven. The cards she lays upon these are the earthly response—in the present time and circumstances. The playing out of time in timelessness is one that humans can often barely distinguish, but these can be the templates of bringing earth and heaven together: the conditions of the times through which we are living, and the eternal hope that is generated by the contemplation of the Great Work.

NOURISHING THE WORLD

Faced with unremitting situations such as Afghanistan or with the prospect of environmental destruction, it is easy to fall into despair, especially when all we hear is the bad news, and rarely the stories of courage and endurance or of kindness and support. When you read Tarot on issues that have little hope or help in them, I would always recommend following them with a meditation, prayer, or blessing—because to leave things as they are, without the blessing of support, merely reduces the knowledge gained from the reading to the thoughtless viewing of a street accident to which we bring no help.

A simple way of doing this is to choose Tarot cards and lay them out in a way that builds in hope, resources, or support for those undergoing traumatic times.

This kind of work is done in the spirit of support and witness, and not as a kind of godlike spell craft whereby we attempt to alter circumstances by our will alone. By standing with a community, a person, a species, a tree, or a group in prayer or meditation, we lend them courage, we acknowledge their need for justice and order, and we witness to the dignity of fellow living beings. Additionally, we can also put our commitment into practice, helping to contribute to associations who support the vulnerable and parts of the environment that have no representation, by donation, by volunteer work, and in numerous ways suited to our circumstances. We are all neighbours within the household of the earth, one with the other, and *every* part of our world counts. Ours are the hands, feet, and voices that are here now, when those of others may have little or no agency.

Perhaps the most important thing in this work of nourishing is to regard the being or group as they essentially are, and not simply as an afflicted being or persecuted group. When we witness to the dignity of someone, we are witnessing to their essence or soul: this inviolable kernel at the heart of all life is what gives them power to continue living. If we concentrate only on the poverty, the despair, or the powerlessness of the being, we just reinforce the prevailing conditions.

From this, we arrive at the following method of building a meditational layout with which we can do our own mending of the world.

1. Placing the cards of the cardinal virtues: Temperance, Strength, Justice, and Prudence/Wisdom (this can be the Hermit or World card) as the corners in a square to help stabilize the situation:

Temperance to bring things into more moderate ways, with less extreme factors reacting. It provides the love and care that nourishes.

Strength to boost forbearance, courage, perseverance, and endurance in hard times. It provides the skill and the light that shines upon all.

Justice to promote truth, clarity, justice, and even-handedness. It provides a level playing field where truth can be active.

Prudence/Wisdom to bring wisdom, insight, and resourcefulness. It provides the stability where providential help can spring forth.

2. Next, chose one card to represent the presiding spirit of the individual, group, species, community, or country. Place this in the centre. You can choose to light a candle next to the card to indicate its living spirit. This spirit is not political but rather is the nourishing and foundational heart of this being or group—it has no sides, no other agenda than to represent the soul of the group, community, or land.

3. Now visualise a central well of help around that central card of the presiding spirit, by placing the cards around the central point that you feel will enable or help those undergoing troubles: these can be cards that provide different kinds of resources. This might include the resourceful ancestors of those who are suffering (10 Pentacles), the goodwill of nations nearby (10 Cups), the Champions who will work for them (Knight Swords), the songs and cultural stories that keep hope in people (6 Cups), or the ability to regroup and be restored (4 Swords + The Star) and to rejoice again (3 Cups). The resources are as various as the cards of your deck.

4. Set all these cards up and begin to meditate on the patterns at work here. As you meditate, be aware of the central well as a place from which people, animals, species, and others can draw to become refreshed or given new heart. If you need to add or change particular cards to the well, place and change them as you need. Visualise the nourishment and support that accumulates in the central well of the cards you're setting out.

5. You can leave these cards set up overnight or much longer, regularly meditating upon the nourishment, help, and hope that are brought, both in time and out of it.

Here is a meditational layout I have been working with this week for an old friend whose life has changed radically due to mental health issues. His family have asked me to hold him in prayer.

FIG. 33 *Nourishing the soul*

I chose the Chariot as my friend's significator, since I wanted to witness to his essential dignity and his ability to steer his own life, which is how I have always thought of him, since we first knew each other. Around the outside, I have laid the four cardinal virtues at the corners, while around him, I have laid four cards that witness to him as a child (6 Cups), a young man (Knight of Wands), as a mature man (King Cups), and as an old man (10 Pentacles). By selecting these, I am holding his entire life experience and holding who he really is in my heart, even though his true self is buried beneath the clouds of mental illness that have been triggered by world events. I have been visualising the cardinal virtues as rivers that flow into the central well where his card is situated, nourishing him with clarity of mind and the ability to stand strong, allowing the gentle light of wisdom to shine on him, and mediating waters of healing to pass into the places that most need them. It is not for me to make anything happen or create changes; I have just been witnessing to him as a whole person, whose soul can be nourished by love and held in the heart of a friend who has known him for years.

BRINGING THINGS TO A PLACE OF REST OR NON-SUFFERING

Very often, we cannot help or bring things to a place of ultimate resolution. Some problems and concerns will need more steps upon the path, more healing and considerable resourcefulness, or they may lie entirely out of our remit. In such cases, we can do nothing more than pray or use the following Tarot ritual to take our issues out of time and place them into the hands of the spiritual powers, into the mercy of the ancestors, and into the encompassing mercy of the gods and holy ones who lie at the heart of the universe. For those who are stuck in situations where resolution is not possible, whether it be miscarriages or extenuated delays of justice, the unaccountable alienation or loss of family members, or the onset of complex conditions for which there is no cure: for these things, there often cannot be any closure or resolution.

In this Tarot ritual you are enabled to bring things to a place of rest or non-suffering, by witnessing that you yourself can do no more, and that you are handing over the issue to higher powers for the issue to receive help or rest. The ritual does not aim to change anything by your will or determination, although subtle changes may be experienced by its subject afterwards. When the issue concerns a person or being who has no agency or cannot give consent, as in the example below, shuffle a significator into the deck and do an Opening of the Book (p. 229). This respects the person, group, or issue that you are praying about; again, we are not aiming to change them or prescribe any particular goal for them, except to witness their struggle and lend whatever support is available to them. Take your time with this ritual: it shouldn't be rushed. Here, I have given a version of the ritual for a single person to perform, but you could do this in a group with some people representing the chosen Major Arcana, who might each receive and pray with the issue card, before turning toward the candle and leaving the issue card before the flame.

Method:

1. Select a card to represent the issue that is not resolvable at this time.

2. Select three Major Arcana cards to represent the higher or spiritual powers or the elder ancestors who look kindly upon us, or the archetypes that are wise and merciful, who can bring their love to those things beyond our personal agency: these cards can be consciously chosen to represent those powers who you feel would be most capable of holding the issue in their merciful love. Note that all the cards in this ritual, which will be turned to face different ways, are considered to be upright, unless any exceptions are required.

3. Clear a space on a table or tray and set a lighted candle to the far side of the space.

4. In front of the candle, lay the three chosen Major Arcana cards so that they face the issue card.

5. Lay the unresolved issue card so that it faces each of the three Major Arcana in turn. Be aware of what happens when the issue card connects in turn with each of the Majors.

6. Now, turn the three Supporter cards to face the candle: they now take the issue into the sanctuary of the candle flame, where it can come to a place of rest or non-suffering. You may also place the issue card behind the candle, if you wish, leaving the candle to burn down safely with the three Supporting cards and issue card / significator set about it at a safe distance.

Example:
Susan is devastated at losing her intelligent elderly sister's conscious mind to dementia. Susan knows there is nothing more she can practically do for Molly, except to love and care for her at home while she can. She is prepared to accept help when the condition escalates.

FIG. 34 *Susan's Tarot ritual for Molly*

In this instance, since the ritual is for a person rather than an issue, Susan selects the Queen of Swords to signify her sister's mind, but, rather than chose cards *for* her sister, she lets the Queen of Swords find the help that Molly would have self-chosen in an Opening of the Book (p. 229)—this respects Molly's autonomy. Interestingly, the significator falls immediately between 7 Cups and reversed 10 Wands— the very cards that speak of the fragmentation or kaleido-scopic vision of the imagination, as well as of the laying down of burdens. Susan takes these three cards as assent from Molly, since they speak tellingly of the dementia. But she doesn't want to place these as supporters. A little farther down either side of the Queen of Swords, Susan finds the Magician, the World, and the Fool. As a taromancer herself, Susan knows that these cards are those that close and open the Major Arcana sequence, and the realisation floods her with the sense that while dementia is seen mostly as a condition that closes and cuts off people, for Molly this may be just the ending of one sequence and the beginning of another adventure.

Susan notices that all three supporter cards are carrying wands or sticks, as if they all are prepared to help bridge this issue. Turning the significator to face the Magician, she experiences him as the embodiment of all who have a keen intelligence, a being whom Molly might regard as formidable enough to deal with her condition. The World is a being who can walk between the physical and spiritual sides of reality and can bring things to a conclusion: there is spaciousness enough here for Molly. The Fool feels like an ancestor of theirs who left his homeland, jumping ship to come to Britain over a hundred years ago. He was a spontaneous figure who went with the flow, and whom everyone in the family says Molly much resembles in appearance.

When Susan turns the three supporters around to face the candle, she cries because she experiences them each as advocates for her sister. She makes her own prayer for Molly too, placing her significator behind the candle.

ICONS OF A MYTH

Looking to the future, when times will have changed entirely, I often wonder whether the *Waite-Smith Tarot's* very ubiquity might lead, in some future time, to an archaeologist or archaeo-anthropologist concluding that it was once used as part of a religious group. If so, I ask, to what kind of religion or spirituality would Tarot have belonged? You might already see the Tarot as a series of timeless icons who stand ready to support the querents for whom you read, or you may see them as divining tools that speak for fate, destiny, and fortune, answering your questions about future tendencies and movements.

There is nothing that the Tarot doesn't speak about, for it can stretch as wide as you wish.

Ancestors and elders of many generations have left handholds and waymarks for us who follow them, trusting that the coming generations will take up their advice and wisdom for their own times. Many of them must have thought like Socrates, who tried to mentor his young and ambitious friend Alcibiades from making huge mistakes by saying to him, "I wish you may persevere. But I am terribly afraid for you; not that I in the least distrust the goodness of your disposition, but perceiving the torrent of the times, I fear you may be borne away with it, in spite of your own resistance, and of my endeavours in your aid."[20] It is very easy to be swept away by the "torrent of the times," despite our determination to stand firm. We cannot do that without engaging with the powers beyond time, asking them to stand with us and strengthen our resolve, deepen our love, and hold us in their regard.

What the ancestors and elders have handed down for us to take up and work with is a trust: they have given Tarot into our hands, and our best act of love is to uphold it in the best way we can. While the household of the earth may still be learning how to be cooperative rather than competitive, and how to see things in terms of "us" rather than "them and us," our task as taromancers is to spread our reading cloth as wide as it needs to go, to help open blocked pathways, to include the resources that can maintain hope and strength, and to raise the lantern of wisdom that it may shine ahead. As we read, we can cooperate with all the help that a provident universe sends to us, with intelligence, skill, and perseverance.

In chapter 1, we began with this version of the household of the earth wherein we saw ourselves as at the centre of a set of nesting boxes:

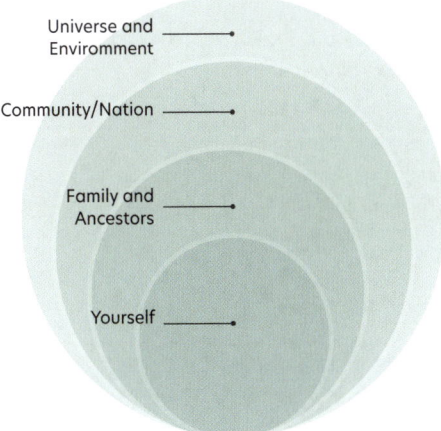

FIG. 35a *An individual's view of the world*

Universe and Enviromment ⎯⎯⎯

Community/Nation ⎯⎯⎯

Family and Ancestors ⎯⎯⎯

Yourself ⎯⎯⎯

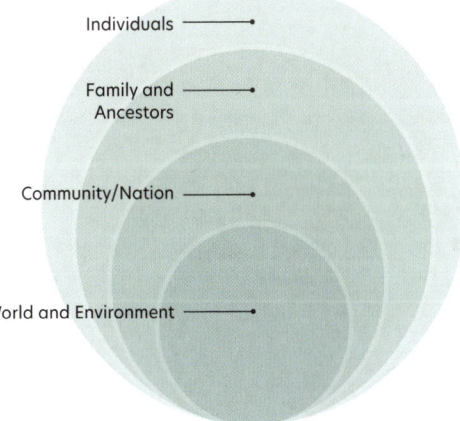

FIG. 35b *A time changer's view of the world*

Individuals ⎯⎯⎯

Family and Ancestors ⎯⎯⎯

Community/Nation ⎯⎯⎯

World and Environment ⎯⎯⎯

What changes when we turn things around, like this? The answer to that is the challenge for us all.

Now, in place of a blessing, I leave you with three questions on which to read for yourself, so that you and your work may become the blessing:

Show me the mythic pattern that I can constellate in my life as a time changer in changing times.

How do I serve the household of the earth?

What wisdom do I bequeath so that the household of the earth may be better honoured?

NOTES

1. Caitlín Matthews, *Untold Tarot* (Atglen, PA: REDFeather, 2018), 179.

2. Caitlín Matthews, John Matthews, and Gareth Knight, *The Lost Book of the Grail* (Rochester, VT: Inner Traditions, 2019).

3. A. E. Waite, *The Key to the Tarot* (London: Rider, 1911).

4. Hierocles, *Ethical Fragments*, trans. Thomas Taylor (Chiswick, UK: C. Whittingham, 1822).

5. Margot Neale, ed., *Songlines: Tracking the Seven Sisters* (Canberra: National Museum of Australia Press, 2017), 25.

6. Yod is a Hebrew letter, and in Kabbalah it signifies the power of divine energy coming to earth.

7. Matthews et al., *The Lost Book of the Grail*.

8. Walter Wink, *Unmasking the Powers* (Minneapolis: Fortress, 1993).

9. Albrecht Mahr is an expert in German family constellations who first coined the term "the Knowing Field." Like the term "morphogenetic fields," created by the British biologist Rupert Sheldrake to stand for the interconnected intelligence that is found in flocks of birds or groups of animals, "the Knowing Field" applies to human beings in concert with each other, whether in families, groups, or the universe.

10. Caitlín Matthews, *The Art of Celtic Seership* (London: Watkins, 2021).

11. Alison Coudert, *Leibnitz, Locke, Newton and the Kabbalah*, https://archive.org/stream/coudert/coudert_djvu.txt, accessed 13 June 2022.

12. Linda Hogan, *Dwellings: A Spiritual History of the Living World* (New York: W. W. Norton, 1995), 45.

13. Sallustius, *On the Gods and the World* (Sturminster Newton, UK: Prometheus Trust, 2006).

14. Although, when we attempt to reconfigure or modernize a traditional myth, we stand to break its core pattern or truth; if we try to "make it work for our times," we can also bankrupt its meaning.

15. Caitlín Matthews, *Singing the Soul*.

16. Daan Van Kampenhout, *The Tears of the Ancestors* (Phoenix, AZ: Zeig, Tucker & Theisen, 2008).

17. K. S. Yang and David Y. F. Ho, "The Role of Yan in Chinese Social Life," in *Asian Contributions to Psychology*, ed. A. C. Paranjpe, David Y. F. Ho, and R. W. Rieber (New York: Praeger, 1988), 263–81.

18. Tarot commentator Paul Huson favors the Hermit card, while my late teacher Gareth Knight favored the World.

19. Matthews, *Untold Tarot*, 142–45.

20. Plato, *Know Thyself: Plato's First Alcibiades and Commentary*, 2nd ed., trans Thomas Taylor and Floyer Sydenham (Westbury, UK: Prometheus Trust, 2011), 135c.

17. "The Role of Yan in Chinese Social Life" by K. S. Yang & Y. F. David.

18. Tarot commentator, Paul Huson favours the Hermit card, while my late teacher, Gareth Knight, favoured the World.

19. Caitlín Matthews, *Untold Tarot*, pp. 142–5.

20. 135c, *The First Alcibiades*, Plato from Thomas Taylor & Floyer Sydenham, *Know Thyself*.

SELECT BIBLIOGRAPHY

Coudert, Allison P. *Leibnitz, Locke, Newton and the Kabbalah*. https://archive.org/stream/coudert/coudert_djvu.txt. Accessed 13 June 2022.

Dorff, Rabbi Elliot N. *The Way into Tikkun Olam: Repairing the World*. Nashville: Jewish Lights, 2008.

Hierocles. *Ethical Fragments*. Translated by Thomas Taylor. Chiswick, UK: C. Whittingham, 1822.

Hogan, Linda. *Dwellings: A Spiritual History of the Living World*. New York: W. W. Norton, 1995.

Huson, Paul. *Mystical Origins of the Tarot*. Rochester, VT: Inner Traditions, 2004.

Knight, Gareth. *The Magical World of the Tarot: The Fourfold Mirror of the Universe*. Newburyport, MA: Samuel Weiser, 1996.

Matthews, Caitlín. *The Art of Celtic Seership*. London: Watkins, 2021.

Matthews, Caitlín. *Psychic Protection Handbook*. London: Piatkus, 2005 (titled *Psychic Shield* in the US).

Matthews, Caitlín. *Singing the Soul Back Home*. London: Eddison Books, 1995.

Matthews, Caitlín. *Untold Tarot*. Atglen, PA: REDFeather, 2018.

Matthews, Caitlín, John Matthews, and Gareth Knight. *The Lost Book of the Grail*. Rochester, VT: Inner Traditions, 2019.

Neale, Margot, ed. *Songlines: Tracking the Seven Sisters*. Canberra: National Museum of Australia Press, 2017.

Rees, Ian. *The Tree of Life and Death*. London: Aeon Books, 2002.

Sallustius. *On the Gods and the World*. Sturminster Newton, UK: Prometheus Trust, 2006.

Seed, John, and Joanna Macy. *Thinking like a Mountain: A Council of All Beings*. Gabriola Island, BC: New Catalyst Books, 2007.

Taylor, Thomas and Floyer Sydenham, trans. *Know Thyself: Plato's First Alcibiades and Commentary*. 2nd ed. Westbury, UK: Prometheus Trust, 2011.

Van Kampenhout, Daan. *The Tears of the Ancestors*. Phoenix, AZ: Zeig, Tucker & Theisen, 2008.

Waite, A. E. *The Pictorial Key to the Tarot*. London: Rider, 1911.

Wink, Walter. *Unmasking the Powers*. Minneapolis: Fortress, 1993.

Yang, K. S., and David Y. F. Ho. "The Role of Yuan in Chinese Social Life: A Conceptual and Empirical Analysis." In *Asian Contributions to Psychology*. Edited by A. C. Paranjpe, David Y. F. Ho, and R. W. Rieber, 263-81. New York: Praeger, 1988.

ABOUT THE AUTHOR

Caitlín has spent a lifetime working within the native and hermetic mysteries of the Western esoteric tradition. She is the director of studies for the Foundation for Inspirational and Oracular Studies, which is dedicated to the sacred arts, the oral and mythic traditions, and ancient sources of inspiration. She is the author of many books, including *Untold Tarot*, *The Da Vinci Enigma Tarot*, *The Art of Celtic Seership*, *The Celtic Book of the Dead*, *Celtic Devotional*, and *Psychic Shield*. Caitlín has had a shamanic practice in Oxford, UK, for the last 32 years, where she addresses the causation of ancestral fragmentation, soul loss, and vocational confusion. She teaches internationally for institutions and groups, revealing the doors and pathways of practical spirituality. www.hallowquest.org.uk